The Torture and Prisoner Abuse Debate

Recent Titles in
Historical Guides to Controversial Issues in America

Gun Control and Gun Rights
Constance Emerson Crooker

The Pro-Life/Choice Debate
Mark Herring

Genetic Engineering
Mark Y. Herring

Same Sex Marriage
Allene Phy-Olsen

Three Strikes Laws
Jennifer E. Walsh

Juvenile Justice
Laura L. Finley

The Welfare Debate
Greg M. Shaw

The Gambling Debate
Richard A. McGowan

Censorship
Mark Paxton

The Torture and Prisoner Abuse Debate

Laura L. Finley

Historical Guides to Controversial Issues in America

GREENWOOD PRESS
Westport, Connecticut • London

Library of Congress Cataloging-in-Publication Data

Finley, Laura L.
  The torture and prisoner abuse debate / Laura L. Finley.
       p. cm. — (Historical guides to controversial issues in America, ISSN 1541–0021)
  Includes bibliographical references and index.
  ISBN 978–0–313–34292–9 (alk. paper)
 1. Torture—United States.   2. Political prisoners—Abuse of—United
States.   I. Title.
  HV8599.U6F56   2008
  364.67—dc22   2008012634

British Library Cataloguing in Publication Data is available.

Library of Congress Catalog Card Number: 2008012634
ISBN: 978–0–313–34292–9
ISSN: 1541–0021

First published in 2008

Greenwood Press, 88 Post Road West, Westport, CT 06881
An imprint of Greenwood Publishing Group, Inc.
www.greenwood.com

Printed in the United States of America

The paper used in this book complies with the
Permanent Paper Standard issued by the National
Information Standards Organization (Z39.48–1984).

10 9 8 7 6 5 4 3 2 1

Contents

Acknowledgments   vii

1   Introduction: Describing the Problem   1

2   Torture and Its Origins   15

3   Prison Abuse in the U.S. Pre-Civil Rights Era   23

4   The Central Intelligence Agency and Torture   37

5   Domestic Prison Abuse Today   69

6   Abuse in Guantanamo Bay, Afghanistan, and Iraq   109

7   Summing Up the Torture Debate   149

*Timeline of Significant Events in the History of Torture
and Prisoner Abuse*   163

Further Readings   171

Bibliography   173

Index   181

Acknowledgments

"How depressing" was the most frequent comment I received when I told people about the book I was writing. Reading for more than a year about the horrific track record of my country in regard to ensuring the basic human rights of those in detention was at times shocking, and certainly not uplifting. Yet it was also interesting, provocative, and, even more, important. This is exactly the type of subject many authors of nonfiction are looking for when they research, and I am thrilled to have had the opportunity to do so. I sincerely hope that this book can make some good out of all of the violence.

There are many people to thank: Most notably, my husband, Peter, who as always supported me through the entire process; and my beautiful four-year-old daughter, the budding singer, actress, dancer, and environmentalist. You are a wonder and a joy. You are already making the world a better place. As I wrote, I held two full-time jobs, teaching at Florida Atlantic University and helping make social change to end domestic violence at Women In Distress of Broward County. To all my students and colleagues, thanks for listening to me.

And thanks to Sandy Towers and the rest of the editorial staff at Greenwood for allowing authors the autonomy and flexibility needed to craft what we hope to be useful reference guides on critical topics.

1

Introduction: Describing the Problem

This introduction provides readers with an overview of the current debate about torture. It begins with a description of the infamous Abu Ghraib photographs and outlines the circumstances leading up to their publication. It highlights the Bush administration's position on abuse allegations from the Guantanamo Bay prison in Cuba, various prisons in Afghanistan, and locations in Iraq. It also examines the opposing viewpoint, which holds that the United States has and currently is torturing prisoners and detainees at locations overseas, as well as outsourcing torture to other nations known to do so. In addition, the chapter discusses public support for torture, as well as for the death penalty and harsh interrogations and conditions for prisoners domestically.

THE ABU GHRAIB PHOTOGRAPHS

Abu Ghraib, 20 miles west of Baghdad, was a notoriously brutal Iraqi prison under the leadership of Saddam Hussein. First created in 1959 by an Iraqi ruler, General Abdul Karim Kassem, the prison was intended to be one of the finest and most secure in all the world. When Saddam Hussein's Arab Baath Socialist Party attempted to assassinate Kassem, the construction dragged to a halt. Hussein was ordered to be executed, but he escaped from prison in 1967 and, in 1968, led a coup that overthrew the Iraqi regime. He then took over the prison project, and the facility opened in 1970. The number of detainees grew over the following two decades, and despite being designed to hold only 1,500 inmates, it is said to have once held as many as 40,000. Hussein actually encouraged public reports of the brutality that occurred at Abu Ghraib, as he felt it ensured compliance. Up to 30,000 prisoners were hanged there, and inmates suffered devastating diseases due to overcrowding and its corollary effects.[1] Yet it will forever be infamous as the scene of scandalous abuse of prisoners at the hands of American soldiers.

CBS first aired the horrible photographs on its program *60 Minutes* in April 2004. Although those shown were certainly horrifying, the station claimed it had dozens more, many worse than those they did show. In fact, Congress was shown 1,800 additional photographs.[2] "The images set the national and international media on fire. In newspapers and magazines, on television channels, news broadcasts, the radio waves, and most of all, the Internet, other pictures that CBS had chosen to withhold began circulating. On Friday, April 30, they were broadcast on the Arab satellite TV channels, Al-Jazeera and Al-Arabiya, although no images, not even of death or mutilation, could have been more offensive to Muslims."[3]

Anticipating the outrage that would follow the public broadcast of the photos, CBS had, at the request of the Pentagon, waited two weeks before it aired them, and did so only when it became clear that a report about the Army's internal investigation by Major General Antonio M. Taguba had been leaked to Pulitzer Prize–winning journalist Seymour Hersh. The Taguba report was not, however, the first time the abuse of detainees by Military Intelligence had been the subject of official inquiry. Major General Donald Ryder had previously concluded that the detention system was in serious need of immediate attention because deficient training and manpower had created a climate ripe for abuse.[4]

As had been predicted, the nation was aghast when the horrifying pictures of prisoner abuse were first aired. How could such atrocities have occurred, and most of all, how could U.S. soldiers have been involved in such heinous behavior? Without a doubt, the pictures were disturbing, and they indeed prompted an ongoing national dialogue regarding the definitions of torture and cruel and inhuman treatment, as well as an examination of U.S. compliance with international guidelines regarding these issues. And yet, although it has been almost four years since the airing of the pictures, some argue little has changed.

The photographs show naked, contorted bodies arranged in a pyramid. They show hooded men masturbating while a soldier smiles and points. They show a dead body packed on ice, and smiling soldiers giving the thumbs-up. They show dogs straining at the leash and a nude man cowering—and the same man, later, bleeding. They show a ghostly figure, hooded and draped with a blanket, standing on a narrow box, wires running from his hands. But on their own, these pictures from the American military prison at Abu Ghraib tell us almost nothing. They offer a glimpse of horror, but they cannot explain what is happening, or why, or who benefits, or who is responsible.[5]

Several of the photos that received the most attention were taken on a single night at Abu Ghraib. It was September 8, 2003, and guards were targeting seven men accused of inciting a riot in the prison. It started out, according to Specialist Matthew Wisdom, with Staff Sergeant SSG Frederick, Sergeant Davis, and Corporal Graner hitting the prisoners who had been brought to the Tier 1A area of the prison for interrogation. None of them appeared to be posing any danger to the military personnel, according to Wisdom, who left after he delivered the prisoners to the Tier. After that, the guards lined the prisoners up against a wall. According to Private Lynndie England, SSG Frederick started to move one of the prisoner's arms up and down as if he was masturbating, then asked England to pose for a picture with the prisoner. This is the infamous photograph of England pointing at the man's genitals and giving the thumbs-up. One of the prisoners in the photos, Nori Samir Gunbar al-Yasseri, described what happened: "When we were naked [a guard] ordered us to stroke, acting like we're masturbating and when we start to do that he would bring another inmate and sit him down on his knees in front of the penis and take photos which looked like this inmate was putting the penis in his mouth."[6] The inmates were then forced to pile up into a pyramid while more pictures were taken. Corporal Graner placed the men into position and then posed with Specialist Sabrina Harman behind the pile.

Some of the most horrifying photographs of abuses at Abu Ghraib show a figure that has been dubbed the Statue of Liberty. Several prisoners have claimed it could be them in the picture, which shows a man standing on a Meals-Ready-To-Eat (MRE) box with wires attached to his fingers, toes, and penis.[7]

A particular element that was surprising to many was the inclusion of women as abusers.

The pictures from Abu Ghraib show smiling American women holding prisoners on leashes, posing with piles of nude, hooded figures, mocking and pointing at the genitals of stripped, helpless men. All this received a great deal of comment in the US press when the photos were released. To some it was seen as an additional shock that women (presumably, the gentler sex) should be engaged in such appalling behavior. Others explained that women were useful in the interrogation of Iraqi men because Arab culture deemed it particularly shameful for men to submit to women.[8]

In May 2004 more damaging visual images emerged, also connected to Abu Ghraib. A group claiming they were acting in retaliation for the abuses shown in these images videotaped their beheading of American contractor Nicholas Berg.[9]

THE BUSH ADMINISTRATION RESPONSE

Although they expressed horror at the pictures, the Bush administration line was that the soldiers acted alone, and that they alone needed to be punished. The acts were considered to be onetime incidents perpetrated by soldiers who had lost their sense of moral decency, caught up in a difficult situation in a foreign country and surrounded by the enemy. Even torture opponent Senator John McCain has offered what Garry Wills has called the "original sinless" argument. The argument is that the United States is using torture on prisoners and detainees overseas for the first time ever, and only because it is the only way to get the information needed to keep the entire nation safe. Until September 11, 2001, the argument goes, the United States always treated enemies with fairness and humanity, and in ways consistent with human rights legislation.[10]

The administration has maintained that what they have authorized falls short of violating any international law. When asked about torture in November 2005, President Bush said, "Any activity we conduct is within the law. We do not torture."[11]

More than just the Bush administration, others have promoted the position that the United States does not torture prisoners. Conservative shock jock Rush Limbaugh chalked the abuse up to simply normal behavior. Even more, "torture is feminist," he argued on his May 3, 2004, show. "Have you noticed who the torturers are? Women! The babes!... It looks just like anything you'd see Madonna, or Britney Spears do on stage." It's also a display of gay sexuality: "We have these pictures of homoeroticism that look like standard good-old American pornography."[12] Limbaugh's guest, Oliver North, infamous for his role in the Iran-Contra affair, concurred. Later, Limbaugh opined: "And we hear that the most humiliating thing you can do is make one Arab male disrobe in front of another...and especially if you put a woman in front of them and then spread those pictures around the Arab world. Maybe the people who executed this pulled off a brilliant maneuver....Nobody got hurt.... Sounds pretty effective to me if you look at us [sic] in the right context."[13]

THE OTHER SIDE

Others have argued the pictures clearly demonstrate that abuse was endemic in Iraq. According to this perspective, more than merely showing the acts of rogue individuals, the events at Abu Ghraib were the result of decisions made at the highest levels that supported the use of torture and cruel, inhuman, and degrading treatment. "Abu Ghraib is the fully predictable image of what a torture culture looks like. Abu Ghraib is not a few bad apples. It is the apple tree."[14]

This side maintains that the Bush administration's denial that the nation has ever used torture and cruel, inhuman, and degrading treatment is not only absurd but prevents major human-rights policy initiatives from ever being implemented. As Naomi Klein, author and columnist for the *Nation,* put it, "Every time Americans repeat the fairy tale about their pre-Cheney innocence, these already hazy memories fade even further. . . . Inside U.S. collective memory, the disappeared are being disappeared all over again."[15] Jones refers to this as "democrisy." Democrisy is "the stain of hypocrisy that attaches to regimes that are avowedly democratic in character, that allow comparative freedom and immunity from naked state violence domestically, but that initiate or participate in atrocious actions beyond their borders."[16] According to Jones,

Democratic states *"wouldn't* do" something atrocious; therefore they "don't." Any suggestion that they regularly have done it, and continue to do it, is viewed as intemperate or ungrateful at best, dangerous or extremist at worst. The result is an effective "culture of impunity" in which the atrocities committed by Western states and their allies are systematically ignored, explained away, defined out of existence, or openly celebrated—anything to preserve them from serious and objective criticism.[17]

Regardless of who specifically is depicted in them, the Abu Ghraib photographs certainly seem to indicate that someone with expertise was directing the torture.[18] That expertise came from a long history of honing our legal arguments and our specific techniques.

THE LEAD-UP TO ABU GHRAIB

The directives to administer abuse came immediately after the September 11 terrorist attacks. On September 11, 2001, right after he made an evening address to the nation, President Bush told his White House counterterrorism staff, "Any barriers in your way, they are gone." When Defense Secretary Donald Rumsfeld interjected that there might be legal restraints on some actions that could be taken in regard to counterterrorism, the president responded, "I don't care what the international lawyers say, we are going to kick some ass." Only five days after the 9/11 attacks, Vice President Dick Cheney commented that the government needed to "work through, sort of, the dark side." He said, "A lot of what needs to be done here will have to be done quietly, without any discussion, using sources and methods that are available to our intelligence agencies, if we're going to be successful. That's the world these folks operate in. And so it's going to be vital for us to use any means at our disposal, basically to achieve our objective."[19]

The president's speech at the Pentagon on September 17, 2001, outlined his approach to the war on terror, and allowed wide latitude in interpretation of what is and is not acceptable treatment of detainees during the war.

All I can tell you is that Osama bin Laden is a prime suspect, and the people that house him, encourage him, provide food, comfort, or money are on notice.... We're going to find those who—those evil-doers, those barbaric people who attacked our country and we're going to hold them accountable.... I know that an act of war was declared against America.... I know that this is a different type of enemy than we're used to. It's an enemy that likes to hide and burrow in, and their network is extensive. *There are no rules.* It's barbaric behavior. They slit throats of women in airplanes in order to achieve an objective that is beyond comprehension. And they like to hit, and then they like to hide out. But we're going to smoke them out. And we're adjusting our thinking to this new type of enemy.... It's going to require a new type of thought process. And I'm proud to report our military, led by the Secretary of Defense, understands that; understands it's a new type of war, it's going to take a long time to win this war... to get them running and find them and hunt them down.

This speech, as well as other comments and memos coming from the White House, were interpreted by the Central Intelligence Agency (CIA) as authorizing an array of treatments of prisoners, including the transfer of suspects to nations notorious for torture. In late 2001, the Justice Department gave the CIA a narrow interpretation of the United Nations anti-torture convention that sanctioned use of "sleep deprivation...and deployment of stress factors" for interrogating al Qaeda suspects—as long as they did not reach the level of "severe physical or mental pain."[20]

Two months later, on November 13, Bush issued a sweeping order, drafted by the vice president's counsel, David S. Addington, for detention of al Qaeda suspects under "such conditions as the Secretary of Defense may prescribe." Those conditions included denying these detainees access to any court, whether U.S. or international. Instead, their cases were relegated to military tribunals, which, the president said, would be "full and fair."[21]

On January 9, 2002, John Yoo of the Justice Department's Office of Legal Counsel wrote a 42-page memo asserting that the Geneva Conventions and the U.S. War Crimes Act did not apply to the Afghanistan conflict. Yoo argued Afghanistan was a "failed state." His memo placed al Qaeda and the entire Taliban regime into a new category, beyond soldier or civilian, called "illegal enemy combatants," which, according to the Bush administration, put them outside the scope of the Geneva Conventions. According to Yoo, even Article 3, common to all four of the Geneva Conventions, which bars "cruel treatment and torture" or "humiliating and degrading treatment," did not apply because the conflict was "between a State and a transnational terrorist group."[22] Author Kristian Williams commented, "Just as Soviet leaders turned to torture in times of crisis, as the CIA had once reported, so President Bush, on the fateful day of 9/11, moved from fear in the morning, to flight in the afternoon, to tough talk and torture orders in the evening."[23]

Interviews with some of those accused in the Abu Ghraib scandal lend support to the notion that abuse of prisoners and detainees was not only condoned, but encouraged. Shortly after the airing of the photos, *Newsweek* interviewed Brigadier General Janis L. Karpinski. She claimed that the military police (MPs) were being made to take the fall for the prisoner abuse scandal, and that only a month prior to the abuse allegations, an intelligence team from Guantanamo had come to Abu Ghraib and had explained specific techniques that were to be used to obtain information from detainees during interrogations. Staff Sergeant "Chip" Frederick stated that he had been keeping a journal since investigators first approached him on January 14 to inquire about abuses. In it, he documented the fact that commanders had ignored several requests to clarify operating procedures. When he told a commanding officer that detainees were being confined, naked, in three-by-four-foot cells with no running water or toilet, he was told, "I don't care if they have to sleep standing up."[24]

In regard to the second set of pictures—those that allegedly prompted the decapitation of Nicholas Berg—some have maintained they served only as a means of distraction from the much-needed debate about U.S. torture and prisoner abuse.

The uncensored video was posted on scores of websites, allowing viewers to watch the gruesome details of the decapitation, and a deluge of letters to *National Review's* weblog demanded more photos. The beheading immediately deflected attention from the burgeoning torture scandal and allowed apologists for the administration to claim that Abu Ghraib was fully justified by the barbarism of the enemy. On Capitol Hill, senators ceased criticizing the government and the administration claimed the right, indeed the duty, to withhold the remaining pictures in case they incited further revenge killings. The major papers took up the cry, the *New York Post* kicking off an article on the killing with the line "What cruel sick bastards" and calling for a resumption of major combat.[25]

In his analysis of the Abu Ghraib scandal, author Rajiva commented, "Fiction is needed to sustain the national self-perception of an unspotted nation defending itself righteously from total evil, and, as usual, it was concocted almost immediately by the avatar of the American street, Rush Limbaugh."[26] Limbaugh declared, "If anybody—and I don't care who they are—if anybody tries to tell you that these pictures from this prison are responsible for the death of Nick Berg, I want you to stand up, and I want you to tell them to stuff it. This is just al Qaeda being who they are. Al Qaeda beheaded Daniel Pearl before there was any knowledge of whatever went on in this prison in Baghdad."[27] Others who garner more widespread respect than Limbaugh offered a similar perspective. Senator Joseph Lieberman made the argument, "Prison abuse must not blur the enormous moral differences between us and those we fight in Iraq, and in the worldwide war on terrorism."[28]

Part of the difficulty in ascertaining which "side" is correct is in defining the concepts. Like pornography, of which a Supreme Court justice commented that he could not define it but "knew it when he saw it," torture and cruel, inhuman, and degrading treatment are difficult to define precisely, and their meanings are open to some degree of debate. "Torture is defined in law as the deliberate infliction by state officials of 'severe pain, whether physical or mental.' Such pain, the law defines, can be inflicted in a single act—like the use of electric shocks or a threat to kill someone's family. But torture, as defined, can also mean a pattern of treatment that, little by little, destroys the prisoner's mind."[29]

Mossallanejed described four components of torture: (1) It is severe pain or suffering, either physical or psychological, that has been purposely inflicted on a person; (2) it has a goal, whether that be as a form of punishment, to extract information, or to obtain a confession; (3) it is perpetrated by a public official; and (4) it is not sanctioned by law. Yet he also commented,

Despite its usefulness, the above definition is far from adequate. It does not address state and religiously sanctioned tortures, which are prevalent in many parts of the world. In Iran, Saudi Arabia, Sudan, Nigeria, Pakistan, Mauritania, Bangladesh, and some other countries, the law permits flogging people who drink alcohol or do not observe the dress code of the government. Men and women, especially women, are stoned to death for the crime of adultery. Here, governments turn ordinary people into torturers by inciting them to throw stones at the victims. They are told to bury men up to their bellies and women up to their breasts and start throwing stones; they are instructed to choose stones which are neither too small nor too large in order to prolong the victim's agony. This type of torture is a part of the criminal code of some fundamentalist countries. Another religiously sanctioned form of torture is the act of suttee: the burning alive of a widow on a funeral pyre alongside the dead body of her husband.[30]

Shue identified several types of torture. In terroristic torture, the victim's suffering is a means to an end. Interrogational torture is intended to extract information, and has, at least theoretically, a built-in end point. That is, once the information has been obtained, the torture would conclude. Shue describes three categories of possible victims of torture: the ready collaborator, the innocent bystander, and the dedicated enemy. The first two are unlikely to have information that would prove helpful. The dedicated enemy could possibly have useful information, but is the least likely to provide it, given the level of commitment to the enemy group.[31]

International bodies to date have identified certain acts that decidedly constitute torture. The Human Rights Committee has declared beatings, forcing inmates to stand for long periods of time, and holding persons incommunicado to be torture.[32] The U.N. Committee Against Torture specified in May 1997 that the following practices constitute torture: restraint in very painful positions; hooding under special conditions; sounding of loud music for prolonged periods; sleep deprivation for prolonged periods; threats, including death threats; violent shaking; and using cold air to chill.[33] In addition, torture experts recognize that the application of methods that might not individually constitute torture might well be considered torture when used together and against particular cultural groups.

Using the vagaries and subjective elements of international human rights law as well as U.S. law regarding torture and cruel, inhuman, and degrading treatment, the CIA has instituted a practice, called rendition, whereby detainees are shipped to other nations known to torture for their interrogation. In November 2001, just two months after 9/11, President George W. Bush, standing next to President Jacques Chirac of France, declared that Allied nations needed to do more than express sympathy in the war on terror. It was incumbent on all U.S. allies "to perform." He added, "You're either with us or against us in the fight against terror." The United States thereby demanded support in the war on terror. Nations across the globe were already offering assistance with intelligence and in other ways, however.

This practice, too, has been subject to much debate. Some maintain the CIA's practice is in clear violation of the law, while others argue that the wording of the law exempts these actions. CIA Chief Porter Goss called his agency's interrogation techniques "unique," but has said, "This agency does not do torture. Torture does not work."[34] "Since September 11, 2001, the [United States] has increasingly taken advantage of the generosity of other regimes, many of which are well-known for their brutality. Terror suspects are arrested in their home countries at the request of U.S. officials, or kidnapped from wherever they happen to be and flown to somewhere willing to employ harsh methods. This allows the U.S. to maintain that the prisoners are not really under its control."[35] In researching the number of renditions that occurred after 9/11, Stephen Grey found that hundreds were carried out by the

CIA and the U.S. military. Studies of case files at Guantanamo showed that, contrary to popular belief, the majority of those in custody had been rendered from outside the Afghanistan combat zone.

Dragged for months or even years from prison to prison, from country to country, with no hope of release, no hope of appearing in court, or no hope of facing concrete charges, rendition for many became a tunnel with no light at the end. And for those held within its confines, the torture of rendition came not from the tactics of the interrogators. Those pains could be endured. The system itself was the torture. Ordered and authorized from the top of the White House, the rendition program had become a torture program.[36]

In late 2007 lawyers for Guantanamo detainee Majid Khan filed suit in a federal court requesting that the Bush administration preserve evidence of how Khan had been tortured by the CIA for more than three years in their custody. Khan's attorneys met with him in mid-October and found him with a large scar on his arm from trying to gnaw through to an artery. Khan had been held as a "ghost detainee," and thus no one was allowed to make contact with him. According to the suit, Khan admitted anything his interrogators demanded, regardless of its truth.[37] In December 2007, media reports revealed that hundreds of videotaped interrogations made in 2002 had been destroyed by the CIA in 2005, despite specific requests that the agency maintain the records. A Justice Department inquiry was launched to assess whether the destruction of the tapes was an attempt to cover up evidence of torture or coercive interrogations.[38]

PUBLIC SUPPORT OF TORTURE

While what exactly constitutes torture or cruel, inhuman, or degrading treatment has been debated, what is clear is that Americans cited greater support for use of harsh methods in the war on terror after the September 11th attacks. Less than one week after the attacks, a university professor offered his ethics class four choices as responses. They could execute the perpetrators on sight, bring them back to the United States for trial, try them through an international tribunal, or interrogate and torture those involved. The majority of students said it was appropriate to execute the perpetrators on sight or to torture them to obtain information.[39] One month after the attacks, the *Washington Post* reported impatience with the Federal Bureau of Investigation (FBI) over the interrogation of four suspected terrorists arrested after 9/11. "We're into this thing for 35 days and nobody is talking," said a senior FBI official, adding that "frustration has begun to appear." The agent admitted that the FBI was considering using torture to elicit information. "We are known for humanitarian treatment.... But it could get to that spot where we could go to pressure... where we won't have a choice, and we are probably getting there."

Support also emerged for rendition. A law enforcement official suggested that suspects be extradited to Morocco, where interrogations were notoriously brutal. The interrogators there, who work for the king, were trained by the CIA. A week later, the *Los Angeles Times* reported serious discussion of torture in intelligence circles.

Interestingly, support for torture spanned the political spectrum. In *Newsweek,* columnist Jonathan Alter wrote: "In this autumn of anger, even a liberal can find his thoughts turning to... torture...." and "Some torture clearly works." Alter advocated psychological techniques or the transfer of suspects to our "less squeamish allies." Panelists on PBS Television's *McLaughlin Group* suggested detainees be sent to the Philippines or Turkey for interrogation, as those countries were well-known for their brutality. Harvard law professor Alan M. Dershowitz told CBS Television's popular *60 Minutes* that torture was "inevitable."

By mid-November, the *Christian Science Monitor* reported that 32 percent of Americans supported torturing terror suspects, and torture had become a common discussion topic in both public and private places.[40] Another poll found 46 percent of Americans supported the use of torture.[41] Surveys eliciting more detailed information found 62 percent approved threatening to transfer prisoners to countries known to use torture, 69 percent supported threatening prisoners with dogs, 73 percent agreed it was acceptable to force prisoners to stand naked and chained for lengthy periods of time, 82 percent supported "waterboarding" (strapping prisoners to boards and forcing their heads underwater so they feel as though they are drowning), and 85 percent approved of having female interrogators make physical contact with Muslim men, which is prohibited by Muslim religious practices at certain times.[42]

Over time, the debate became less concerned with whether the United States had ever used torture, as the public could no longer ignore the mountain of evidence. A CNN/USA Today/Gallup poll in November 2005 found 74 percent of the 515 people polled thought that U.S. troops or government officials had tortured prisoners in Iraq or other countries.[43] Yet many still believe this kind of treatment may be justified in the war on terror. Several polls taken since the publication of the Abu Ghraib photographs show that Americans support torture and cruel, inhuman, and degrading treatment in certain circumstances. A *Newsweek* poll found 44 percent of 1,002 adults surveyed believed it was justifiable to use torture "sometimes" or "often" in order to gain information. More than half (58 percent) supported torturing a detainee if it could prevent another major terrorist attack.[44]

Regardless of what Americans believe, international agreements and even U.S. law clearly prohibit torture and cruel, inhuman, and degrading treatment. From the Universal Declaration of Human Rights in 1948 and the Geneva Conventions of the following year to the International Covenant on Civil and Political Rights (ICCPR) of 1966, the more recent Convention Against Torture (CAT) ratified by the United States in 1994, and many other conventions and treaties, numerous international documents delineate the specific acts that are unlawful and to whom they apply. This includes domestic prisoners as well as prisoners of war. In addition, U.S. legislation such as the War Crimes Act (WCA) also makes torture and cruel, inhuman, and degrading treatment punishable by lengthy jail sentences and, in some cases, death. Chapter 5 offers a more detailed look at these laws and agreements.

Another issue that should be part of the new discussions about torture and cruel treatment of captive persons is domestic abuse allegations. Unfortunately, this has not really been part of the conversation, despite mountains of evidence that people in the United States are subject to abuse every bit as horrific as that occurring overseas. The abuse occurs at all levels of the criminal justice system, from police interrogations to detention. And it happens to people of all ages and demographic groups, although research has clearly demonstrated that racial and ethnic minorities are more likely to suffer abusive treatment at the hands of law enforcement officials or jailers.

Police have long used harsh techniques to elicit evidence and confessions, as chapter 2 documents. Conditions in prisons and detention centers across the country can themselves be said to constitute torture, apart from the treatment that inmates endure. This is perhaps at its worst in "supermax" prisons. Juveniles fare no better, and there is tremendous evidence of abuse occurring in juvenile detention centers and boot camps. Women are most at risk for sexual abuse, especially since they are often guarded by males. Yet males, too, are subject to various forms of sexual harassment and abuse, and many times jailers not only ignore the abuse but even encourage it.

Another current debate surrounds use of the death penalty. The Supreme Court ruled in *Furman v. Georgia* that the death penalty was unconstitutional as it was then applied. At the time, most states held one trial in which both guilt as well as sentencing occurred. The Court held that this led to far too arbitrary application of the death penalty and was consequently cruel and unusual. The Court did not, however, decide that the death penalty was, in and of itself, cruel and unusual. Rather, they required each state wishing to maintain execution as a punishment option to submit a revised plan for the assignment of the sentence. In sum, then, the issue of whether the death penalty itself violates the Eighth Amendment prohibition on cruel and unusual punishment remains unclear.

As this book was being written, the Supreme Court heard arguments about the constitutionality of lethal injection. States using that method had temporarily stopped executions while they awaited the court's decision. On April 16, 2008, the Supreme Court ruled that the three-drug combination used in lethal injections is not cruel and unusual. This ruling set the stage for Kentucky, the test state, and at least ten others to resume executions immediately. The Court previously determined the electric chair and gassing are unconstitutional. The arguments for and against the death penalty, as well as in favor of and opposing lethal injection specifically, are presented in chapter 4. Suffice it to say, though, that this is an issue of considerable controversy, as much of America professes support for the death penalty. As they do with torture of terror suspects, many people believe that these criminals are the "worst of the worst," and consequently deserve whatever treatment is imposed.

The sad reality is that torture and abuse of prisoners and detainees is common domestically and overseas. This has been true for some time. Only by seeing the connections between abuse abroad and abuse at home can we truly look to eradicate it.

NOTES

1. Christianson, S. (2004). *Notorious prisons.* London: First Lyons Press.

2. Harbury, J. (2005). *Truth, torture, and the American way.* Boston: Beacon.

3. Rajiva, L. (2005). *The language of empire: Abu Ghraib and the American media.* New York: Monthly Review, p. 11.

4. Ibid.

5. Williams, K. (2006). *American torture and the logic of domination.* Cambridge, MA: South End Press, p. 1.

6. Ibid., p. 8.

7. Ibid.

8. Ibid., p. 236.

9. Rajiva (2005).

10. Klein, N. (2005, December 26). "Never before!" Our amnesiac torture debate [Electronic version]. *The Nation.* Retrieved from http://www.thenation.com/doc/20051226/klein.html.

11. Lewis, A. (2005, December 26). The torture administration [Electronic version]. *The Nation.* Retrieved from http://www.thenation.com/doc/20051226/lewis, p. 2.

12. Rajiva (2005), p. 28.

13. Ibid., p. 27.

14. Ibid., p. 51.

15. Klein (2005), p. 2.

16. Jones, A. (2004). Introduction: History and complicity. In Jones, A. (Ed.). *Genocide, war crimes and the west: History and complicity* (pp. 3–30). London: Zed, p. 9.

17. Ibid., p. 11.

18. Mayer, J. (2005, February 14). Outsourcing torture. *The New Yorker.* Retrieved April 25, 2007, from http://www.newyorker.com.

19. Williams (2006), p. 113.

20. Ibid., p. 113.

21. Ibid., p. 114.

22. Ibid., pp. 113–114.

23. Ibid., p. 113.

24. Ibid., p. 16.

25. Rajiva (2005), pp. 55–56.

26. Ibid., p. 85.

27. Ibid., p. 85.

28. Ibid., p. 85.

29. Ibid., p. 85.

30. Mossallanejed, E. (2005). *Torture in the age of fear.* Milton, Ontario: Seraphim.

31. Shue, H. (2004). Torture. In Levinson, S. (Ed.), *Torture: A collection* (pp. 47–60). New York: Oxford University Press.

32. Watt, S. (2005). Torture, "stress and duress," and rendition as counterterrorism tools. In Meeropol, R. (Ed.), *America's disappeared* (pp. 72–112). New York: Seven Stories Press.

33. Rose, D. (2004). *Guantanamo: The war on human rights.* New York: The New Press.

34. Herald Wire Services. (n.d.). CIA Chief: Methods don't include torture [Electronic version]. *Miami Herald.*

35. Williams (2006).

36. Grey, S. (2006). *Ghost plane.* New York: St. Martin's Press, pp. 21–22.

37. Rosenberg, C. (2007, December 9). Filing: Detainee "tortured." *Miami Herald,* p. 3A.

38. Johnston, D. (2007, December 9). Destroyed tapes fuel new questions over CIA tactics. *Miami Herald,* p. 3A.

39. Argetsinger, A. (2001, September 17). At colleges, students are facing a big test. *Washington Post,* p. B1.

40. McLaughlin, A. (2001, November 14). How far Americans would go to fight terror. *Christian Science Monitor, 1,* and Rutenberg, J. (2001, November 5). Torture seeps into discussion by news media. *New York Times,* p. C1.

41. Morin, R., & Deane, C. (2004, May 28). Americans split on how to interrogate: Majority polled oppose using torture. *Washington Post.*

42. USA Today/Gallup Poll results. (2005, January 12).

43. Princeton Survey Research Association. (2005, November 10–11). *Newsweek Poll.* Retrieved from http://www.pollingreport.com.

44. Ibid.

2

Torture and Its Origins

Cruel forms of punishment and torture are certainly not American inventions. Indeed, a peek at world history reveals a long line of brutal activities directed at persons guilty of, or merely accused of, criminal activity. "The progress of mankind has been shadowed by the grisly history of torture and execution. For every shining triumph of human endeavor there has been a dark example of state-sanctioned depravity. Each illustration of courage and wisdom goes hand in hand with an unbecoming horror of human design."[1] During the Middle Ages and even into the twentieth century, there was no international agreement on what precisely constituted torture. Nor were there any specific prohibitions on its use, given that many states used it as a regular part of their judicial practice.

The word torture comes from the Latin word for twist, referring to both the manipulation of a person mentally as well as the physical contortions of their body. In the Middle Ages, the strappado, a ladderlike device that stretched the extremities and joints into abnormal positions, exemplified the meaning of the word. The shackled "stress positions" currently used in the war on terror exemplify the ancient meaning of the word as well.

Torture acquired its present meaning, referring to pain inflicted by government officials, in France about 800 years ago. Then, either the church or the government applied "the torture," sometimes to extract confessions and even to elicit testimony. The English adopted the French noun in about 1550. In 1591, William Shakespeare is credited with first using "torture" as a verb.[2]

THE ROMAN LEGACY

In the late Roman empire, sadistic rulers like Nero, Tiberius, and Caligula, who retained almost absolute power, made torture commonplace. "For these monsters, torture was almost a hobby."[3] Torture was a penalty in itself, or sometimes a prelude to death or banishment. It was used for both civil and criminal offenses. For instance, creditors were allowed to torture their debtors. Later, Christian emperors decreed heresy was punishable by flogging. More than just whipping, the Roman flogging whip, or *flagellum,* would often kill.

Other brutal regimes across the globe used torture. In particular, hideous execution techniques were a hallmark of the most notoriously harsh leaders. "Of all the forms of capital punishment that scar history, China's *ling chi,* or 'death of a thousand cuts,' has the mark of a psychopathic inventor."[4] In *ling chi,* the condemned was tied seminaked to a rough wooden cross while slivers of flesh were cut from the breasts, arms, and thighs. The initial attention was focused on the joints, followed by the amputation of fingers, toes, nose, ears, and limbs. It ended with a stab to the heart and immediate decapitation.

THE MIDDLE AGES

By the Middle Ages, torture and executions in Europe no longer used the most instinctive, animalistic ways to harm and kill. Rather, they were conceived to increase the suffering of the victim. That death was occasionally the result was neither surprising nor upsetting. Although today most people only support capital punishment for the most severe physical crimes, in this era the list of capital crimes was more inclusive. Capital crimes of the era included murder, as well as the far more mundane poaching, stealing fruit from trees, damaging orchards, forgery, and debt. The most commonly used form of punishment was hanging. In England the other favored option was branding. The trend was toward immediate punishments rather than anything that took time. Only a few people were imprisoned as their actual sentence.[5] Prisoners were held at Newgate Prison before they were to be hung, and people swarmed by to gawk at the more notorious of the condemned. James MacLaine, dubbed "The Gentleman Highwayman" for the respect he displayed to his young female victims, received 3,000 visitors. The prison chapel housed the Condemned Sermons on Sundays, which were ticketed events that the public could attend to watch the proceedings that involved the most infamous criminals. To many in medieval Europe, suffering was just as important as death. That is, offenders were to be brutalized as a means of redemption. Preferred methods varied somewhat across Europe. Criminals in

France and Germany were broken on the wheel, an ancient form of execution some believe dates back almost as far as the invention of the wheel, some 2,000 years B.C. In this horrific process, a large wheel was laid on a scaffold and the prisoner tied across it. His arms and legs were attached to its outer rim. The executioner used an iron bar to attack the prisoner's limbs, generally breaking each in multiple places. The wheel was propped up so observers could get a better view of the prisoner's agony. "Sometimes the injuries already sustained were sufficient to cause death. If the victim lingered for too long, the executioner wielded the bar against the chest several times."[6]

In Spain, capital punishment was administered by the garrote. The garrote was similar to hanging, except the victim kept both feet on the ground. The executioner simply strangled the person using rope. Later, a post with a hole bored through it was used. The prisoner would stand or sit before the post, with the rope looped around his neck and threaded back through the post. Standing behind, the executioner pulled hard, which killed the prisoner. Later versions of the garrote had a stick on which the rope was twisted and consequently tightened. Then there was an iron collar with a screw that was gradually wound into the victim. Executioners increased their efficiency when they attached a small blade to the garrote, which would sever the spinal cord. The Iron Maiden was another implement used for tortures and executions. An upright coffin with inner spikes, it pierced organs like the eyes and lungs of the victim who was locked inside. The spikes were too short to cause a quick death. Consequently the prisoner lingered in agony for many hours.[7]

During the Inquisition, torture became even more normalized. It was during this time that the techniques of torture became more specialized. Many of these remain today. It generally involved two phases: In the first stage, called territion, jailers worked to induce uncertainty, anxiety, and fear. Among other strategies, they would show a prisoner the torture chamber and implements and allow him to hear the screams of other prisoners being tortured. Next came the physical abuse. Prisoners were beaten with various devices, boiled, and purposely exposed to others with deadly diseases like smallpox.[8]

Judicial Torture

Many European nations in the Middle Ages utilized torture as an integral part of their judicial processes. "For half a millennium the law courts of continental Europe tortured suspected persons to obtain evidence. They acted openly and according to law. Investigation under torture was a routine part of criminal procedure in late medieval and early modern times." Because it was built into the system, use of torture was regulated. "The law of torture developed as an adjunct to the law of proof, that is, to the rules that governed the quality and quantity of evidence needed to convict someone accused of a serious crime." Judges administered the rules regarding to whom, how, and when torture was to be applied. Consequently, the system has come to be known as judicial torture. In essence, judges used torture as a way "to unearth crimes."

"By quaestio [torture] we are to understand the torment and suffering of the body in order to elicit the truth," commented Roman jurist Ulpian. Greeks and Romans did not consider some judicial testimony true unless it was coerced under torture. "The torture of slaves, for example, was not merely customary, but compulsory."[9] There has always been class bias when it comes to torture, whereby prominent persons were typically beheaded in swift fashion while ordinary persons awaited far more brutal techniques, including being broken on the wheel, burned alive, or quartered.[10]

The European law of proof emerged in the city-states of northern Italy in the thirteenth century. This system replaced the earlier system of proof, known as the ordeals, which was conducted by the church. As the ordeals were viewed as God's decision and God could not err, they were supposedly a system of proof that was absolute.

The "trial" of the ordeal began with a religious ritual that lasted up to three days. The accused was required to pray, fast, undergo exorcism, and perform other rites before attempting to prove his innocence. When the preparation was complete, authorities boiled a pot of water. The victim had to put a hand, or arm up to the elbow, into the scalding liquid. Three days later, the condition of the wound was evaluated and used to determine guilt or innocence. If the wound appeared to be healing, the accused was said to have won God's blessing and was considered innocent of all charges. If the wound was open and sore, the man allegedly had been deserted by God and consequently was guilty.[11]

Other trials used cold water. The accused was bound by ankles and feet and lowered into a river or harbor with a rope tied around his waist. A knot was tied in the rope some distance from the body. If it was wet when the man was hauled up, he was innocent. If the water, generally considered to be holy, had repelled the body and the knot was dry, he was guilty.[12] Eventually, jurists realized that this system was indeed subject to error. Although it might have been God's decisions, humans implemented them. After years of using the ordeal, Europeans sought a replacement that was more absolute and more objective. The law of proof spread across the continent with the rest of the era's criminal and civil legal procedures. Torture was used as a means of eliciting information from criminals. Investigation under torture was reserved for cases of serious crime, for which the sanction was death or maiming.[13]

The jurists and judges who created and administered this system were not clueless about the possibility that torture could lead to coerced evidence or confessions. In fact, they crafted rules intended to safeguard against abuses and make tortured confessions reliable. The Italians who refined the European law of proof said any convictions would require the testimony of two unimpeachable eyewitnesses who could speak to the severity of the crime. "Such evidence would be, in the famous phrase, 'as clear as noonday sun.'"[14] Without this type of evidence, a criminal court could not convict a defendant who contested the charges. Nor could a court convict someone only on circumstantial evidence. If the accused voluntarily confessed, then the court was allowed to make a conviction without eyewitness testimony. In essence, the rules of probable cause were intended to restrict investigation under torture to persons highly likely to be guilty.

"By insisting on certainty as the standard of proof, the European jurists solved one problem by creating another. They made the judgment of mortals acceptable in place of the judgment of God, but they bound themselves to a law of proof that as a practical matter could be effective only in cases involving overt crime or repentant criminals."[15] Clearly, crimes are not all overt, nor are they always committed by individuals who will confess and repent before the court. Many worried that the confession rule invited "cruel and stupid subterfuge." In many courts in the thirteenth century, jurists were easily able to coerce confessions from people against whom they already had strong suspicions. The law of torture grew up to regulate this process of generating confessions.

The new system authorized torture as a means of obtaining information only after there was sufficient support that a suspect was guilty, much like modern-day probable cause. Circumstantial evidence could be used to develop this probable cause. Other rules were in place as well. "Torture was not supposed to be used to wring out an abject, unsubstantiated confession of guilt. Rather, the examining magistrate was supposed to use torture to elicit from the accused the factual detail of the crime—information that, in the words of a celebrated German statute of 1532, "no innocent person can know."[16] The examiner was forbidden to engage in so-called suggestive questioning, or questions that lead a person to answer in a specified way. The information that the suspect admitted under torture was supposed to be verified to the extent feasible. "Thus, for example, if the accused confessed to the crime, he was supposed to be asked what he had done with the loot and the weapon or whatever, in order that these objects, when fetched, could corroborate the confession."[17]

For a variety of reasons, the safeguards provided by the law of proof and the law of torture never proved adequate. It was difficult if not impossible to detect whether the magistrates conducting the investigation engaged in suggestive or leading forms of questioning, either purposefully or accidentally. If the accused knew something about the crime but was still innocent, what he did know might make any confession seem credible. In some jurisdictions the requirement of verification was not enforced or was enforced indifferently. In the end, the European states conceded that the long experiment with torture was a failure. Throughout the eighteenth century, they banned the use of torture from their legal system.[18]

The flaws in the law of torture were identified as early as the Middle Ages, with a growing and vocal body of critics emerging during the Renaissance. Within two months of taking the throne in 1740, Frederick the Great virtually abolished torture. Other European states followed suit swiftly, and by the early nineteenth century torture was abolished across all of Europe. Although some of the criticism was related to concerns about fair application and human rights, in reality, much of the change was due to the increasing use of incarceration for serious crimes.[19]

TORTURE IN ENGLAND

Unlike the rest of Europe, English courts never used the system of judicial torture. This was not due to any greater enlightenment; rather, their system was already crude and cruel. While the other Europeans had the system of proof in place, however flawed it might be, the English replacement for trial by ordeal was the jury trial. But this was not a jury trial like we know today. Instead, men living near the scene of the crime were assembled to give a verdict. Unschooled and without regulations, they simply gave verdicts based on what they already knew about the suspect or the situation.[20]

Part of the modern debate about torture emanates from the concept that the punishment should fit the crime. This notion existed in ancient cultures, emerging in such treatises as the Code of Hammurabi, but it took on new form during the Enlightenment.

The principle that the severity of punishment should fit the severity of the crime has been recognized in virtually every criminal code in the history of Western civilization, from Hammurabi to the present time. Although legally prescribed correctional practices have changed dramatically throughout this history (e.g., society no longer legally sanctions putting out offenders' teeth and eyes, breaking their bones, and severing hands and feet), the basic idea of the Talion principle has remained fairly constant to the present time. The problem with the Talion principle, from the very beginning, was not in figuring out how severe the punishment should be. The principle is clear: The punishment should be no more or less severe than the offense. The real difficulty comes in determining how harmful various behaviors actually are, when considered as offenses against the whole society.[21]

One of the most well-known and influential thinkers in the field of criminology was Cesare Beccaria, an Italian born into nobility in 1738. Beccaria's work helped change the thinking about the role of punishment and the type of punishment that was appropriate for a given offense. In 1764 he published his first work, *An Essay on Crimes and Punishment,* anonymously due to his concern that his ideas would not be accepted in Italy, with its antiquated system of law. Beccaria argued that crime was the result of a rational calculus each individual made in an attempt to maximize pleasure and minimize pain. Punishment should deter offenders because it should be just enough to show them that the "pain" or "costs" associated with their offense would be greater than the benefits. Beccaria opposed torture, cruel treatment, and the death penalty because he felt overly harsh punishments did not fit into the rational calculus most people used.[22]

THE DEATH PENALTY

Capital punishment dates back to the Code of Hammurabi from Babylon, which authorized execution for 25 offenses. Interestingly, while many criticize the length of this list, it was actually intended to limit the number of offenses that could be punishable by death, as prior to the code pretty much anything could be and was. Under the Draconian Code in ancient Greece, death was essentially the only penalty for offenses. Things were slightly less severe in the Roman republic, which authorized lighter punishments for juveniles. The class bias in Roman law was tremendous, however, since a slave could be executed for killing a freeman but not the reverse. Class bias continued throughout Europe, where the upper class was subject to "painless" beheadings while the lower classes were generally hung. Other times members of the lower class were drawn, quartered, dismembered, burned at the stake, or broken at the wheel.[23]

The Middle Ages featured public executions, and a carnival-style atmosphere characterized the events. The first real opposition to the death penalty emerged in the eighteenth century, but the resistance was somewhat muted and generally tied to religion—that is, only God should determine when someone is to die.[24]

In sum, torture has been a feature of historical jurisprudence. Modern torture methods differ from the tactics used in the Middle Ages in that they tend to leave less obvious physical damage, focusing instead on psychological means to elicit information and confessions. It is clear, however, that the classical tortures are still utilized in varying degrees, and that the psychological methods developed over time and in various nations have left a horrifying legacy. Most notably, all methods of torture are passed along to new generations through warfare and other forms of contact between nations.

NOTES

1. Kelleway, J. (2000). *The history of torture and execution.* New York: The Lyons Press, p. 6.

2. Ibid., p. 4.

3. Ibid., p. 20.

4. Ibid., p. 28.

5. Christianson, S. (2004). *Notorious prisons.* London: First Lyons Press.

6. Kelleway (2000), p. 46.

7. Ibid., p. 56.

8. Ibid.

9. Christianson (2004).

10. Kelleway (2000), p. 36.

11. Ibid., p. 36.

12. Vito, G., & Simonson, C. (2004). *Juvenile justice today* (4th ed.). Upper Saddle River, NJ: Prentice Hall.

13. Kelleway (2000).

14. Ibid.

15. Ibid., p. 95.

16. Ibid., p. 96.

17. Ibid., p. 96.

18. Ibid., p. 96.

19. Langbein, J. (2004). The legal history of torture. In S. Levison (Ed.), *Torture: A collection* (pp. 93–103). New York: Oxford University Press.

20. Ibid.

21. Crews, G. (2004). Justice and the origin of corrections. In Stanko, S., Gillespie, W., and Crews, G. (Eds.), *Living in prison: A history of the correctional system with an insider's view* (pp. 25–42). Westport, CT: Greenwood, p. 27.

22. Pfohl, S. (1994). *Images of deviance and social control: A sociological history* (2nd ed.). New York: McGraw-Hill.

23. Lifton, R., & Mitchell, G. (2002). *Who owns death? Capital punishment, the American conscience, and the end of executions.* New York: Perennial.

24. Ibid.

3

Prison Abuse in the
U.S. Pre-Civil Rights Era

This chapter begins with an overview of the torture and abuse of slaves, including the lynching of black men after the Civil War. It also addresses police-perpetrated abuse, including the "third degree" as well as significant court cases that shaped interrogation processes in the United States. Also included is an examination of abuse occurring in prisons. In addition, the chapter addresses the earliest uses of the electric chair. Finally, the chapter includes information about a significant report on abuse known as the Wickersham Commission Report.

TORTURE OF SLAVES

"Why has the word 'torture' been so rarely employed in U.S. interrogation jurisprudence? The explanation might [be] that torture has never been sanctioned under the common law as it was in the civil law system—or simply because the word is so provocative. Common law courts had no official torturers trained to administer carefully measured doses of pain to test pleas of innocence."[1] Yet in reality torture was very much part of the treatment of prisoners. In particular, harsh treatments and torture was widely used against blacks in the South. Slaves were whipped as punishment for myriad offenses, be they real or imaginary. John Brown, a former slave, listed the most common ways slaves were tortured: whipping, branding, flopping with the flopping paddle, spiced washes following whipping, the picket, and bucking. All of these except for bucking were tactics used by the British. Other common forms included the standing handcuffs (hanging from the rafters) and forced standing (crucifixion). In the slave picket, masters suspended slaves by their wrists from a tall pole, then yanked them up with a pulley. The left foot was drawn up and tied to the right thigh, toes pointing downward. A sharpened stump was placed beneath the victim. If the victim rested his foot on the sharp point, a bystander would force the foot downward, often puncturing the heel or sole of the foot all the way to the bone.[2]

Bucking has also been called the "parrot's perch." The victim sits with knees bent, hands tied and brought down over the knees until the chin rests on the knees. A thick stick is then slipped over the elbows and below the crook of the knees. The victim is rendered absolutely immobile and soon experiences powerful strains and muscle spasms. Bucking was used widely because it allows for easy transportation of a prisoner, and it has a long history. Romans used to carry Christians into amphitheaters in this way. The ancient procedure persisted in the Mediterranean region until the twentieth century. By the 1930s, bucking was a common practice throughout the Americas. In the early nineteenth century, the French painter Jean Debret drew a remarkable portrait of a Brazilian master beating a bucked slave, a picture that was reproduced many times in American antislavery pamphlets. Debret portrayed what John Brown described. Bucking was also a standard military punishment in the United States in the 1850s. In New York, Sing Sing Prison guards also practiced bucking around 1860. Guards there practiced the true parrot's perch, "suspending the poles with the prisoner's head swinging downward."[3]

Shortly after the Civil War, a survey of prisons and reformatories in North America found prisons commonly used whips and dark cells as their primary means of torture. However, northeastern U.S. prisons used other tortures, notably bucking, showers, and the yoke. Sing Sing officials experimented in this period with alternatives to whipping. Techniques came and went, including bucking, gagging, the ball and chain, the iron hat, the iron jacket, and the yoke or crucifixion. The latter two were positional torture devices that came from the Chinese. Yokes were four-inch-wide long iron bars, the heaviest weighing 40 pounds, with staples for the neck and arms. The prisoner's arms were stretched along the bar's length. Even a short stint on a yoke could leave one immobilized for weeks. The iron jacket was a bulky device fixed around the neck and worn by the inmate day and night.[4]

LYNCHING

After the Civil War and into the 1930s, black men were lynched regardless of their guilt, mostly in the South but elsewhere as well. Black men who were arrested were frequently assaulted by police on the way to or in jail as well. Indeed, it was difficult to discern the line between vigilante and official justice. Vigilante justice only disappeared completely with the beginnings of the civil rights movement of the 1960s. After the Civil War, the South had to integrate a huge new population. By no means were all ready for the change in citizenship status, and a good portion of the white population wanted to maintain their social and political dominance. For many, the solution was to further develop tactics of terror and torture, both within the legal system and outside of it, that maintained white's superiority.

Black men who violated, or were even thought to have violated, the customs and institutions that kept them in a subordinated position lived in constant threat of lynching. "The lynching itself was a dreadful ritual of beating, burning, and humiliation. The dead, mutilated body was hanged for all to see and to remember—the 'strange fruit' of Lillian Smith's celebrated novel. The tortured body served the double purpose of affirming the God-given racial superiority of all whites against any black and of intimidating black men who might think of challenging the reigning social order."[5] Like today's debates about torture, lynching in earlier decades was part of a culture of violence that included support from numerous institutions. Local police and courts were expected to assist in upholding the system, as were people in all varieties of professions, such as bus drivers and railroad conductors. "Although the term 'lynching' rightly summons visions of mob violence, law enforcement officials were often implicated, sometimes as participants, more often as sympathetic observers."[6] It has been estimated that at least half of the lynchings carried out in the 1930s were conducted with the participation of law enforcement, and in 90 percent of the others police either condoned or failed to denounce the actions.[7] In all, more than 3,000 men and some women were lynched between 1880 and 1920.[8]

The Supreme Court dealt a blow to lynching as a form of justice in 1936, when the Court heard *Brown v. Mississippi*. Three black tenant farmers were accused of murdering a white man with no evidence against them except their confessions. The confessions had been produced via torture from police. Within 10 days of their arrest, they were convicted of capital murder. Law enforcement, accompanied by a crowd of white men, came to the black men's homes, hung them from trees with ropes, and repeatedly brought them down for questioning. This was repeated, with whipping in between, until the men confessed. Although the rope burns were clearly visible during the trial, the tortured confessions were admitted as evidence. The Supreme Court overturned the convictions, and Justice Hughes pronounced, "It would be difficult to conceive of methods more revolting to the sense of justice than those taken to procure the confessions of these petitioners, and the use of confessions thus obtained as the bases for conviction and sentence was a clear denial of due process."[9] This case set a new precedent for state courts but did not completely outlaw all forms of torture, nor did it specify what, precisely, constituted cruel forms of punishment or a denial of due process.

After *Brown,* the Supreme Court struggled with a series of cases regarding police interrogation. For example, how many hours could police grill a suspect? The court determined 36 hours was impermissible, but did not delineate a lower boundary. In another decision, the Court said police could not strip off a defendant's clothes and keep him naked for hours. Nor could they threaten to bring in a suspect's ailing wife if he failed to cooperate. A number of other ruses were invalidated as well, including threatening to cut off financial aid to a defendant's children and having them taken away from her if she failed to answer questions; and isolating a defendant in a distant place so his friends and family could not see him, contact him, or work toward his release.[10]

POLICE-PERPETRATED TORTURE

Lynching was not the only form of torture used in the United States during this era. One police tactic introduced after the Civil War was called the "sweat box." The sweat box was a cell next to a huge stove in which all kinds of items (bones, rotting vegetables, shoes, etc.) were burned. The combination of the heat and the stench was so rotten it allegedly could make anyone share the most secret information.[11]

Police used a number of tactics that, when added together, were called the third degree. The third degree was employed in order to elicit information and coerce confessions. The phrase originated from Major Richard Sylvester of Washington, D.C., the president of the International Association of Chiefs of Police. In 1910, Sylvester described three police duties: arrest (the first degree), transportation to jail (the second degree), and interrogation (the third degree).

Soon, Americans used the phrase *third degree* to refer solely to violence used to obtain confession or information about a crime—in short, torture. But to the public, torture also meant scarring injuries, and if police were really practicing the third degree in interrogations rooms across the United States, where was the evidence of wounds and scars on the suspects' bodies? Many American police chiefs denied that police practiced the third degree.[12]

Pretty much anything was allowable as part of the third degree. Police used fists, rubber hoses, blackjacks, and other implements in order to literally pound out confessions. Compounding the depravity was the fact that police regularly lied about how prisoners came to have bruises and other injuries, often saying they fell down stairs.[13]

"Sweating" criminal suspects referred to lengthy interrogations conducted under extreme circumstances. It was a practice widely used by police in the United States in the 1920s and 1930s. In his book *Torture and Democracy,* Darius Rejali described a 1924 case in which Washington, D.C., police interrogated a Chinese American, D. C. Wan, in a hotel room for eight days until he confessed. In 1925, Louisiana police held two men for 38 days, obtaining confessions on the 34th day. Rejali commented, "One could no doubt find earlier examples. To start, it is enough to know that in the years following World War I, sweating became a common police practice in the United States."[14]

THE DEATH PENALTY AS TORTURE

Yet another means of torture emerging from this era was capital punishment by the electric chair. Death penalty scholars Robert Jay Lifton and Greg Mitchell commented,

As long as there have been people on earth, those in authority—familial, tribal, or governmental—have executed wrongdoers in their midst. America has embraced the death penalty since colonial times, and probably before that. Of course, much has changed concerning the institution of capital punishment over these centuries, but what is most striking, in pondering this rich if bloody history, is how much remains the same. Methods of execution evolve—we no longer crucify criminals or stone them to death—but almost every theme, argument, and issue surrounding the death penalty today was sounded or debated in the past.[15]

The first execution in America was in 1608, when George Kendall was hung for plotting to betray the colony. According to Lifton and Mitchell, by the end of the eighteenth century at least 1,500 executions had occurred. After the Revolutionary War, opposition to the death penalty began to grow. The abolitionist movement was largely influenced by the work of Italian jurist Cesare Beccaria, who held that the purpose of punishment should be deterrence, not vengeance. Beccaria maintained that the death penalty was not a deterrent but instead a momentary spectacle. In the United States, physician and signatory to the Declaration of Independence Benjamin Rush adopted Beccaria's arguments, and added to them a moral objection.[16]

Although the Supreme Court is still grappling with the issue of whether the death penalty is in and of itself cruel and unusual, they determined the electric chair as a form of capital punishment was unconstitutional. The origin of the electric chair can be traced back to a battle between Thomas Edison and George Westinghouse. The two were in competition to determine the nature of the socket that is now common on the walls of our homes. One man wanted it to yield direct (DC) and the other alternating (AC) current. At the time this competition was occurring, several states were actively seeking alternatives to hanging for offenders to be executed. Many doctors opposed lethal injection, and Edison promoted AC equipment as a quick and painless means of execution, which had already been suggested by the magazine *Scientific American* in 1876. In the process of testing his machine, Edison and his allies killed dozens of dogs, cats, and horses.[17]

The New York state legislature was the first to authorize the use of an electrocution machine, and in 1880 the state executed William Kemmler. Versions of the execution differ, with proponents saying it was relatively quick and providing suggestions to make it more so. Opponents argued Kemmler's execution was barbaric, and that the horrific stench and the length of time it took Kemmler to die was unacceptable. The process continued regardless, and during the seventh execution at Sing Sing in 1893, Charles Mc-Elvaine did not die after being shocked for 55 seconds straight.[18] "Witnesses to electrocution...almost always notice that it is a less than tidy procedure, physically and morally.... Inmates usually buck in the seat and strain mightily at restraining straps; vomit, defecate, or urinate, or all three; lapse into convulsions and facial contortions; and sometimes emit cries, the cords on their neck standing out like steel ropes."[19] In 1946, the execution of 17-year-old Willie Francis in Louisiana was especially gruesome. Although he was electrocuted, Francis survived. His lawyers maintained that a second round of electrocution was in violation of the Eighth Amendment to no avail, and Francis was executed a year later.[20]

Over time, preferred methods of execution change. Gassing prisoners was considered a more humane method of execution, and the first inmate killed by cyanide in a gas chamber was executed at San Quentin in 1924. "Considering how the Nazis had put cyanide gas to use, it was strange that after World War II there was not more association with Hitler's Germany. Instead, the use of the gas chamber thrived during the 1950s, the latest manifestation of ever-present pressure in America to become more up-to-date, more technologically advanced."[21]

In 1982, Charles Brooks Jr., was the first to be executed by lethal injection. Lethal injection was a supposedly more humane way to execute a prisoner. He or she was simply given injections of sodium thiopental, pavulon, and potassium chloride and then allegedly went to sleep, never to wake again. This method was not as humane as it was once thought to be, as evidenced in the botched execution of Jimmy Lee Gray in 1983. Gray thrashed around violently for eight minutes, in the process bashing his head on an iron pipe.[22] This method was recently tested in the Supreme Court and found to be constitutional.

ELECTROSHOCK TORTURE

Other nefarious uses for electroshock emerged in the twentieth century. American and Argentinean police forces used electrotorture in the 1920s. The method fulfilled their need for a "clean" form of torture—one that left few, if any, physical marks. Although not necessarily used by all police agencies, those that did utilized electrotorture with their own niche.

Until 1925, Dallas used the "electric monkey"—so called because it was used "especially against Negroes"—which consisted of a storage battery with two terminals. The prisoner held one pole, and the other was pressed against his spine, giving what police called "a needle in the back." Between 1922 and 1926, the Seattle police chief used a cell with an electrically wired carpet. When the carpet was on, "sparks fly and the prisoner leaps, screaming in agony, into the air . . . it is not fatal, its effects are not lasting, and *it leaves no marks.*"[23]

In Helena, Arkansas, in 1929, local sheriff J. C. Barlow charged James McAllister, an African American, with the murder of his stepson. McAllister was strapped and shocked in what can only be called an improvised electric chair. McAllister confessed to the crime and was convicted, then subsequently appealed his conviction, claiming his confession had been coerced. The judge demanded to see the chair, which was rolled into the courtroom. Sheriff Barlow testified that he had inherited the device from his predecessor; in other words, it came with the office. Barlow did admit he had rebuilt the chair and used it on three suspects.[24]

There are other examples of police using electric chairs for interrogation. Most of the examples occurred in the South. In Alabama, police whipped a suspect at Atmore Prison Farm, and then bound him in the electric chair used for executions at Kilby Prison. After eight days and nights in the chair, he implicated four men charged with murder.[25]

WATER TORTURE

Drawing on the innate fear of drowning, water has also been used in many different forms of torture. During the Spanish-American War in 1902, U.S. soldiers put funnels in the mouths of Filipinos and forced massive amounts of water into their organs. The practice was so commonplace that William Howard Taft, governor of the Philippines, admitted to the Senate that the "water cure" was normal practice. Although it is not entirely clear how the Americans learned this practice, it is likely that they adapted it from the Filipinos, who knew it from Spanish colonial history. "What is certain is that no one remembered that it was one of the most fearful tortures of the Inquisition. President Roosevelt called it a 'mild torture.' War critics were outraged, but, painful as the torture was, Americans could not see damage, and pumping and choking took root among soldiers and policeman."[26]

In the nineteenth century, American jailers used to punish prisoners by choking them under long showers. At Sing Sing, guards released a solid stream of cold water from a great height, literally beating the prisoners with water. It was said to be similar to standing before a fire hose. The impact caused extensive bruises and eventually unconsciousness. In 1858, guards at Auburn Prison showered Simon Moore for 30 minutes. Moore collapsed and died. To avoid unwanted scandal, New York prisons reduced the shower heights and eventually abolished water punishments in 1882. Innovative prison officials realized fire hoses could deliver water with great force, which enabled them to serve as effective substitutes for the earlier tall showers. In the late nineteenth century, American fire hoses could deliver water with pressures tested to 350 psi. In the early 1860s, the "shower bath" was a standard punishment at San Quentin. Prison guards stripped prisoners, tied them to the "ladder," and "sprayed a stream of cold water from a one-and-one-half-inch hose under great pressure against the victim's face, breast, and exposed genitalia." Prison records show a minimum of 42 Hispanics received this shower punishment between 1872 and 1875, although Anglo prisoners also received the punishment. At San Quentin, flogging was abolished in 1880 and the shower bath in 1882. But the practice was not forgotten. In 1918, for instance, military officers used fire hoses to beat imprisoned Molokans, a small religious sect of conscientious objectors, when they refused to stand for reveille. The hosing lasted for two hours.[27] During World War I, conscientious objectors who had been imprisoned described being subjected to the water cure. In the 1920s, police subjected prisoners to pumping, which meant "having an ordinary water hose thrust into the mouth or down the throat, the faucet opened and the stomach flushed."[28]

CHEMICAL TORTURE

Another tactic was to cover the suspects' or inmates' bodies with dangerous, sometimes lethal, chemicals. Louisiana's Pentonville Prison was the first to use pepper spray in 1856, when they sprayed it on prisoners held in confined spaces. The governor blew smoke that contained cayenne pepper down the hallway to where a specific prisoner was located. Another tactic, used during the Civil War, was to confine prisoners in cells next to furnaces that generated dark smoke. This low-tech approach still persists in some countries. In Sri Lanka, for example, torturers burn chilies over a fire and blow the irritant smoke into the eyes of the prisoners. At the turn of the century, Folsom Penitentiary in California created a "Chloride of Lime Cell"—a cell whose floor was soaked with chloride of lime. Chloride of lime has a biting acrid smell, much like bleach, and within minutes the fumes affected the prisoner's breathing, burned the lining of his nose and throat, and stung his eyes. Soviet army guards also used this procedure in military prisons. In the 1920s, Chicago police pioneered the technique of pumping tear gas into small cells. Others placed a box over a prisoner's head and released a canister inside the box. Technological advances now allow torturers to apply mace, pepper spray, or tear gas directly into keyholes or into the mouth or face of prisoners. This technique appeared first in Israeli prisons in the 1970s, then in American and Canadian prisons in the 1980s.[29]

OTHER FORMS OF TORTURE

One of the prisons most notorious for abuse in the 1800s was New York's Sing Sing. In 1833, an inmate named Colonel Levi S. Burr, who was serving time for perjury, published an exposé that outlined the abuse occurring at the facility. Subsequent investigations found some inmates had been lashed 400 times with cat o' nine tails, and jailers hit prisoners with hot pokers for the slightest infractions. As noted, Sing Sing was strongly identified with use of the electric chair. Between 1891 and 1963, 614 executions took place at Sing Sing, more than at any other prison in the United States.[30]

THE WICKERSHAM COMMISSION

Without a doubt, brutal forms of interrogation were common across the United States in the early part of the twentieth century. Suspects were slapped, beaten, whipped, and poked in back rooms, in rural precincts, and in secret locations. In 1931, the National Commission on Law Observance and Enforcement of the American Bar Association (ABA) issued a comprehensive account of police brutality in American cities entitled *Report on Lawlessness in Law Enforcement.* The commission, dubbed the Wickersham Commission after its chair, George Wickersham, gathered hundreds of affidavits and news reports to reveal an ongoing, persistent pattern of brutality across the United States. It found that police all over the country used torture. One-third of the cases occurred in rural towns, and 29 major cities were found to use torture. The commission investigated 15 cities for more detailed case studies, finding that police commonly beat and sweated suspects in 10 of them. Knowing some would try to excuse the behavior as the antics of small-town, unprofessional cops, the commission emphasized that these were professional departments. Further, they found that police tortured suspects not in the heat of the moment, but as a calculated effort intended to elicit confessions.

The Wickersham Commission drew national attention to widespread police abuse, and many books were written that cited the contents of the commission's report and made it accessible for the public. Although it was not the first report of police torture, it was so thorough and complete that the facts were difficult to deny. The report built on public intolerance of police torture that had begun to grow over the previous decade. In 1924, George Dougherty, the former deputy commissioner of the New York Police Department, put it plainly: "The bench, jurors, the public are becoming more and more suspicious every day of confessions procured as a result of severe interrogation and examination." In some cases the report resulted in major change, as some entire precincts disavowed use of any torturous interrogations. In other jurisdictions, police simply developed "cleaner" techniques that enabled them to continue their "work" with less scrutiny and without raising alarm.[31]

The Wickersham Commission identified five major cities—New York, Chicago, Cleveland, Dallas, and Seattle—where police generally used a combination of clean techniques to coerce false confessions and to elicit information. The most common techniques used included sweating, which was often conducted through a "relay" of officers, clean beating (use of heavy objects that have no edges, such as clubs, rubber hoses, bags filled with sand, telephone books, etc.), prolonged exposure to powerful lights and electricity, forced positional tortures (keeping the body in excruciating positions for lengthy periods of time), various uses of water and air (including ice-cold baths, forced drinking, volumes of water poured into the nostrils, etc.), sweatboxes (very tiny cells placed close to stoves or other heat-producing sources), drugs and irritants, and the use of devices that constrained prisoners in painful positions. "The police struck areas that were unlikely to leave long-term bruises: slaps to the face and blows over the kidneys, in the abdomen, or in the soft hollows above the hips. They squeezed, twisted, and lifted men by the genitals. They disguised blows as accidents, for example, kicking the shins or pushing the suspect forward unexpectedly."[32]

The Wickersham Commission made a huge impact on American policing and even on legal precedent in the 1930s. Many of the Supreme Court decisions that came between 1936 and 1944 cited the commission's work. The first of these was the *Brown* case, which was already mentioned. In *Chambers v. Florida* (1939), the Court overturned confessions based on mob pressure and persistent questioning over five days, including one all-night session. The

Court condemned "the protracted questioning and cross questioning of these ignorant young colored tenant farmers by state officers and other white citizens in a fourth floor jail room, where as prisoners they were without friends, advisers or counselors, and under circumstances calculated to break the strongest nerves and stoutest resistance." In *Ashcraft v. Tennessee* (1944), the Court struck down confessions secured by relay interrogations under bright lights. In 1941, police interrogated Ashcraft for 36 hours continuously until he confessed to murdering his wife.[33]

PRISON EXPERIMENTS

Today, Americans are generally horrified by the atrocities perpetrated by Nazis during and prior to World War II. The torture of Jews, gypsies, the mentally ill, and many others makes us shudder. Professor Carl Clauberg injected chemicals into the wombs of Jewish and gypsy women, leading to terrible pain and sterilization. Dr. Josef Mengele, the "Angel of Death," was notorious for his experiments on twins. In order to simulate the combat wounds of German soldiers, Dr. Herta Oberheuser rubbed foreign objects, including wood, rusty nails, glass shards, sawdust, and dirt, into the wounds of prisoners. Many experiments involved water, running the gamut from immersing prisoners for lengthy periods in ice water or forcing them to drink saltwater. Other prisoners were infected with deadly diseases, like malaria, or exposed to poisons such as mustard gas. After the war, 15 Nazi doctors were found guilty, with seven receiving death sentences and eight lengthy prison terms. Eight others were acquitted.[34]

We are appalled when we read about these and many other examples of medical experiments conducted at concentration camps. Yet what many do not know is that a good portion of the ideas for these experiments and for the cruel and inhuman treatment of detainees at concentration camps came from the United States.

During the Nuremberg trials of Nazi officials, details emerged about experiments conducted on prisoners in the United States. In 1906, Dr. Richard P. Strong, an American, performed a series of experiments using the cholera virus on prisoners in Manila. His efforts resulted in 13 deaths. A government report defended Strong, saying he made some great discoveries. Strong later became professor of tropical medicine at Harvard. Six years later, Strong used prison inmates as samples in a study of beriberi, a disease that causes paralysis, mental disturbances, and heart failure. Survivors were rewarded with cigars and cigarettes, although not all survived. The Louisiana State Board of Health authorized giving Negro prisoners a steady diet of molasses for five weeks in order to test whether sulfuric acid, an ingredient in molasses, was injurious.[35]

Dr. L. L. Stanley devised hundreds of experiments, using prisoners as subjects, that were intended to see if lost potency in ill and aging men could be reinvigorated. Five hundred San Quentin inmates had testicular implants between 1919 and 1922. Many other experiments took place during wartime. President Franklin D. Roosevelt created the Committee on Medical Research to help discover antidotes to diseases that were devastating the troops, and the government appealed to prisoners' patriotism as a way to encourage them to be research subjects. One of the best-known examples of human experimentation in a state prison is that of Stateville Penitentiary. The work done at Stateville was mentioned frequently by the Nazi physicians who were tried at Nuremberg. Dr. Alf S. Alving of the University of Chicago Medical School began the experiment in search of a cure for malaria in 1944 with more than 400 inmates. Over two intense years, the subjects became painfully sick, experiencing periodic mosquito bites, raging fevers, nausea, blackouts, and other effects. Many of the inmates were paroled upon completion of the study, and after the war Governor Adlai Stevenson commuted the sentences of 317 of the 432 convicts who participated, including 24 murderers and one rapist.[36] Many of the prison experiments remained secret for years. In 1977, the public finally heard about an experiment at Ionia State Hospital in Michigan involving 142 inmates.

The first suggestion that drugs might be useful in getting difficult persons to communicate occurred by accident in 1916. Arthur S. Lovenhart and his associates at the University of Wisconsin, experimenting with respiratory stimulants, were surprised when, after an injection of sodium cyanide, a catatonic patient who had long been mute and rigid suddenly relaxed, opened his eyes, and even answered a few questions. By the early 1930s a number of psychiatrists were experimenting with drugs as an adjunct to established methods of therapy. These fairly quickly spiraled into experiments in how best to interrogate suspects. In 1922, Robert House, an obstetrician from Dallas, began to experiment with scopolamine in order to elicit confessions. He interviewed two prisoners in the Dallas county jail who had been given scopolamine and whose guilt seemed clear. Under the drug, both men denied the charges on which they were held and both, upon trial, were found not guilty. Enthusiastic at this success, House concluded that a patient under the influence of scopolamine lacks the power to think or reason and is incapable of lying. His experiment and this conclusion attracted wide attention, and the concept of a "truth" drug was promptly launched.[37]

The phrase "truth serum" is believed to have appeared first in a news report of House's experiment in the *Los Angeles Record,* sometime in 1922. House resisted the term for a while but eventually came to employ it regularly himself. He published 11 articles on scopolamine in the years 1921–1929. In the

1920s and 1930s, police officials, still attracted by the possibility that drugs might help in the interrogation of suspects and witnesses, turned to a class of depressant drugs known as barbiturates. By 1935, Clarence W. Muehlberger, head of the Michigan Crime Detection Laboratory at East Lansing, was using barbiturates on reluctant suspects, though police work was continually hampered by the courts' rejection of drug-induced confessions except in a few carefully circumscribed instances.[38]

Despite the recognition by major investigative bodies, lawmakers, and the judiciary that cruel interrogations were problematic, as we shall see, these strategies persisted. In particular, experiments on prisoners continued and even escalated in the next era.

NOTES

1. Rajiva, L. (2005). *The language of empire: Abu Ghraib and the American media.* New York: Monthly Review.

2. Rejali, D. (2007). *American torture.* Princeton, NJ: Princeton University Press.

3. Ibid., pp. 306–307.

4. Ibid.

5. Ibid., p. 106.

6. Ibid., p. 106.

7. Myrdal, G. (1944). *An American dilemma: The Negro problem and modern democracy.* New York: Harper.

8. Lifton, R., & Mitchell, G. (2002). *Who owns death?* New York: HarperCollins.

9. Cited in Skolnick. J. (2004). In S. Levinson, (ed.). *Torture: A collection.* New York: Oxford, pp. 108–109.

10. Otterman, M. (2007). *American torture.* London: Pluto Press.

11. Rejali (2007).

12. Ibid., p. 73.

13. Hopkins, E. (1972). *Our lawless police: A study of the unlawful enforcement of the law.* New York: Viking.

14. Rejali (2007), p. 70.

15. Lifton & Mitchell (2002), p. 19.

16. Ibid.

17. Rejali (2007).

18. Ibid.

19. Lifton & Mitchell (2002), p. 49.

20. Ibid.

21. Ibid., p. 50.

22. Ibid.

23. Rejali (2007).

24. Ibid.

25. Ibid.

26. Ibid., p. 280.

27. Ibid., p. 286.

28. Ibid., p. 280.

29. Ibid.

30. Christianson, S. (2004). *Notorious prisons.* London: New Lyons Press.

31. Rejali (2007).

32. Ibid., p. 72.

33. Ibid., p. 74.

34. *The Nazi doctors.* (2007). Retrieved January 12, 2008, from http://www.aus chwitz.dk/doctors.html.

35. Hornblum, A. (1998). *Acres of skin.* New York: Routledge.

36. Ibid.

37. Schaffer Library on Drug Policy. (1950). "Truth" drugs in interrogation. MKULTRA Hearing. Retrieved October 12, 2007, from http://www.druglibrary. org/schaffer/HISTORY/e1950/mkultra/hearing04.html.

38. Otterman (2007).

4

The Central Intelligence Agency and Torture

Torture and abuse became more controversial in the era after World War II. As the world realized the depth of depravity exhibited by Nazi officials, great efforts were made to ensure nothing like it would happen again. International agreements, starting with the Universal Declaration of Human Rights of 1948 and the Geneva Conventions of 1949, outlined rules for humane treatment of all persons, including during times of warfare. Later agreements in the 1960s and 1970s offered additional detail. These are described in the first portion of the chapter. Next, the chapter explores the origins of the Central Intelligence Agency (CIA) and its earliest research into psychological warfare and mind control. Several significant CIA-directed projects are detailed, as are CIA-led training programs authorizing torture. Additionally, the chapter discusses how these techniques were spread to other nations and, consequently, their legacy today in the allegations of abuse and torture at foreign detention facilities.

INTERNATIONAL AGREEMENTS ON TORTURE AND HUMAN RIGHTS

Shortly after World War II, nations across the globe came together to discuss the need for international standards for warfare and the treatment of prisoners. In 1948, much of the world realized the importance of basic human rights, delineating these in the essential and living document called the Universal Declaration of Human Rights. Article 5 of this document explicitly prohibits torture and cruel, inhuman, and degrading forms of punishment.

The Geneva Conventions of 1949 addressed rules of warfare, including humane treatment of prisoners of war, civilians, and others. Article 31 specifies "no physical or moral coercion shall be exercised against protected persons, in particular to obtain information from them or third parties." Articles 12, 14, 17, and 130 address respectful treatment of prisoners of war.

The first effort to address all the elements of torture was the United Nation's General Assembly's adoption of the Declaration of the Protection of All Persons from Being Subjected to Torture and other Cruel, Inhuman, or Degrading Treatment or Punishment on December 9, 1975. Nations were not specifically obligated to follow the declaration, however, since it was non-binding.[1]

Two covenants—The International Covenant on Civil and Political Rights (ICCPR) and the International Covenant on Economic, Social, and Cultural Rights (ICESCR)—further clarified the rights of prisoners and detainees and helped establish the standards for interrogations. Both the ICCPR and the ECRSCR were enacted in 1966 and took force 10 years later. Together these are called the International Bill of Human Rights.

In 1975, the United Nations specifically defined torture:

Any act by which severe pain or suffering, whether physical or mental, is intentionally inflicted by or at the instigation of a public official on a person for such purposes as obtaining from him or a third person information or confession, punishing him for an act he has committed, or intimidating him or other persons. . . . Torture constitutes an aggravated and deliberate form of cruelty, inhuman or degrading treatment or punishment.[2]

This definition was part of the Declaration on the Protection of All Persons from Being Subjected to Torture, which was passed without dissent. In 1984, the definition was adjusted to include actions taken by *anyone* acting in an official capacity, not just public officials.[3]

In 1994, the United States ratified the Convention Against Torture and Other Cruel, Inhuman, or Degrading Treatment or Punishment (CAT), which utilizes the above definition of torture. The CAT also prohibits any form of cruel, inhuman, or degrading treatment. Enacted on June 26, 1987, this is considered the most important document to date dealing with the issue of torture. Ronald Reagan signed the CAT in 1988. It specifies that torture is never justified, even during war or in a state of public emergency. The CAT also clearly prohibits sending a person to a third country where torture might occur. Drawing on lessons learned from Nuremberg and several Vietnam-era situations described in this chapter, an order from a superior officer or a public authority does not justify torture. More than just stipulating responses when acts of torture occur, Article 2 of the CAT requires that member nations take effective legislative, administrative, judicial, or other measures to *prevent* torture.[4]

According to Article 4, all parties to the CAT are required to make torture a violation of their state's criminal laws. The U.S. government has generally said existing state and federal laws already include torture, although they are clearly inadequate.[5]

Article 10 of the CAT requires that member nations ensure education and information regarding the specific prohibitions of torture are fully included in the training of law enforcement (civil or military), medical personnel, public officials, and other persons who may be involved in custody, interrogation, or treatment of individuals who are subjected to any form of arrest, detention, or imprisonment.[6]

Article 11 mandates that member nations keep their interrogation rules, instructions, methods, and practices under systemic review. They must also document their arrangements for custody and treatment of persons arrested, detained, or imprisoned in any territory under the nation's jurisdiction. Signees to the CAT are also obligated to take action to prevent other actions that are cruel, inhuman, or degrading but fall short of this definition of torture.[7]

There have been attempts internationally to articulate the role of non-military and non-government personnel regarding treatment of prisoners. The UN General Assembly adopted a Code of Conduct for Law Enforcement Officials in 1979, which prohibits the infliction, instigation, or toleration of any act of torture or other cruel, inhuman, or degrading treatment or punishment. Doctors, nurses, and health personnel have often been involved in torture, whether of their own volition or under coercion. When they refuse, medical personnel have been tortured and persecuted for their adherence to medical ethics. In 1975, the World Medical Association (WMA) met and established the Declaration of Tokyo, which provided medical doctors with guidelines on torture of prisoners and detainees. The preamble says, "The utmost respect for human life is to be maintained even under threat, and no use made of any medical knowledge contrary to the laws of humanity." The WMA further clarified the role of medical personnel in regards to prisoners in 1981, when it announced, "It is unethical for physicians to participate in capital punishment." The above developments, along with the WMA's concerns for human rights, led to the establishment of the Principles of Medical Ethics, which were adopted by the UN General Assembly on December 18, 1992, and which also consider torture and cruel, inhuman, and degrading treatment a gross violation of medical ethics.[8]

This document consists of six principles. Principle 1 requires medical personnel, particularly physicians, not to discriminate against those who are imprisoned or detained. Under Principle 2, it is considered a "gross contravention of medical ethics" for medical professionals "to engage, actively or passively, in acts which constitute participation in, complicity in, incitement to or attempts to commit torture or other cruel, inhuman or degrading treatment or punishment." Principle 4 prohibits medical professionals from applying their knowledge and skills to either certify prisoners for specific punishments or to assist in interrogations. Only if it is medically necessary are medical personnel authorized to restrain or assist in restraining prisoners, according to Principle 5.[9]

According to the above listed document, senior law enforcement officers, members of the judiciary, and doctors and medical staff who do not intervene when they become aware of torture and abusive treatment are in violation of international human rights guidelines, and "provide silent endorsement and so contribute to the blanket of immunity necessary for the torturer to have confidence in his task." All the people who issue orders or fail to control the actions of subordinates, who devise and implement training of personnel (or fail to do so), and who determine and implement policy are also responsible when torture and cruel, inhuman, and degrading treatment occur.[10]

The United States established early on that that it would not fully cooperate with international efforts to ban torture and cruel, inhuman, and degrading treatment. The United States made 19 reservations to the CAT, while no other country made a single reservation. One reservation was to the Article 16 prohibition of cruel, inhuman, or degrading treatment. Government officials maintained the nation was bound only to those things prohibited by the U.S. Constitution, and argued that the Constitution did not address these topics specifically, nor were they to be considered cruel and unusual punishment and thus covered by the Eighth Amendment. The United States also demanded the same reservation with Article 7 of the ICCPR. Further, the United States specified torture as an act conducted with the intent to inflict severe physical or mental pain or suffering. Another reservation was that the prohibitions only applied to acts directed against persons in the offender's direct custody or physical control.[11]

"Often ignored in the celebrations of the Convention against Torture is the fact that while it is quite strong in substance, it is remarkably weak in enforcement. The central enforcement procedure in the treaty is a requirement that states submit reports to the Committee against Torture, an international body created by the treaty to oversee the Convention. But failure to abide by even this minimal commitment is frequently ignored." Oona Hathaway, author of numerous scholarly pieces on international law and human rights, studied what types of countries have ratified the Convention against Torture. He found that countries that sign and ratify treaties that outlaw torture do not have better torture practices than those that do not; in fact, countries that have worse torture ratings are slightly more likely to ratify the Conventions.[12]

The CAT was clearly intended to prohibit all forms of physical and psychological torture. American torture techniques taught at training schools and used overseas (described later in this chapter) were in clear violation. Consequently, lawyers in the Department of Justice's Office of Legal Counsel (OLC) rewrote the CAT's broad definition of torture and its provisions in order to absolve the administration The U.S. government's narrow redefinition of torture soon found its way into two U.S. criminal laws, and thus later became the basis for Washington's policy on prisoner interrogation during the war on terror.

Through this process, the United States, in effect, accepted just half the UN Convention Against Torture—affirming only the ban on physical methods. This decision, unnoticed when Congress finally ratified the convention in 1994, would effectively exempt the CIA's interrogation methods from international law. This clever diplomatic maneuvering meant that U.S. practice could diverge, even dangerously so, from international standards.[13]

The OLC provides legal advice to the president and to agencies under the president's direction. In particular, the Central Intelligence Agency (CIA) and its activities over the prior three decades were of great concern and were a major impetus for the reservations.

THE CIA AND MIND CONTROL

The CIA was created in 1947. Only in recent years has it become clear that the agency has long been involved in questionable experiments, prohibited forms of interrogation, and training others to torture prisoners and detainees. In fact, the agency was granted extralegal powers in the new "crusade" against Communism. The 1947 Act that created the agency contained a small clause granting the CIA the power to "perform such other functions and duties related to intelligence affecting the national security as the President or the National Security Council (NSC) may direct." From the agency's inception, this clause has been used to justify overt action, as directed by the president, outside the bounds of conventional law. On December 9, 1947, the NSC met again to discuss anti-Soviet propaganda efforts. This time the NSC directed that "in the interests of world peace and US national security, the foreign information activities of the US Government must be supplemented by covert psychological operations." The CIA was considered to be the logical agency to conduct this type of operation because of their ability to keep the actions secret. The Central Intelligence Act, passed two years later, exempted the agency from normal financial controls regulating the expenditure of public funds. In order to protect the details of its programs, the agency was not required to disclose to Congress its "organization, functions, names, officials, titles, salaries, or numbers of personnel employed." Thus, in addition to having extralegal powers, the CIA was to operate under a veil of secrecy.[14]

Given its unique status, the CIA was the primary agency charged with mind-control research during the Cold War. Although two congressional inquiries, the Rockefeller Commission and the Church Committee, revealed some information, the bulk of what is known today about the CIA's quest for mind control stems from a 1975 Freedom of Information Act (FOIA) request by American journalist John Marks for documents relating to agency-sponsored human experimentation. After nearly three years of delays, the CIA delivered to Marks more than 16,000 pages of documents concerning various top-secret CIA behavioral control programs. These files are on view today at the National Security Archive in Washington, D.C.[15]

One of the agency's earliest activities was to engage in experimentation designed to find a truth serum or other form of eliciting information or confessions. It began with an examination of the techniques used by Nazi officials in Germany. The Navy recruited Dr. Kurt Plotner, who directly oversaw human experimentation at Dachau, to continue his interrogation research within the United States under the title Operation Paperclip. Other Nazi doctors for whom the United States had no use were tried at Nuremburg. A new code of ethics was produced after the trials, known today as the Nuremburg Code. Article 1 declares that "the voluntary consent of the human subject is absolutely essential." Article 4 states that "the experiment should be so conducted as to avoid all unnecessary physical and mental suffering and injury." Subjects must always have the ability to terminate involvement in the experiment, according to Article 9, if they have "reached the physical or mental state where continuation of the experiment seems to him to be impossible." Sixteen of the doctors tried were found guilty of violating these basic principles. Seven were executed. Clearly unaffected by the lessons of Nuremburg, the U.S. government continued to experiment on humans, all in the name of national security. In 1947, the U.S. Navy launched Operation Chatter after receiving reports citing "amazing results" of Soviet drug research. Under this program, mescaline was tested upon volunteers at the Naval Medical Research Institute in Bethesda, Maryland, as well as on unwitting subjects in parts of western Europe.

As the Iron Curtain came down across Europe in 1948, the human mind became a Cold War battleground. Just as the War Department had mobilized physicians to develop radar and atomic weapons during World War II, so the CIA now recruited psychologists to discover new means of mind control.... Soviet scientists had already launched an intense effort to crack the code of human consciousness, so the CIA now felt forced to mount a massive program that soon made it a powerful patron in the infant field of behavioral science.[16]

The CIA's early investigations examined the potential of d-lysergic acid di-ethylamide, or LSD. LSD had been discovered by accident in 1943 by Dr. Albert Hoffman, a Swiss chemist working for the Sandoz Pharmaceutical firm. The drug is several times more potent than other mind-altering drugs like mescaline. Hoffman, a staff chemist, took a small dose himself and "soon thought I was dying or going crazy." When his research was published four years later, it attracted a great deal of attention from various espionage agencies, and the army sent a representative to speak to Hoffman about the possibility of producing large quantities of LSD to test its use as a military "incapacitating agent." Though these plans proved impractical, Sandoz sent LSD to the Food and Drug Administration, and Hoffman believed they distributed it to the CIA. The Soviets were also studying LSD. Simply put, "In an attempt to discover how and why LSD worked as it did, and what anti-dotes could be used against it, the CIA sank hundreds of thousands of dollars into a whole new field of research."[17]

The CIA was disturbed by the suggestion that the Soviets had superior methods of mind control and became consumed with beating them at their supposed game. Yale Psychologist Irving Janis was likely the first to warn the intelligence community of the Soviets' use of hypnosis to elicit false confessions, which were later used in show trials. Janis recommended that the intelligence community conduct a serious investigation of how they could place a suspected person under a trance and then elicit a sense of guilt and, consequently, a confession.[18]

A key incident that convinced the CIA that the Soviets had superior mind-control techniques occurred in 1949. American Robert Vogeler, an assistant vice president of the International Telephone and Telegraph Company (ITT), was arrested en route between Budapest and Vienna. He immediately confessed to committing sabotage and espionage against the Hungarian people, although his confession was clearly false. Since his claims were so outlandish and he repeated them over and over, some suggested he was not in control of his own mind. Vogeler's wife added fuel to the fire, claiming he was using language he had never before used. The Vogeler trial prompted speculation of communist mind control. The U.S. State Department suggested he was either coerced or drugged. The *New York Times* ran an article alleging Soviet confessions were due to drugging, torture, or "black psychiatry."[19]

The CIA's own research team confirmed what Janus was saying and what the Vogeler case suggested. In a 1950 analysis of Stalin's 1937 show trials, they found confessions they deemed "inexplicable" unless they had been induced by artificial means.[20] The CIA justified the development and implementation of extreme methods to counter the Soviet threat. In 1952, the chief of medical staff at the agency commented, "The Communists were utilizing drugs, physical duress, electric shock and possibly hypnosis against their enemies. With such evidence, it is difficult not to keep from becoming rabid about our apparent laxity. We are forced by this mounting evidence to assume a more aggressive role in the development of these techniques."[21] Edward Hunter of the *Miami Daily News* coined the phrase "brainwashing" in 1950, and then authored a book with that title in 1960. It was later revealed that Hunter was paid by the CIA. In a scene that would foreshadow those made by the Bush administration, a secret panel appointed by President Dwight D. Eisenhower and chaired by Lieutenant Jimmy Doolittle determined the Cold War was a "new paradigm." They advised the president, "It is now clear that we are facing an implacable enemy whose avowed objective is world domination by whatever means and at whatever cost. There are no rules in such a game.... If the US is to survive, longstanding American concepts of 'fair play' must be reconsidered."[22]

Between 1950 and 1962, the CIA conducted secret research into controlling the mind. Their experimentation cost a billion dollars annually, "a veritable Manhattan Project of the mind." Allegedly in response to the Communist challenge, the CIA worked to "probe two key aspects of human consciousness—the mechanisms of mass persuasion and the effects of coercion on individual consciousness. This complex, at times chaotic, mind-control project had two goals: improved psychological warfare to influence whole societies and better interrogation techniques for targeted individuals." Gradually, the two goals diverged. One became public and the other disappeared "into a covert netherworld." Research into methods of psychological warfare and mass persuasion was conducted through the U.S. Information Agency and the academic field of mass communications. Over time, it became a legitimate topic of diplomacy and scholarly study. "By contrast, as it probed the impact of drugs, electric shock, and sensory deprivation on individual consciousness, interrogation research moved ever deeper inside a clandestine complex of military, intelligence, and medical laboratories."[23]

After experiments with hallucinogenic drugs, electroshock, and sensory deprivation, this work then produced a new approach to torture that was psychological, not physical, perhaps best described as "no-touch" torture. The agency's discovery was a counterintuitive breakthrough—indeed, the first real revolution in the cruel science of pain in more than three centuries. To test and then propagate its distinctive form of torture, the CIA operated covertly within its own society, penetrating and compromising key American institutions—universities, hospitals, U.S. Agency for International Development, and the armed forces. As the head agency within the larger intelligence community, the CIA has long been able to draw upon both military and civil resources to amplify its reach and reduce its responsibility. Moreover, the agency's attempts to conceal these programs from executive and legislative review have required manipulation of its own government through clandestine techniques, notably disinformation and destruction of incriminating documents.[24]

In April 1950, then–CIA director Roscoe Hillenkoetter launched Operation Bluebird. Bluebird's aim was to discover more effective methods for interrogation through use of a team that included a psychiatrist, a polygraph expert, and a hypnotist. Under this project, Boris Pash, formerly employed in Operation Paperclip, reviewed Nazi interrogation techniques, including the use of electroshock, drugs, hypnosis, and various surgical procedures. Operation Bluebird also conducted the first CIA experiments with the newly discovered hallucinogenic drug LSD. Pash directed tests on 12 subjects before expanding the program to more than 7,000 unwitting U.S. soldiers at Maryland's Edgewood Chemical Arsenal. In August of 1951 the project was renamed. The CIA's Office of Scientific Intelligence started Project Artichoke. Artichoke was designed to examine use of hypnosis in conjunction with drugs to facilitate interrogations. Artichoke generally used American subjects—notably seven patients at a drug-treatment facility in Lexington, Kentucky, who were kept on dangerous doses of LSD for 77 straight days.[25] Tests using LSD were the most common, although other drugs were tested on "volunteers" as well, including PCP, marijuana, cocaine, mescaline, and heroin.

In 1953, CIA director Allen Dulles hired two noted doctors, Harold Wolff and Lawrence Hinkle, to study "brainwashing" being conducted by the Communists. "Dulles had seen films in which American pilots held prisoner in Korea had recited unbelievable confessions, apparently voluntarily. Had the Communists developed special new techniques for mind control, techniques that apparently left no marks? Dulles wanted to know."[26] QKHILLTOP, a project to study Chinese Communist brainwashing techniques and to develop interrogation techniques, began in 1954. Most of the work is believed to have been conducted by the Cornell University Medical School Human Ecology Study Programs.[27]

During the Korean War, the Clandestine Services Department of the CIA established two secret projects, code-named ULTRA and NAOMI, "to investigate whether and how it was possible to modify an individual's behavior by covert means." MK-ULTRA absorbed the work of QKHILLTOP as well.[28]

MK-ULTRA was directed by scientist Dr. Sidney Gottlieb of the CIA's Technical Services Division. Gottlieb reported to Assistant Deputy Director of Plans (a euphemism for covert operations) Richard Helms. Helms played a key role in the mind-control effort for the next 20 years, protecting behavior-modification research from both internal review and external attack.[29]

Until its funding, totaling some $25 million, was withdrawn in 1963, MK-ULTRA supervised 149 projects and 33 more subprojects all focused in some way on the control of human consciousness. CIA investigators studied everything from hallucinogenic mushrooms to BZ. In an attempt to create the perfect CIA operative, the agency conducted experiments in brainwashing, hypnosis, electroshock, personality assessments, and a host of other techniques. "Most, if not all, of these initiatives proved useless; the vision of a simple, one-step drug to facilitate everything from police investigations to the unmasking of foreign spies was considerably more difficult to realize than the agency had expected."[30]

MK-ULTRA involved universities and hospitals, where scholars and practitioners served as researchers as well as test subjects. Much of the activity was conducted covertly, given that academic and medical researchers are generally hesitant to get overtly involved in this type of project. From the beginning of the project, Helms and CIA Director Dulles agreed that 6 percent of a project's budget could be spent without any formal contractual obligation. By the late 1950s, medical researchers were using MK-ULTRA funding for experiments at Mt. Sinai, Boston Psychopathic, and Columbia University hospitals. In the early stages, Dulles complained there were no human subjects on which they could try their new techniques.

To overcome this critical shortage, the agency adopted testing methods marked by cruelty, illegality, and with surprising frequency, failure. Seeking unwitting subjects, the CIA injected not only North Korean prisoners, but also spiked drugs at a New York City party house, paid prostitutes to slip LSD to their customers or agency cameras at a San Francisco safe house, pumped hallucinogens into children at a summer camp, attempted behavior modification on inmates at California's Vacaville Prison, and collected powerful toxins from Amazon tribes. For 'terminal experiments'—those that were pushed to possibly fatal limits—agents trolled Europe for dubious defectors or double agents deemed 'expendable.'[31]

One track of experiments involved examining the impact of sensory deprivation. Canadian psychologist Dr. Donald Hebb of McGill University quickly became one of the leading scholars on sensory deprivation, with most of his work funded by the United States. From 1951–54, Hebb received a U.S. defense grant for $10,000 to study sensory deprivation. He used student volunteers to study the effects of isolating humans for days in a black box. After two or three days of lying in a soundproofed cubicle wearing goggles and thick gloves for 24 hours straight, Hebb found that subjects lost their sense of identity. Some described scary hallucinations. "The CIA's Technical Services Division (TDS) was remarkably quick to recognize the implications of Hebb's experiments among the hundreds of projects backed by millions of dollars in secret funding from three governments."[32] They moved quickly to do their own sensory deprivation work.

Previously, a CIA medical officer had blocked some sensory deprivation projects, calling them immoral and inhuman. "But the stakes were too high for moral concerns to stop this critical pursuit. In another non-coercive experiment at the National Institute of Mental Health (NIMH) in 1955–56, Dr. John C. Lilly, later famed for his work with dolphins, immersed two volunteers 'in a tank containing slowly flowing water,' with a blacked out mask enclosing not just their eyes but their entire head. After just three hours with sensory stimulation limited to 'some faint sounds of water from the piping,' both subjects went from 'normal' problem-solving and thinking patterns to experiencing powerful and emotional visual hallucinations. Once intelligence officials learned about his work, they 'swooped down on Lilly…interested in the use of his tank as an interrogation tool,' and pressured him to immerse 'involuntary subjects' until they were 'broken down to the point where their belief systems…could be altered.' Lilly evidently did a little of this work, but because he grappled with the ethics of doing so, he made himself and a colleague the sole subjects until 1958. He realized at that point that intelligence agencies had no interest in sensory deprivation or its 'positive benefits' and resigned from the NIMH."[33]

In 1957, a team of four Harvard psychiatrists conducted an experiment similar to Lilly's. The project was funded by the ONR's covert behavioral program under the auspices of polio research. Rather than immersing volunteers in water, 17 paid volunteers were immersed in a tank-style respirator much like an iron lung. A specially built mattress inhibited their movement and tactile contact. Minimal artificial light and the constant dull running of the respirator's motor were the only sensory triggers. One subject, after 17 hours, "began to punch and shake the respirator" and "tried to break out of the tank." At least four volunteers left the experiment early due to anxiety and panic, and only five lasted the entire 36 hours. Half of the subjects had hallucinations.[34]

Although useful in understanding the effects of sensory deprivation, none of these experiments provided the answers the CIA desired. In order to be effective in interrogations, the CIA needed to know how useful these measures would be with prisoners, and in other cases where someone could not escape. A colleague of Hebb's, Dr. D. Ewen Cameron of McGill University, was working on studies involving sleep deprivation, electroshocks, drug use, and hypnosis. The CIA, in conjunction with the NIMH, sent a representative to approach Cameron about reproducing these studies with patients at the Allan Memorial Institute, McGill's psychiatric center. Cameron submitted a grant application to study breaking down a patient's behavior by using electroshock, intense repetition of a verbal signal (such as repeated messaging about parental rejection, incestuous longings, or other noxious language), partial sensory isolation, and 7–10 day hypnosis. The grant was approved within days of his submission in January 1957, and Cameron received $20,000 to support MK-ULTRA Subproject 68. Between 1957 and 1963, approximately 100 patients admitted to the Allan Institute with moderate emotional problems became unwitting subjects to the study, which allegedly was about treating schizophrenia. Subjects included a new staff psychiatrist and a new mother seeking help for postpartum depression. Although Cameron claimed his work showed tremendous results, by 1963 the CIA terminated the project. By then, Cameron had been branded as a crackpot, and his colleague Hebb called him "criminally stupid." Follow-up studies three years later found long-term effects. Of the subjects who reached the more advanced stages of Cameron's de-patterning, 60 percent still suffered from amnesia, and 23 percent had serious physical complications. In 1980, the press revealed the CIA's funding of Cameron's work, and nine of his former patients filed a lawsuit. They settled out of court for the legislated maximum amount, $750,000.[35]

THE MILGRAM EXPERIMENT

During these years of covert experimentation, another track of research investigated self-inflicted pain. Lawrence Hinkle and Harold Wolff of Cornell Medical Center, founders of the Human Ecology Society, conducted studies in 1953–54 using LSD as well as other "police practices" designed to elicit behavioral control. The CIA funded the Human Ecology Society at $5 million for three years. One study involved testing LSD on 26 sexual psychopaths at Ionia State Hospital in Michigan. They determined, however, upon investigation of KGB and Chinese Communist techniques, that isolation, induced anxiety, lack of sleep, chronic hunger, and uncomfortable temperatures were more useful in making prisoners cooperate with interrogators. This track of research coincided with that of Yale psychologist Stanley Milgram. Although there is no direct evidence linking Milgram's work to CIA funding sources, many assert it is probable if not likely that the agency funded his work. Milgram was closely tied to the ONR, and Yale's senior psychologist was Irving Janus, who had previously authored the Air Force study of Soviet mind control. In 1961, the National Science Foundation gave Milgram $24,700 to study the dynamics of obedience.[36]

Milgram tested forty "ordinary" residents of New Haven, Connecticut, to see if they would torture a helpless "victim" with escalating electric shocks when commanded to do so. Milgram carefully staged the experiment so that participants indeed felt as though a legitimate authority had told them to torture their victim. At Yale's elegant Interaction Laboratory, a uniformed experimenter seated the subjects before a machine labeled "Shock Generator Type ZLB" in the Yale Interaction Laboratory. The experimenter ordered the subjects to activate 30 switches, ranging from 15 to 450 volts. At 75 volts, the victim, who was not actually being shocked, gave a "little grunt." At 315 volts, he screamed violently. After 330 volts, the victim fell silent. Compliance varied based on the specific instructions the subjects were given and the setup of the experiment. When the volunteers heard but could not see the victim, 65 percent of them flicked the switches on command all the way to the supposedly fatal maximum level, 450 volts. If the volunteers were asked just to assist, but not to act, almost 100 percent complied. If, by contrast, a nonauthority figure, such as someone without a white lab coat, gave the commands, obedience was zero. Applying his findings to the My Lai massacre and other famous atrocities, Milgram suggested that participants employ a variety of mental techniques to justify their participation in acts of horror. They tend to view these acts as administrative, not moral, decisions.

The effect of the experiment was dramatic, both on subjects and their victims. In some subjects, the test induced what Milgram called "extreme levels of nervous tension," and they began to tremble, stutter, and sweat. One subject, a very poised businessman, according to Milgram, was reduced in just 20 minutes to "a twitching, stuttering wreck, who was rapidly approaching a point of nervous collapse."[37]

Milgram rejected the explanation that the subjects were sadistic monsters, given their normal psychological profiles before the experiment. Instead, he concluded that social convention led normal individuals to accept authority and ignore the victim's pain. "Whether his analysis was valid or not, one result of this research was clear: At the end of each simulated-torture session, ordinary New Haven citizens walked out of the Yale Laboratory with a check for $4.50 and the disturbing knowledge that they, like Gestapo interrogators, could inflict pain and even death on an innocent victim."[38]

Enormous controversy followed the publication of Milgram's experiments, and even he questioned the ethics of what he did. The American Psychological Association (APA) denied Milgram membership for one year when a Yale colleague complained that the work was potentially harmful to its subjects.

Milgram later moved on to Harvard, where he was actually denied tenure. He was quickly hired and promoted to full professor at the City University of New York, however, where the new graduate dean was Mina Rees, recently retired deputy director of the ONR.

THE CIA AND LSD

Although obviously there were a variety of experiments conducted, those involving LSD dominated the CIA's mind-control research. One CIA officer testified before the Senate that "we were literally terrified" by reports of Soviet use of LSD "because this was the one material that we had ever been able to locate that really had potential fantastic possibilities, if used wrongly." MK-ULTRA's chief scientist, Sidney Gottlieb, said, "The impetus for going into the LSD project specifically rested in a report, never verified...that the Russians had bought the world supply."[39]

Gottlieb often freelanced, devising his own LSD tests on unsuspecting subjects. In November 1953, he spiked the drinks of colleagues during a meeting at a Maryland lodge. One of the other CIA scientists, Dr. Frank R. Olson, suffered an immediate mental breakdown. Several days after taking the drug, Olson either jumped or was pushed from the 10th floor of New York's Statler Hotel, where the agency had confined him for observation. The CIA covered up this crime for the next 20 years, reporting Olson's death to his family as a suicide. Gottlieb told internal agency investigators that Olson's death was "just one of the risks running with scientific experimentation." He received a mild reprimand for "poor judgment," but continued to play a prominent role in drug experiments. In 1975, an investigation of the CIA headed by Vice President Nelson Rockefeller finally revealed that Olson's death was drug induced. The report claimed that Olson might have had a history of emotional instability, thus reducing their responsibility. Olson's family announced it planned to sue the government until President Gerald Ford apologized formally to them in the Oval Office and authorized a payment of $750,000.

As it became clear that drugs were not necessarily the best vehicle to achieve mind control, the CIA shifted to more academic-based behavioral research. In 1950, after just a few months of investigation, the CIA transferred the psychological part of the research to locations outside the agency. One of the first contracts was to a department of psychology at an unnamed university. The contract was made through the Office of Naval Research (ONR) for $300,000. Within two years, ONR had 117 contracts with 58 universities.

Of the billions expended on mind-control research in the 1950s, the intelligence community allocated $7 million to $13 million annually for behavioral studies at major universities. Most of the time, the funds were channeled through private foundations, some legitimate and others merely fronts. These included the Ford and Rockefeller foundations. One of the main conduits was the Bureau of Social Science Research (BSSR), which was established at the American University in 1950.[40]

THE CIA AND TORTURE

Many of these studies were clearly about torture. Some studies conducted by the BSSR at U.S. universities (with Air Force funding) explored "the relative usefulness of drugs, electroshock, violence, and other coercive techniques during interrogation of prisoners." Most of the early findings were classified, but some of the BSSR's later work was actually published in leading academic journals, notably an article for a 1960 issue of *Sociometry* titled, "Social-Psychological Needs and Involuntary Behavior as Illustrated by Compliance in Interrogation." A year later, this same research team published a compilation of essays by various contributors with a large and reputable publisher, John Wiley. The compilation was called *The Manipulation of Human Behavior*.[41]

By the early 1960s, the CIA was ready to move out of the lab and begin applying the findings of these various experiments in the field. In 1963, however, the CIA's inspector general uncovered the secret MK-ULTRA project and condemned it. The CIA suspended MK-ULTRA, but powerful backers won permission to continue experiments at lower levels for another decade.[42]

The CIA continued the research, re-named Project MK-SEARCH, for another decade. The purpose of MK-SEARCH was to develop, test, and evaluate capabilities for the covert use of biological, chemical, and radioactive material systems, as well as to continue examination of psychological forms of interrogation. Researchers sought to develop ways to train U.S. personnel to resist coercive interrogation as well as to determine whether the Soviets, Koreans, or Chinese really could brainwash prisoners, much like the strategy depicted in Richard Condon's controversial 1959 film, *The Manchurian Candidate*. In the film, a prisoner of war (POW) is programmed to assassinate a U.S. presidential candidate. CIA-funded researchers studied Korean, Chinese, and Soviet interrogation. They conducted approximately 200 experiments examining the use of hypnosis, stress, electroshock, coma, sensory deprivation, sedatives, hallucinogens (including LSD), drugs that induced symptoms to mimic diseases or disabilities, and sensory deprivation to improve interrogation. Because this group found torture and the threat of death to be useless as a means to obtain information, they experimented with the use of psychological stressors, which were considered to be legitimate and effective means to obtain information. Although the CIA still denies it, there is some evidence that experiments with radiological materials were conducted as well.

After the CIA completed much of its research into nonphysical forms of torture, their findings were compiled into a document called the *Kubark Counterintelligence Interrogation Manual* in 1963.

For the next forty years, the *Kubark* manual would define the agency's interrogation methods and training programs throughout the Third World. Synthesizing the behavioral research done by contract academics, the manual spelled out a revolutionary two-phase form of torture that relied on sensory deprivation and self-inflicted pain for an effect that, for the first time in the two millennia of this cruel science, was more psychological than physical.[43]

The agency disseminated these practices across the globe, first through U.S. Agency for International Development's (AID) Office of Public Safety to police departments in Asia and Latin America. During the 1980s, they utilized the U.S. Army Mobile Technology Training Teams in Central America to disseminate their strategies. "In battling communism, the United States thus adopted some of its most objectionable practices—subversion abroad, repression at home, and torture."[44]

The *Kubark* manual explained that effective interrogation involved inducing the subject to regress to a far weaker personality. Interrogators were to reduce a subject's sense of identity and of the familiar until the situation became "mentally intolerable." The best way to do this, according to the manual, was to attack the subject's sense of time. From the moment of arrest, interrogators were told to create "existential chaos." The more complete the sensory deprivation, the easier it is to obtain cooperation from a subject. In the first stage of interrogation, *Kubark* authorizes interrogators to use hooding or sleep denial to disorient the subject. Attacks on personal identity, including personal or sexual humiliation, can intensify the disorientation. Once the subject is disoriented, interrogators can then use techniques designed to make the person feel as though they are responsible for their own suffering. This might include prolonged standing with arms extended.

One year after the *Kubark Counterintelligence Interrogation Manual* was published, the CIA found an ideal guinea pig to test the manual's techniques. Yuri Nosenko was a KGB colonel who defected to the United States on February 14, 1964. To prove he was a bona fide defector, Nosenko divulged sensitive information to agency officials about covert KGB operations. Nosenko disclosed the names of more than 20 Soviet sleeper agents in the West and revealed that the KGB had bugged the American embassy in Moscow. Nosenko also claimed that he had personally inspected the KGB file on Lee Harvey Oswald. According to the file, he said, the KGB was not involved in JFK's assassination. Rather, the file suggested that Oswald was a hired assassin for a group of right-wing American millionaires who wanted to silence the liberal president permanently. Nosenko's charges caused major concern in the agency. The CIA was divided, as some felt Nosenko was telling the truth and others thought he was a Soviet double agent sent by Moscow to infiltrate the CIA. CIA Director Richard Helms ordered Nosenko interrogated using the procedures outlined in *Kubark*. Nosenko was kept in an isolated cell, but after three months the pressure increased. He was moved to a cell where there was nothing but a single light bulb burning 24 hours per day. After 500 days Nosenko still had not confessed, so he was moved to a specially built steel vault. There he suffered from a nervous breakdown, experiencing hallucinations. After 700 days he still had not confessed, and the CIA began to starve him. They also played music through earphones they forced Nosenko to wear 23 hours per day. Nosenko was dosed with LSD and other mind-altering substances, but still pronounced he was a genuine defector. Helms reluctantly released Nosenko after he had spent 1,277 days in captivity. "Nosenko's exit left the CIA without a subject to use for testing DDD [Debility, Dependency, and Dread] methods and training novice agents. This problem was, again, short-lived. By the late 1960s, the CIA had created a DDD interrogation school at 'The Farm,' a 3753 hectare training site in rural Virginia."[45]

Calling it the CIA's "premier course," Bill Wagner, a former agent, attended the three-week interrogation program at The Farm in 1970. Competition for admission was so strong among ambitious young agents that many secured slots by volunteering for the role of "captives." For weeks, these volunteers, following the *Kubark* method, "were deprived of sleep, kept doused with water in cold rooms, forced to sit or stand in uncomfortable positions for long periods, isolated from sunlight and social contacts, given food deliberately made unappetizing (oversalted, for instance…), and subjected to mock executions."[46] Even for hardened agents participating in a controlled training exercise in their own agency, *Kubark*'s prescriptions were so devastating that at least 10 percent of the volunteers dropped out and many later refused to take the course when their turn came. "By the time this controversial program was shut down during Congress's investigations of the agency in the mid-1970s, an entire generation of CIA agents and interrogators had been trained in psychological torture."[47]

It was not just the CIA that was sponsoring research into various forms of torture and mind control. The U.S. military also studied brainwashing, but instead of focusing on the use of illicit drugs, the Pentagon worked to develop and test physical and psychological techniques that were ostensibly supposed to assist soldiers in "resisting communist coercion." The U.S. Air Force set up a special "prison camp school" at Chinhae, South Korea, in May of 1953. Students there were "taught the psychosis of prisoner-of-war life," according to

Captain Keith D. Young, head of the school. The harsh regimen at Chinhae, crafted from methods used by the Soviets and Communist China, involved food deprivation, endless physical exercise, and solitary confinement. In July 1953, just two months after the Korean school opened, the Defense Department expanded their stress-inoculation training. A new school was founded at Camp Mackall, North Carolina, where both navy and army soldiers were forced to endure isolation, sleep deprivation, and self-inflicted pain.[48]

It was the Air Force, however, that established the most brutal torture for cadets. "In the 1950s, following enactment of the POW Code of Conduct, the Chinhae course was phased out and replaced by a program at Stead Air Force Base in Nevada. By 1955 the Stead school was considered the toughest 'torture school' in the armed forces. The school adopted the nickname SERE, an acronym for Survival, Evasion, Resistance, and Escape."[49] Cadets were forced to live off the land, stranded for 10 days in the Sierra Nevada Mountains with just two and a half days worth of rations. Electric shocks and forced standing were common, as were other endurance-based stress positions. Teams of doctors and psychologists worked at Stead to supervise the ordeals. Although the public learned about the outrageous treatment of cadets at Stead, the school continued.

The Air Force also had a SERE school at Fairchild Air Force Base in Washington state, and in 1993, the Air Force Academy in Colorado Springs, Colorado, began a version of SERE as well. Christian Polintan was a popular, straight-A student at the Colorado Springs facility. He told *20/20* he was forced to wear makeup and a skirt and act as the executive officer's "sex toy." He was forced to grope another male student. *20/20* also found 24 cadets who had been sexually assaulted at the academy.[50]

Although the Cold War ended in the late 1980s, SERE programs remained. The Reagan and first Bush administrations kept SERE techniques legal for the CIA and the military by inserting narrow definitions of torture into the UN Convention Against Torture and various domestic statutes. After 9/11, SERE tortures were transmitted to Afghanistan, Iraq and Cuba by interrogators who had passed through these schools themselves, and by health care workers and instructors with SERE backgrounds. SERE techniques have now become so commonplace that interrogators later charged with murdering detainees have successfully defended themselves in court by claiming that their actions were no worse than what American soldiers themselves endured during training.[51]

In the early 1960s, the U.S. Navy opened two SERE schools: a cold-weather facility at Naval Air Station Brunswick in northwest Maine and a warm-weather school at Warner Springs, California, outside San Diego in the Cleveland National Forest. In 1961, a sailor died when he suffocated inside an isolation box during the course at Warner Springs. Six years later, another student suffered a fatal heart attack during an evasion exercise. Despite the deaths, the Warner Springs SERE school remained open.[52]

During the Vietnam War, the Office of Public Safety (OPS) trained officers at the International Police Academy (IPA). The course manuals used by the IPA are still sealed, but student exams are available and reveal that students had been taught torture techniques.

THE WORST OF THE WORST: PHOENIX

One of the nastiest torture programs was in place during the Vietnam War as well. Counterterrorism programs in Vietnam, already known for kidnapping, abusing, and assassinating Viet Cong leaders, expanded in 1967 under the covert Phoenix program. "With limitless funding and unrestrained powers, Phoenix represented an application of the most advanced interrogation techniques to the task of destroying the Vietcong's revolutionary underground. From its overall strategy to its specific interrogation techniques, Phoenix was the culmination of the CIA's mind-control program." The CIA maintained Phoenix was a counterinsurgency program. However, "it soon devolved into a brutality that produced many casualties but few verifiable results."[53] Phoenix and allied programs allowed the CIA to continue its research into the effects of coercion on human consciousness. No longer restricted to isolated drug trials or simulated psychology experiments, the agency was now operating a nationwide network of interrogation centers that used torture to generate intelligence and provided a limitless supply of human subjects.

Phoenix involved two main components: Provincial Reconnaissance Units (PRUs) and regional interrogation centers. PRUs killed Vietcong Infrastructure (VCI) members and tortured civilians in attempts to gain information about the VCI. CIA interrogators also tortured civilians at the regional interrogation centers. One PRU officer recalls wrapping a detonator cord around the neck of a prisoner and wiring him to a detonator box so that his head was blown off. If a prisoner survived an encounter with the PRU, he was sent for more interrogation at a National Interrogation Center (NIC) in Saigon or a Provincial Interrogation Center (PIC). The most violent interrogations were conducted at PICs, where prisoners were held in solitary confinement in cells the size of closets. Interrogators, many of whom had been trained at Fort Bragg in the United States, frequently used brutal physical torture tactics. A popular saying among the CIA-trained interrogators was *Khong danh cho co,* or "If they are innocent, beat them until they become guilty." Reports detailed prisoners' having electric shocks applied under their fingernails, and one boy had been electrocuted with some device attached to his penis.

In addition to these forms of torture, the CIA used Phoenix prisoners as live human subjects for experimentation.[54]

In one Phoenix-directed experiment, the CIA provided electroshock machines and personnel to conduct electroconvulsive treatment at Bien Hoa Mental Hospital near Saigon. In another experiment at Bien Hoa in 1968, a CIA crew, including a skilled neurosurgeon, inserted tiny electrodes in the brains of three Vietcong prisoners, then used radio frequencies to attempt to induce the men to use violence. The subjects defecated and vomited, but did little else. After a week, they were shot by Green Berets and their bodies were burned.[55]

K. Barton Osborn, who worked with the Phoenix program in 1967–68, described several horrifying incidents. In one, a six-inch dowel was inserted into the ear canal of a detainee. It was tapped through his brain until he died. He described detainees having electronic equipment attached to their vaginas and testicles to shock them into submission. Osborn further testified he had been taught all of these techniques during his time at Fort Holabird and that they could be found in the *Defense Collection Intelligence Manual*. The U.S. Army Intelligence Command investigated Osborn's claims and, though they nitpicked the details, never denied the brutality of Phoenix. A 1968 review of Phoenix in Central Vietnam found widespread use of truncheons and electric shocks for interrogations. While most advisers claimed they did not personally participate in any of the atrocities, they were aware of them and did nothing.[56]

In 1977, former CIA agent Frank Snepp published a best-selling memoir of his experience in Vietnam. With graphic detail, Snepp described the months he spent torturing a captured North Vietnamese man, Nguyen Van Tai. CIA and Vietnamese interrogators found that this dedicated Communist had one "psychic-physical flaw"—a dreaded fear of the cold. The CIA, using its technique of sensory deprivation, kept Tai in solitary confinement inside an all-white, windowless room with just one feature—heavy-duty air conditioners—for more than four years. After none of their tactics seemed to work, Snepp himself, assigned to the case as lead interrogator, maintained the frigid air conditioning and found, through two or three sessions daily, only two flaws to be exploited in Tai's personality—most important, a longing to return to his wife and child. Playing on this weakness, Snepp varied Tai's interview times randomly "so as to throw off his internal clock" and taunted him with the hope of reuniting with his family. These techniques finally worked, and Tai started talking. Just before Saigon fell, however, a "senior CIA official" suggested that Tai should be "disappeared." Tai was then hauled onto an airplane and thrown out over the South China Sea.[57]

Perhaps the most famous incident of torture occurring in Vietnam has come to be known as the My Lai massacre. Lt. Gen. W. R. Peers reported to the secretary of the army on March 14, 1970, the events of the horrifying morning of March 19, 1968. He described how an American, assisted by an ARVN (Army of the Republic of Vietnam) interpreter, interrogated detainees. One technique used to obtain information involved a field telephone with leads attached to various parts of the body that produced electric shocks. Peers also reported that the ARVN interpreter severely kicked and beat detainees, while an American, probably the same one who used the field telephone, inflicted knife wounds on the backs of the detainees' hands and then rubbed salt into the wounds. The discovery of American torture in Vietnam was shocking, and it led to a broader investigation. On May 21, 1971, in a report to the White House, Major General Kenneth J. Hodson, the army judge advocate general, confirmed that American interrogators occasionally used electrical devices to torture Vietnamese during intelligence operations. Certainly the evidence suggests torture was used more than "occasionally," although exactly how often it was employed may never be known due to deficiencies in the reporting of war crimes. Until March 5, 1966, American commanders in Vietnam were only obliged to report war crimes committed by hostile forces. They were not obliged to report any war crimes, including torture, performed by U.S. forces and allies. After 1966, field commanders were obliged to report all war crimes, whether by hostile or U.S. forces. It was not until 1970 that the new rules accounted for the possibility that the commander himself may have been involved, as Lieutenant William Calley was at My Lai.[58]

After almost four years of murky operations, Congress and the press finally exposed the Phoenix program in 1970. William Colby, chief of pacification in Vietnam, testified before the Senate Foreign Relations Committee that, in 1969 alone, Phoenix had killed 6,187 members of the 75,000-person Vietcong infrastructure. Colby later said the number was 20,587, but the Saigon government argued Phoenix killed almost double that, totaling 40,994 Vietcong.[59]

At the end of the Vietnam War, the public, disturbed by the failure in Vietnam and reports of harsh CIA tactics, demanded reform. A number of Congressional inquiries examined alleged unlawful monitoring of antiwar activists and, although they found ample room for criticism, did not specify that the agency had overstepped the law. A special Senate committee, led by Frank Church (D-Idaho), held hearings that probed aggressively for CIA abuses. This inquiry, however, did not probe in depth, and thus barely scratched the surface of the torture training programs and mind-control experiments.[60] In 1973, under the orders of Richard Helms, now the agency's director, most of the documentation of the agency's mind-control activities was destroyed. Other programs like Phoenix were exposed as well, although it is likely that all the details have still not emerged. Following revelations of MK-ULTRA and other unethical CIA practices, President Gerald Ford issued the first Executive Order on Intelligence Activities in 1976. The Executive Order, among other things, prohibited "experimentation with drugs on human subjects, except with the informed consent, in writing and witnessed by a disinterested third party, of each such human subject and in accordance with the guidelines issued by the National Commission for the Protection of Human Subjects for Biomedical and Behavioral Research." Subsequent Executive Orders by presidents Jimmy Carter and Ronald Reagan expanded the directive to apply to any forms of human experimentation: "No agency within the Intelligence Community shall sponsor, contract for, or conduct research on human subjects except in accordance with guidelines issued by the Department of Health, Education, and Welfare. The subject's informed consent shall be documented as required by those guidelines."[61]

DISSEMINATING TORTURE

The CIA techniques outlined in *Kubark* did not die out, however. They moved through two phases of dissemination. First, they were implemented covertly in police-training programs in Asia and Latin America. From 1962 to 1971, the CIA worked through the Office of Public Safety (OPS), a division of U.S.AID that posted police advisers to developing nations. Established by President John F. Kennedy in 1962, in just six years OPS grew into a global anti-Communist operation with an annual budget of $35 million and over 400 U.S. advisers assigned worldwide. By 1971, the program had trained over one million police officers in 47 nations, including 85,000 in South Vietnam and 100,000 in Brazil. In Brazil in the 1960s, the CIA directly trained interrogators. They introduced the Brazilians to field telephone torture, even supplying small hand-held magnetos (*pimentinhas*).[62]

Hidden amidst the larger OPS effort, CIA interrogation training created police agencies across the Third World that became synonymous with human rights abuses. This was especially true in South Vietnam, Uruguay, Iran, and the Philippines.[63] Indeed, "the most notorious Office of Public Safety adviser of the 1960s and 1970s did not work in South-East Asia, but in Latin America. While Phoenix interrogators shocked, bludgeoned, and starved their way through tens of thousands of Vietnamese civilians ostensibly protected by the Geneva Conventions, the United States also spent more than US$51 million on police training in 'America's backyard.'"[64]

Later, implementation of the CIA's torture techniques occurred through collaboration with army teams that advised local counterinsurgency forces, largely in Central America. "Throughout this thirty-year effort, the CIA's torture training grew increasingly brutal, moving by degrees beyond the original psychological techniques to harsh physical methods through its experience in the Vietnam War." Allegations that U.S. AID's International Police Academy taught or encouraged torture emerged in the 1970s, but a General Accounting Office investigation in 1976 determined there was no support for them. In contrast, Amnesty International found widespread use of torture in 24 of the 49 nations hosting OPS police-training teams. An examination of students' theses also revealed evidence of torture training. A 1968 thesis by a Greek student described using drugs or instrumental aids for an effective interrogation, and a 1971 paper by a South Vietnamese student discussed four types of torture: use of force, threats, indirect physical suffering, and mental or psychological torture. "In retrospect, Phoenix proved a seminal experience for the U.S. intelligence community, combining both physical and psychological techniques in an extreme method that would serve as a model for later counterinsurgency training in South and Central America."[66] In the 1970s, Noam Chomsky and Edward Herman made the argument that the United States was a universal distributor of torture tactics. In their book, *The Washington Connection and Third World Fascism,* Chomsky and Herman likened the exportation of torture tactics to the solar system. The United States was at the center of the solar system, and 26 "planets" circled around the sun, representing the nations that were receiving American military aid and police training in the 1970s.[65]

Army Intelligence launched Project X in 1965–66, which was designed, according to a confidential Pentagon memo, "to develop an exportable foreign intelligence package to provide counterinsurgency techniques learned in Vietnam to Latin American countries." For the next quarter of a century, the army transmitted these extreme tactics, by both direct training and through training manuals, to the armies of at least 10 Latin American nations. Under Project X, the U.S. Army Intelligence Center and School in Arizona sent thousands of counterinsurgency-training handbooks to all "nonresident foreign students" who had been nominated by "missions, military groups, attaches, and other US military agencies in the US advisory-training efforts in friendly foreign countries." By the mid-1980s, counterintelligence operations in Colombia and Central America bore "an eerie but explicable resemblance to South Vietnam."[66]

The Philippines also provides an important lesson about the consequences of CIA psychological torture. From 1972 to 1986, torture was a critical component of President Ferdinand Marcos's martial-law rule. Filipino interrogators combined the agency's psychological techniques with a "lurid physical brutality to terrorize, not just their many victims, but an entire society." Under the Marcos regime, 3,257 people were killed and an estimated 35,000 people were tortured. Eventually, however, the torturers became a burden and blight on the military and the nation. In the 1980s, a group of military leaders formed a clique called the Reform the Armed Services Movement (RAM). Led primarily by officers who were experienced in torture, RAM attempted its first coup against Marcos in 1986, and then five more against his successor, President Corazon Aquino. The movement went underground after a coup in 1989, which lasted until a peace accord in 1995. The Philippine torture methods are so similar to the CIA's it is highly likely that the agency trained Marcos's interrogators. In 1978, a Philippine human-rights newsletter reported that the Marcos regime's top torturer, Lieutenant Colonel Rolando Abadilla, was studying at the Command and General Staff College in Fort Leavenworth, Kansas. A year later, another human-rights group claimed that his understudy, Lieutenant Rodolfo "Rudy" Aguinaldo, was on his way to the United States "for six months to one year for additional training under the Central Intelligence Agency."[67]

The murder of an American police adviser in Uruguay finally exposed Public Safety's involvement in torture and led to the abolition of that torture training program. American police adviser Dan A. Mitrione was kidnapped by Tupamero guerillas in Montevideo, Uruguay, and was executed, point blank. Although initially described as an ordinary family man from Indiana who was sent to Uruguay to encourage responsible and humane policing when the story broke in 1970, later investigations revealed that Mitrione may himself have been a torturer. Cuban double agent Manuel Hevia Cosculluela, who worked with the CIA and with Mitrione in Montevideo, said Mitrione demonstrated torture while training Uruguayan police rookies. According to Cosculluela, Mitrione preached that "trainees should use the right amount of pain at the right time, and that interrogation was a complex art of humiliation and breaking down a detainee's sense of reality." Three months before Mitrione's death, Congress heard testimony about the use of torture in police training in Brazil. It took four years for Congress to stop these OPS operations in Brazil.

Although these reforms were well intentioned, Congress had failed to probe for the source of the training. The investigations had exposed some elements of the CIA's mind-control project, but there was no public pressure to restrain the agency's propagation of psychological torture. Furthermore, by the time Congress began investigating the OPS, the CIA had already stopped using it as a cover for its foreign operations, shifting its torture training to the Army's Military Adviser Program.[68]

In 1975, former CIA officer Philip Agee published his memoir, *Inside the Company,* which described his time as an operative in Uruguay. In the book, he explains how he first became aware of the CIA's use of torture in December 1965, when he was in the headquarters of the chief of police.

He initially heard a strange low sound, then moaning. The moaning turned to screams, and Agee realized not only was a man being tortured down the hall, but that it was he who had likely supplied the man's names to his interrogators. Agee was so disturbed that he published the real names of hundreds of CIA officers, and he was hounded for what was perceived as a betrayal. President George H. W. Bush, a former head of the CIA, proclaimed that, while he could forgive many people, he could never forgive Philip Agee. The book even inspired a law prohibiting operatives from revealing what they know. Agee passed away in 2008. Stephen Grey, author of *Ghost Plane,* commented,

Despite his betrayals, Agee exposed a conflict at the heart of intelligence gathering. His story reminds us that when the terrorist attacks of September 11, 2001 led to the lifting again of restrictions on covert CIA warfare, the agency's officers were not evolving some new "thinking out of the box" experimental methods. They were dusting off the old manuals. The Romans and the British used to outsource their imperial tasks. And during the Cold War, the outsourcing of the CIA's difficult jobs had been just a matter of routine.[69]

The U.S. government also provided aid to brutal regimes that tortured. The U.S. government, under the Carter and Reagan administrations, provided financial aid, military support, and military training to brutal governments in El Salvador. More than $6 billion had been provided by 1990. Between 1979 and 1984, between 20,000 and 30,000 people were killed and thousands more "disappeared"—kidnapped, tortured, murdered, and discarded. According to author Kristian Williams, "these atrocities began right away and intensified with US assistance."[70]

    "Among Washington's torture training programs, few were as disastrous as the CIA effort in Iran. After launching a coup in 1953 that restored the shah to direct rule, the CIA helped consolidate his control. By 1959, American and Israeli advisers were involved in the reorganization of the 'Iranian secret police.' The agency helped established the most lethal of the shah's secret police, the Savak, and even trained its interrogators." "As opposition to the shah grew in the 1970s, Savak tortured dissidents cruelly and indiscriminately, fueling angry Iranian student protests in Europe and the United States against the brutality of the shah's police and their detention of fifty thousand political prisoners."[71] Savak's torture techniques, and the role of the CIA in training the perpetrators, were widely publicized when the Shah fell from power in 1979. Three hundred former Savak agents were tried for murder, yet "despite such sordid detail, there was little public reaction in the United States to revelations about the CIA's ties to the shah's secret police."[72]

    In addition to providing guns and money, the U.S. has shared its knowledge and tactics through training schools. One notorious example is the

U.S. Army School of the Americas (SOA), which was developed as a training institute. Since it was formed in 1946, the SOA has trained more than
60,000 Latin American soldiers in counterinsurgency strategy, sniper techniques, commando tactics, psychological operations, military intelligence,
and interrogation. The school was originally based in Panama, but was relo-
cated in 1984 to Fort Benning, Georgia. Faced with serious public criticism, it
officially closed in 2001, but was immediately re-opened as the Western Hemisphere Institute for Security Cooperation (WHISC).[73]

SOA/WHISC graduates are notorious for their brutality. The list of alumni
includes Argentine dictators Roberto Viola and Leopoldo Galtieri, who ruled
that country during the infamous Dirty War in 1981 and 1982, as well as
former Guatemalan dictator Fernando Romeo Lucas Garcia and several high-
ranking Guatemalan leaders known to have orchestrated the rape, torture,
murder, and genocide of that country's Mayan population. The country that
has sent the most students to the school is Columbia. Compilations of SOA
manuals have repeatedly shown that techniques taught at SOA/WHISC were
in violation of international law as well as U.S. policy.[74] Between 1989 and
1991, the SOA issued 693 copies of the handbook as texts in intelligence
courses for students from 10 nations, including Bolivia, Columbia, Peru,
Venezuela, Guatemala, and Honduras. In addition to the SOA manuals, the
U.S. government has authored and produced "torture textbooks."[75] Simultaneous to the dissemination of the SOA manuals, the Army Intelligence
Center at Fort Huachuca, Arizona, ran a mail-order operation as part of Project X, sending complete training packets to foreign officers nominated by
their U.S. counterparts. Interrogation was central to this curriculum.[76] Only
one of these handbooks remains, the *Human Resource Exploitation Training
Manual—1983,* used in Honduras. The manual instructed interrogators to
use threats in ways that make the subject feel he is to blame and to manipu-
late the subject's environment so as to disrupt patterns of time, space, and
the senses. The manual details many techniques, such as the use of blindfolds
and restraints, solitary confinement and sleep deprivation, the manipulation
of temperature and light, the restriction of bedding and access to the toilet,
and, "anticipating General Miller by almost 20 years, the importance of co-
ordination between interrogators and guards."[77] Although the CIA manual
largely addresses psychological threats and acknowledges that physical torture
weakens the "moral caliber of the [security] organization and corrupts those
that rely on it," it does acknowledge that threats of physical torture might
be necessary. In essence, the 1983 Honduras handbook reads in many places
almost verbatim from the *Kubark* manual.

In October 1984, a CIA manual instructing Nicaraguan rebels in techniques of guerilla warfare was given to the U.S. House Intelligence Committee.

This manual, *Psychological Operations in Guerilla Warfare,* was compiled in late 1983 by "John Kirkpatrick," a pseudonym used by a Phoenix veteran and adviser to the Contra rebels who had worked under CIA contract. The handbook states that unpopular government officials can be "neutralized" with the "selective use of violence" and recommends the hiring of criminals to carry out "selective jobs." Reagan first sought to downplay the importance of the manual, claiming that to "neutralize" a person meant nothing more than "you just say to the fellow that's sitting there in the office, 'You're not in the office any more.' "[78] A 1988 article in the *New York Times Magazine* about the abuse occurring in Nicaragua prompted Senate hearings that revealed the 1963 and 1983 CIA manuals. As with Bush administration today, key officials defended the manuals, arguing the techniques described were "harsh" but did not constitute torture.[79]

Eight years after the end of the Cold War, the public first heard the details of the CIA's torture training. In January 1997, the *Baltimore Sun, Washington Post,* and *New York Times* published extracts from the agency's Honduran handbook, *The Human Resource Exploitation Training Manual—1983.* They described it as the latest edition of a thousand-page manual that had been distributed to Latin American armies for 20 years. Under the headline "Torture was taught by CIA," one press account stated: "A newly declassified CIA training manual details torture methods used against suspected subversives in Central America during the 1980s, refuting claims by the Agency that no such methods were taught there." Although these press descriptions of torture were disturbing, public reaction was still mixed.

Citizens and civic groups remained silent. Editorials did not call for an investigation. Congress did not react. Above all, there was no pressure on the CIA to repudiate or reform the techniques revealed in its training manual. Throughout this decade of media expose, congressional criticism, and public protest, attention focused on sensational post-Phoenix excesses such as assassination and physical abuse, leaving the more complex issue of psychological torture largely unexamined. In effect, the public debate complemented the national security bureaucracy's own resolution of the torture question after the Cold war—purging the Phoenix-style physical abuse but preserving the original psychological paradigm as legal and even necessary.[80]

CHANGING PERSPECTIVES?

At the same time the U.S. government tacitly tolerated torture by its Third World allies, several European groups launched a global movement to monitor, respond to, and prevent human-rights abuses. The international community proposed both treaties to ban torture and therapy to treat its victims.

In 1972, Amnesty International, realizing the limitations of its lawyerly approaches of documentation and petition, appealed to the medical profession for support. A group of Danish doctors responded by examining Greek and Chilean refugees to identify the effects of torture. They discovered a form of post-traumatic stress disorder. Of the 200 victims examined, Danish doctors found nearly 70 percent still had mental symptoms many years after their torture, including nightmares, depression, panic attacks, and low energy. "When you've been tortured," explained one of the Danish researchers, Dr. Inge Genefke, "the private hell stays with you through your life if it's not treated." But, provided with the right therapy, the victims could recover. By 1982, these discoveries inspired the founding of the Rehabilitation and Research Centre for Torture Victims (RCT) in Copenhagen. Within a decade, the RCT built 99 treatment centers in 49 countries, developing a therapy regimen that in one year alone, 1992, treated 48,000 victims. These efforts broadened medical understanding of torture and built international support for its abolition.

At the same time, the United States also resumed active participation in the global human-rights movement through both diplomacy and domestic legislation. In 1991, Congress passed the Protection for Victims of Torture Act, which allowed civil suits in U.S. courts against foreign perpetrators who entered American jurisdiction. The legislation, however, used the same narrow definition of "mental pain" that was drafted during the Reagan administration. In 1994, Congress amended the U.S. criminal code, under Section 2340–2340A, to make torture, again as narrowly redefined by the Reagan administration in 1988, a crime punishable by 20 years' imprisonment.

Ironically, it was the liberal Clinton administration that, in approving the UN convention, acceded to the conservative language of Reagan-era reservations, in essence legitimating torture as an open, accepted practice in the U.S. intelligence community. Through their ignorance of CIA covert practices, Congress and the Clinton White House had granted psychological torture a qualified legality in the very legislation designed to ban its practice.[81]

At the time these legislative changes were occurring, the military moved toward making their interrogation policies more consistent with the Geneva Conventions. In September 1992, the army revised their field manual based on experiences obtained in the Gulf War. The manual advised that torture was "illegal, impractical, and immoral." It acknowledged that torture negatively impacts U.S. forces, since it undermines support for their efforts and discredits the United States in foreign nations. The new manual prohibited the most common forms of physical abuse, including food deprivation, electric shock, beating, and infliction of pain through chemicals or bondage. It also prohibited forcing an individual to sit, stand, or kneel for lengths of time in uncomfortable positions.

The sum of these reforms, civil and military, amounted to a contradictory conclusion of the Cold War. Civil authorities had ratified the UN anti-torture convention in ways that legitimated psychological torture within U.S. criminal law; the Army, by contrast, was complying fully with the Geneva Conventions by making all torture, physical and psychological, crimes under the Uniform Code of Military Justice. In effect, Washington had, by the late 1990s, buried this bundle of contradictions—American civil law versus military justice, U.S. criminal code versus UN convention—only to have them erupt with phenomenal force, just a few years later, in the Abu Ghraib controversy.[82]

Despite years of attention, the American public still has a spotty understanding of the United States's history of torture and prisoner abuse. "With the controversy over Abu Ghraib, however, incidents that once seemed isolated gain renewed significance. They form a clear mosaic of a clandestine agency manipulating its government and deceiving its citizens to propagate a new form of torture throughout the Third World."[83]

NOTES

1. McEntee, A. (1996). Law and torture. In Forrest, D. (Ed.), *A glimpse of hell* (pp. 1–20). New York: New York University Press.

2. Conroy, J. (2000). *Unspeakable acts, ordinary people: The dynamics of torture.* New York: Alfred A. Knopf, p. 37.

3. United Nations General Assembly. (1975, December 9). *Declaration on the protection of all persons from being subjected to torture and other cruel, inhuman, and degrading treatment.* Adopted as Resolution 3452. Retrieved in full from the Office of the High Commissioner for Human Rights from http://www.unhchr.udhr/index.html.

4. United Nations General Assembly. (1984, December 10). *Convention against torture and other cruel, inhuman, or degrading treatment or punishment.* Adopted as Resolution 39146. Retrieved in full from the Office of the High Commissioner for Human Rights from http://www.unhchr.udhr/index.html.

5. Amnesty International. (2000, May). *United States of America: A briefing for the UN Committee against Torture.* New York: Amnesty International.

6. United Nations General Assembly (1984).

7. Ibid.

8. McEntee (1996).

9. Jempson, M. (1996). The agencies involved. In Forrest, D. (Ed.), *A glimpse of hell* (pp. 122–126). New York: New York University Press.

10. Ibid.

11. Amnesty International (2000).

12. Hathaway, O. (2004). The promise and limits of the international law of torture. In S. Levison (Ed.), *Torture: An anthology* (pp. 199–212). New York: Oxford University Press.

13. McCoy, A. (2006). *A question of torture: CIA interrogation, from the Cold War to the war on terror.* New York: Metropolitan.

14. Otterman, M. (2007). *American torture.* London: Pluto Press.

15. Otterman (2007).

16. Ibid., p. 21.

17. Ibid., p. 139.

18. McCoy (2006).

19. Otterman (2007).

20. Ibid.

21. Ibid.

22. Ibid.

23. Ibid.

24. Ibid.

25. McCoy (2006).

26. Rejali, D. (2007). *American torture.* Princeton, NJ: Princeton University Press.

27. Shaffer Library on Drug Policy. (n.d.) "Truth" drugs in interrogation. Retrieved June 2, 2007, from http://www.druglibrary.org/Shaffer/history/e1950/MKULTRA/Hearing04.htm.

28. Ibid.

29. Otterman (2007).

30. McCoy (2006).

31. Ibid.

32. Ibid.

33. Ibid.

34. Ibid.

35. Ibid.

36. Ibid.

37. Ibid.

38. Ibid.

39. Ibid.

40. Ibid.

41. Otterman (2007).

42. Ibid.

43. Ibid.

44. Ibid.

45. Ibid.

46. Ibid.

47. Ibid.

48. Ibid.

49. Ibid.

50. Ibid.

51. Ibid.

52. Ibid.

53. McCoy (2006).

54. Valentine, D. (2000). *The Phoenix program*. Lincoln, Nebraska: iUniverse.com.

55. Ibid.

56. Ibid., p. 68.

57. Snepp, F. (1980). *Interval: The American debacle in Vietnam and the fall of Saigon*. London: Allen Lane.

58. Ibid.

59. Cockburn, A., & St. Clair, J. (1999). *Whiteout: The CIA, drugs, and the press*. New York: Verso.

60. Ibid.

61. Otterman (2007).

62. Rejali (2007).

63. Otterman (2007).

64. Ibid.

65. Ibid.

66. Ibid.

67. Ibid.

68. Ibid.

69. Ibid.

70. Grey, S. (2006). *Ghost plane*. New York: St. Martin's Press, p. 10.

71. Williams (2006).

72. Ibid.

73. Ibid.

74. Harbury, J. (2005). *Truth, torture, and the American way*. Boston: Beacon.

75. Ibid.

76. Ibid.

77. Otterman (2007).

78. Ibid.

79. McCoy (2006).

80. Ibid.

81. Ibid.

82. Ibid.

83. Ibid.

5

Domestic Prison Abuse Today

This chapter describes abuse that has been and still is occurring throughout the U.S. criminal justice system. It begins with a brief overview of the types of abuse that are being perpetrated, then reviews relevant international agreements from the last several decades that were intended to protect prisoners and suspects from unlawful interrogations, abuse, and experimentation. The chapter next focuses on abuse by police, chronicling the most common forms, highlighting the most troublesome cases, and examining competing explanations for abuse by law enforcement officers. Next, a review of abuse that occurs in detention facilities is presented. Included in this review is examination of abuse of men, women, juveniles, minorities, and immigrants. Particular attention is given to the ways prison abuse in the domestic United States has helped set the stage for abuse of detainees overseas. In addition, conditions on death rows, as well as methods used to execute prisoners in the United States, are examined.

Adrian Lomax, author of *The Celling of America: An Inside Look at the U.S. Prison Industry* and a former inmate in Wisconsin, argued that, while torture takes many forms, it is and has always been present in the United States, from police practices to prison environments.[1] Episodes of torture are not just isolated incidents but systemic in nature. For instance, in Los Angeles police allowed their K-9s to bite more than 900 suspects, just as prisoners at Abu Ghraib in Iraq were tortured by dogs.[2] In 1995, a federal judge found routine abuse by staff, excessive use of electronic stun devices, beatings, and brutality at Pelican Bay Prison in California. The judge concluded the violence "appears to be open, acknowledged, tolerated and sometimes expressly approved" by high-ranking corrections officials. Similar to the Pelican Bay decision, in 1999, a federal judge concluded that Texas prisons were pervaded by a "culture of sadistic and malicious violence." Guards were allowing gang leaders to buy and sell other inmates for sex.[3]

In recent years, guards in U.S. prisons have abused inmates in numerous ways, including dousing them with chemical sprays, beating them with fists and batons, stomping on them, kicking them, choking them, slamming them face first onto concrete floors, stunning them with electronic devices, and shooting them. Inmates have suffered broken jaws, smashed ribs, perforated eardrums, missing teeth, and burn scars, in addition to the obvious psychological scars and emotional pain. Some have died. When Florida inmate Frank Valdez died in 1999, every rib in his body was broken. The imprints of boot marks were obvious on his body, and his testicles were badly swollen. Guards admitted they "struggled with him," but denied they had used excessive force. They claimed most of his injuries had been "self-inflicted." Again, the parallels to abuse overseas are obvious.[4]

In Maricopa County, Arizona, Sheriff Joe Arpaio, who often dresses male jail inmates in pink underwear as a means of humiliation, introduced live "jail cam" broadcasts on the Internet in 2000. Three cameras captured the holding and searching cells of the jail. Footage revealed shots of strip searches, inmates bound in "restraint chairs," and even, for a while, unobstructed views of women using the toilet. The broadcasts were eventually copied onto porn Web sites.[5] Yet Arpaio has many defenders who credit him with reforming corrections in Maricopa County and who would never describe these actions as torture or cruel, inhuman, or degrading treatment.

Even more appalling images are available in the documentary film *Maximum Security University*, about California's Corcoran Prison. For years at Corcoran, guards set up fights among prisoners, bet on the outcome, and then often shot the men for fighting, seriously wounding at least 43 and killing 8 just in the period 1989–1994. The film features official footage of five separate incidents in which guards, with no legal justification, shoot down and kill unarmed prisoners.[6] Just this January, a videotape at a California facility captured two officers beating and kicking two inmates. One officer struck an inmate approximately 20 times in the face; another officer is shown kicking a handcuffed inmate in the head.[7]

Even detained children and youth are subject to staff brutality and abuse. They too are kicked, beaten, punched, choked, and sexually preyed upon by adult staff. The Massachusetts juvenile correctional system regularly "punished their charges by forcing them to drink from toilets, to kneel on a stone floor with pencils under their knees, to remain naked for days in dark concrete cells, and to submit to falanga—a form of torture in which the soles of the feet are beaten."[8] The Maryland State Police recently filed criminal assault charges against staff at a youth facility because of an incident in which one guard restrained a youth while three others kicked him and punched him in the face. In January 2004, the U.S. Department of Justice reported on terrible conditions at Arizona's juvenile detentions centers, including sexual abuse of the children by staff members (and fellow inmates) that occurred "with disturbing frequency" and a level of physical abuse that was "equally disturbing."[9] In Panama City, Florida, juvenile boot camps were shut down in 2006 after guards killed Martin Lee Anderson, which was captured on videotape.

Both male and female prisoners face rape and sexual abuse perpetrated by police and prison staff. Women are especially vulnerable, due to the large number of male correctional officers who work at female-only facilities. Correctional officers will bribe, coerce, or violently force inmates into granting sexual favors, including oral sex or intercourse. Prison staff have laughed at and ignored the pleas of male prisoners seeking protection from rape by other inmates.[10]

One common form of torture is the denial of medical attention. Guards are rarely punished, even when they are aware of an inmate's need for medical attention but ignore it. In some cases guards are actually responsible for the inmate's need for medical attention. In 1990, guards at Waupun Correctional Institution in Wisconsin used several belts to restrain inmate Donald Woods to the steel-frame bed in his cell. Wisconsin law requires that a nurse check on inmates who are restrained this way every 30 minutes, due to the potential for health problems. Although Nurse Beth Dittman did check on Woods and found him nonresponsive several times, she never sought help or offered any form of medical attention. Woods died of asphyxiation the next day. Instead of being fired, Dittman was actually promoted. As Lomax explained,

Beth Dittman is no less a criminal than Lynndie England, the Army private who earlier this year pled guilty to abusing detainees at Abu Ghraib prison in Iraq. Yet because Dittman works in a prison inside the U.S. rather than in an American military prison in Iraq, her abuse of the human rights of inmates is treated in a manner strikingly different than the fate meted out to England.[11]

The case described above highlights the complexities of holding perpetrators accountable for abuse of prisoners. Many times, their actions are not defined as torture or cruel, inhuman, and degrading punishment, although they are clearly in violation of international human-rights laws and agreements as well as domestic legislation. Indeed, most of the men and women who work in U.S. prisons are decent professionals who have never physically abused or intentionally degraded an inmate. As in detention centers overseas, absent or inadequate leadership, oversight, and external scrutiny leads to conditions in which abuse is far more likely.

Since the United States ratified the Convention Against Torture (CAT) in 1994 (described in the previous chapter), international human-rights monitor Amnesty International (AI) has continually expressed concern about the nation's use of torture and cruel, inhuman, and degrading treatment. In particular, AI has documented widespread abuse in U.S. prisons. AI has noted a lack of oversight bodies to monitor police and detention centers, as well as inadequate sanctions against police and prison officials who violate human-rights legislation. The United States still falls far short in the prevention of torture and abuse as well as in the documentation of incidents and practices used in prisons, even though Articles 2, 11, and 16 of the CAT require member nations to take effective legislative, administrative, and judicial steps to prevent torture and ill-treatment and to keep systemic review of interrogation rules, practices, and arrangements for custody and treatment of detainees. AI is also concerned that in the United States there are no binding national standards on the use of restraints and stun guns. AI has also expressed concern over the lack of national data on police use of force. The 1994 Crime Control Act required the U.S. Attorney General to collect data and to write an annual report about police use of force, yet Congress did not fund the measure.[12]

AI's gravest concerns are about brutality and inhumane conditions in jails and prisons. Supermax prisons, designed for intense deprivation, electroshock, and other cruel restraint methods, are some of the most problematic. Several jurisdictions have reintroduced chain gangs, which AI calls cruel, inhuman, and degrading. AI is also concerned about the use of restraint chairs, which are described in more detail in this chapter. Prisoners have been restrained in these chairs for minor acts of noncompliance. They have often been hooded and tortured. Prisoners describe being stripped naked, left for hours in their own wastes, and being shocked with stun guns or pepper spray while in these chairs.[13]

INTERNATIONAL AGREEMENTS RELEVANT TO ABUSE OF PRISONERS

In 1947, the Nuremberg Code provided an outline for the fair treatment of and experimentation with prisoners. After the 1947 Nuremberg Code, the next major initiative to protect prisoners from cruel and inhumane treatment as research subjects was the Belmont Report. The report outlined three major ethical principles regarding research with human subjects: respect for persons, beneficence, and justice. The report further articulated the need for informed consent, special protections for those with diminished autonomy, and a requirement to do no harm. Title 45, Part 46 of the Code of Federal Regulations was developed in 1978 and then revised in 2001. It offered still further protection for prisoners.[14]

In 1955, the First United Nations Congress on the Prevention of Crime and the Treatment of Offenders was also held in Geneva, Switzerland. The Congress set forth specific guidelines for the humane treatment of prisoners held in domestic institutions. These *Standard Minimum Rules for the Treatment of Prisoners* were approved by the UN's Economic and Social Council and put into effect in 1957. The *Rules* consist of two parts: Part I deals with the overall management of correctional facilities and applies to all prisoners, and Part II covers special categories addressed in the various sections of Part I. Part I of the *Rules* outlines recommendations regarding prisoners' rights and concerns over the humane treatment of inmates. Part I provisions are to be applied impartially regardless of race, color, sex, language, religion, political or other opinions, national or social origin, or other status. The Part I *Rules* cover a number of topics, including prisoners' registration, separation of categories, accommodation, personal hygiene, clothing and bedding, food, exercise, medical services, discipline and punishment, restraint, information to and complaints by prisoners, contact with the outside world, books, religion, personal property, notification of death, illness, transfer, and removal of prisoners.[15]

According to the *Rules,* at least one person on the prison's medical staff is to be trained in psychiatry. Psychiatric services are supposed to be available for the diagnosis and treatment of mental illness. Medical staff is expected to conduct regular inspections, including examination of the prison's food, overall cleanliness, sanitation, heating, lighting, ventilation, clothing and bedding, and exercise. Prenatal and postnatal assistance must be made available to pregnant inmates.[16]

On March 23, 1976, the International Covenant on Civil and Political Rights (ICCPR), described in the previous chapter, echoed Article 7 of the UN Declaration of Human Rights in prohibiting medical or scientific experiments on subjects without their informed consent. These two instruments paved the way for the development of the UN Human Rights Committee and the December 18, 1982, adoption by the General Assembly of the Principles of Medical Ethics, which prohibits medical personnel from being involved in torture.[17]

The UN also set forth guidelines concerning discipline and punishment. Although the *Rules* acknowledge that discipline and order must be upheld with firmness, they specify that there must be no unnecessary restrictions on inmates except those required to maintain safe custody and well-ordered institutional life. Disciplinary offenses must be brought before an administrative authority and should always be determined by a legal proceeding. Prisoners may be punished only in accordance with the law and never twice for the same crime. The UN prohibited any type of corporal punishment, isolation in a dark cell, or any cruel, inhuman, or degrading punishments for disciplinary offenses. Close confinement or reduction in diet are also not appropriate punishments, unless a medical doctor has examined the inmate and certified in writing that he or she is able to withstand it. Related to issues of discipline, the instruments of restraint (e.g., handcuffs, chains, irons, straightjackets) should never be applied as punishment. The UN does not condone the use of chains or irons as restraints. Moreover, other methods of restraint should only be used during transfers, for medical reasons, or by order of the warden when other means of control do not work.[18]

The November 20, 1989, adoption, and the September 2, 1990, enforcement, of the UN Convention on the Rights of the Child extended the prohibition against torture and cruel, inhuman, and degrading treatment to children and youth. Other international declarations that have influenced some countries to develop domestic legislation prohibiting torture and cruel, inhuman, or degrading treatment of prisoners include: the Declaration on the Elimination of Violence Against Women in December 1993; the Declaration on the Protection of Women and Children in Emergency and Armed Conflicts in December 1974; United Nations Rules for Protection of Juveniles Deprived of their Liberty in December 1990; Body Principles for the Protection of All Persons under Any Form of Detention or Imprisonment in December 1988; Basic Principles for the Treatment of Prisoners in December 1990; Standard Minimum Rules for the Treatment of Prisoners in July 1957; the Code of Conduct for Law Enforcement Officials in December 1979; Basic Principles for the Use of Force and Firearms by Law Enforcement Officials in September 1990; Guidelines on the Role of Prosecutors in September 1990; and the Declaration on the Protection of All Persons from Enforced Disappearance in December 1992.[19]

The imprisonment of women poses unique challenges. "Far from providing adequate protection to women, states all around the world have connived in these abuses, have covered them up, have acquiesced in them and have allowed them to continue unchecked."[20] The United Nations Charter of Human Rights specifies that female inmates should be guarded exclusively by women. Although European countries follow this guideline, the United States has not always followed suit.[21]

PRISON EXPERIMENTS

Sadistic experiments on prisoners are and have been commonplace throughout world history. Prisoners have long been considered expendable, and thus have been the focus of a variety of so-called research projects. The 1960s brought continued growth in human experimentation in prisons, furthered by a new relationship between penal institutions and pharmaceutical companies and little oversight by Food and Drug Administration officials. The government exacerbated the problem in 1962 when, in the aftermath of the Thalidomide disaster, the FDA required pharmaceutical companies to conduct three phases of human trials before allowing a drug to be marketed. Phase I drug testing now required large pools of healthy subjects for non-therapeutic experiments, and the prior practice of using a few hospital patients was judged totally inadequate. Pharmaceutical companies sought out private or university-affiliated physicians who had access to a stockpile of human material—large numbers of people isolated behind prison walls and living in highly regimented conditions proved ideal. A significant bonus for the drug companies and doctors was the fact that the imprisoned masses locked inside these institutions were willing to expose themselves to more risk for less money than the experimental subjects outside of prison walls. "Finally, government overseers would be less likely to visit the fortress-like institutions holding dangerous criminals than tree-lined, ivy-covered college campuses."[22]

Consequently, experiments on prisoners were common, and increasingly dangerous. In the 1960s, more than 130 Oregon prisoners had their testicles irradiated in an effort to discern how much radiation U.S. astronauts could handle during space flights. Many complained, and men from this trial are still emerging with complaints of prostate cancer, vision loss, vascular problems, and sexual identity questions. By the early 1970s, critics of prisoner experimentation emerged with a louder voice. Prominent among them was Jessica Mitford, author of *Kind and Unusual Punishment.* Ms. Mitford emphasized the many ways the United States was departing from the Nuremberg Code and testified before a Senate subcommittee. In the summer of 1974, Congressman Parren Mitchell introduced H.R. 16160, a bill intended to limit the use of inmates in medical research. The bill died in the 93rd Congress.[23]

POLICE OFFICERS AND TORTURE

Police continue to torture suspects during interrogations, despite critical Supreme Court decisions intended to specify the rights of suspects. In *Miranda v. Arizona,* the Court determined that suspects in police custody must be told they have the right to remain silent, that anything said can be used in court, and that they have the right to an attorney. They must be informed that an attorney will be provided if they cannot pay. Suspects can waive their rights, although there is still much debate regarding whether all groups have the necessary capacity to understand what they are waiving. In 2000, the Supreme Court reaffirmed *Miranda,* to the surprise, and chagrin, of many. Police still get around the waiver requirement, however. One way they do so is by substituting "interviewing" for custodial interrogation. Since the interviewee is not yet a suspect in custody and is presumptively free to leave, the detectives may question without giving *Miranda* warnings.

However much we think we deplore deception and trickery by American police, the post-*Miranda* era of deceptive questioning has ushered in an era of psychological pressure as an alternative to physical brutality, which in some instances could surely have been characterized as "torture." This is not to presume that police brutality has disappeared on the streets and in the stationhouses. But physical force is rarely, if ever, used when the police are seeking evidence that can be introduced in a trial.[24]

Psychological techniques dominate modern examples of police-perpetrated torture. Many police tactics, such as use of pressure points or directly applying pepper spray, do not generally leave visible marks, nor do they look to outsiders as bad as they feel. This requires the public to have to believe either one side or another, and many people are far more likely to believe law enforcement officers than someone suspected of a crime (whether he or she is guilty or not). Even more difficult for the public to recognize are patterns of abuse.

In Prince George's County, Maryland, police interrogated Keith Longtin for 38 hours following the murder of his wife. Detectives showed Longtin photographs of his wife's bloody, mutilated, naked corpse and taunted him as he wept. Longtin says that when he tried to leave, a detective "said he was going to handcuff me to the wall and beat the crap out of me if I didn't sit down." Over the course of two days, Longtin was only allowed 50 minutes of sleep, while detectives tag teamed him with their questioning. The first would describe the murder in excruciating detail and the next would ask questions about the crime. Longtin eventually repeated what he had been told. Police reported he "knew" information only the perpetrator would know and he spent eight months in jail before DNA proved his innocence. The case generated a yearlong investigation by the *Washington Post,* which concluded that Prince George's County homicide detectives often coerced confessions. They found interrogations lasting as long as 80 hours, with some including brutal beatings. Another lengthy interrogation involved a 17-year-old black man named Corey Beale. Beale had a learning disability that significantly impacted his ability to understand spoken language. While being interrogated about his knowledge of a murder that occurred at a party he attended, police threw him into a wall and beat him up. Beale served 10 months in jail before he was released because new evidence exonerated him.[25]

In some cases, the police use torture absent any type of investigation. In 1989, Kenneth Watson, a black man, was arrested for leaving the site of an accident. According to inmates present at the time, sheriff's deputies in Monroe, Michigan, taped Watson's mouth shut and chained him to a drain cover on his cell floor. Then, shouting racist slurs, they beat him and kicked him for several hours until he lost consciousness. Watson suffered a broken wrist and fractured skull, as well as assorted cuts and bruises. He sued and, in December 1992, received as $600,000 settlement. No deputies were penalized for the attack.[26]

"Some features of the criminal justice system practically invite abuse. Electroshock stun equipment, for example—stun guns, stun belts, and stun shields—have all the features of ideal torture tools. Portable, easy to use, and with the potential to inflict severe pain without leaving substantial visible marks on the human body, electroshock stun equipment is, Amnesty International believes, particularly open to abuse by unscrupulous law enforcement officials."[27] One of the first uses of stun technology by police emerged during the civil rights era. In April 1962, Alabama police used electric prods to "herd Negro demonstrators." A year later, the *New York Times* showed photos of Alabama highway patrolmen repeatedly shocking 10 Freedom Walkers with electric cattle prods. "As one of the Negroes flinched and twisted in the grip of the four troopers, an elderly toothless white man shouted from a roadside pasture: 'Stick him again! Stick him again!'" It wasn't long before prods appeared in other civil rights conflicts.[28]

The first commercial stun gun, the NOVA XR-5000, appeared in 1985. More than 7,000 law enforcement agencies used Taser stun guns as of 2005. These stun guns give five-second, 50,000-volt shocks either by direct contact with a subject or by firing barbed darts at the subject. They are, according to author Kristian Williams, generally used against "*inarticulate* subjects, with *criminal or institutional* histories, and in cases of *intense public disapproval of those crimes.*" In 1986 prosecutors indicted five NYPD officers on charges of using stun guns between 1985 and 1986 to torture African American and Hispanic youths suspected of drug dealing. In 1985, a San Diego private security guard admitted using stun guns against the homeless and transients. In 1986, the LAPD discovered two officers had repeatedly shocked a Hispanic juvenile who they thought had stolen stereo parts.[29]

In the 1990s, records from one health clinic in the Bronx show that 11 percent of its patients reported "electric torture." Between 2001 and 2005, at least 140 people died after being shocked with Tasers, most of whom were unarmed at the time. In fact, the most common reason police use Tasers, according to a 2002 study, is for verbal noncompliance. In 2004, Denver police allegedly used stun guns on handcuffed prisoners, including at least one pregnant woman. This all occurred while they were in squad cars or chained to the wall of booking rooms.[30]

According to Williams, a lucky opportunity in the 1980s secured the continued used of stun technology. In 1982, the Los Angeles City Council banned police use of chokeholds during arrests. Records indicated that LAPD officers had killed 15 people in the previous seven years while holding them in chokeholds, and the public was outraged. According to reports, "the police department demonstrated laxity in pursuing use-of-force alternatives." Police initially switched to swinging metal batons, but complaints of excessive force doubled. LAPD-related litigation costs soared from $891,000 to $11.3 million. Stun technology was perceived as another alternative.[31]

Proponents of Tasers claim they offer law enforcement an option besides firearms in cases where force is required. Although it may be true Tasers are an additional option, statistics suggest they are not necessarily being used in lieu of firearms. Within two years of having adopted the Taser, it was the most frequently used weapon by Orange County, Florida, sheriff's officers. But, the overall number of times officers used force increased 37 percent. Thus the Taser may provide an additional force option, but may also make it more likely that officers use force when it is not warranted.

A somewhat new but troublesome variety of electroshock weaponry is the stun belt. Stun belts fasten around a prisoner's waist and can be activated by remote control, which sends a 50,000-volt shock through the body for eight seconds. The shock causes the victim's muscles to spasm, often causing him or her to fall. This can, of course, lead to serious injury. The shock is also "fiercely painful, totally incapacitating, and undeniably humiliating." Often, people who have been shocked by a stun belt spontaneously defecate or urinate. Amnesty International has said use of a stun belt, even when not activated, is cruel and unusual. This is because subjects must constantly be aware of the possibility of being shocked. This is, of course, exactly the point, according to some law enforcement agents.[32]

Craig Shelton, an inmate who was being transferred from Hutchinson Correctional Facility to Larned Correctional Mental Health Facility in Kansas described his experience being shocked by a stun belt when he dozed off during the trip:

[I] woke up a short time later to a very intense shocking pain running through my body. This electrical current was so intense that I thought I was actually dying. I had not been causing any trouble, I was belly chained, shackled, seat belted in, and there was a fence between the officers and me, so there was absolutely no reason for them to be using this device on me. The rest of the trip to Larned Correctional Mental Health Facility is kind of a blur to me.... When we arrived at Larned, I was unloaded from the van and taken to a holding cell.... Once I was in the cell, several officers came into the cell and again I was shocked by the stun-belt. This electrical blast knocked me to the floor, and I could hear the officers that were around me laughing and making jokes.[33]

Pepper spray is another tool widely used by law enforcement because it is easy to carry, easy to use, and poses little risk to the officer. The spray, which comes from cayenne pepper, causes the eyes to tear and close involuntarily. It creates a painful burning sensation on the skin and mucus membranes, and it causes the airways to swell, restricting breathing. Even mild exposure can be incapacitating. "For all of these reasons, and because it leaves little in the way of long-term evidence, pepper spray is liable to be abused, and makes a convenient tool for torturers."[34]

Another tactic used occasionally by police involves simulated or real asphyxiation. Police officers put the prisoner's head into a cheap plastic bag, tie the bottom, and then remove it before the prisoner asphyxiates. American police called this technique "bagging." Latin Americans, who have also used the technique, call it *la bolsa* (the bag), while others refer to it as the "dry submarine" or *submarine seco,* a Spanish expression from the 1970s. Bagging was frequently used by Chicago police during the 1970s and 1980s. The technique was used elsewhere as well. In 1980, New Orleans police chained several detainees to chairs, beat them with fists and books, and, in two cases, bagged them.[35]

Perhaps the worst example of police-perpetrated torture was inflicted on Haitian immigrant Abner Louima. On August 9, 1997, Louima was arrested outside a Brooklyn nightclub following an altercation between police and some of the club's patrons. Louima was not involved in the conflict, but police mistook him for another man who had been fighting. The officers who transported Louima to the precinct stopped twice on the way to the station and beat him. Later, inside the station house, Officer Justin Volpe removed Louima from his cell and led him to a bathroom. While another officer held Louima down, Volpe shoved a broken broom handle into his rear end, and then into his mouth. Louima was returned to the holding cell, where he waited in pain until other inmates complained that he was bleeding. He was then moved to a hospital, where a nurse reported the abuse to Internal Affairs. Louima's injuries included a ruptured bladder, a torn colon, and broken teeth.

Officer Volpe was arrested and charged with assault. He pleaded guilty and was sentenced to 30 years. Officers Thomas Weise and Thomas Bruder were charged with obstructing justice. "Justin Volpe's attack on Abner Louima is particularly well-known, but it is, unfortunately, far from unique." Like the

Louima case, most of the modern cases of known U.S. police brutality are retributive and have not taken place during interrogations. "Had the brutality practices on Mr. Louima been carried out in connection with an interrogation, rather than as retribution for a false belief that Mr. Louima had punched Officer Volpe, it would surely qualify as torture."[36] As the Louima case highlights, torturers utilize a

continuous theme of sexualized abuse, encompassing a startling range of practices: penetration of the genital and anal openings, using the perpetrators' bodies, sticks, bottles, truncheons, and (at Abu Ghraib) a chemical light; groping of the breasts, genitals, or buttocks; forced prostitution; coerced abortions; obscene gestures or sexually graphic remarks; mutilation of the genitals by crushing or electrocution; and rituals of humiliation involving strip searches and body cavity searches, prolonged nudity, pornographic poses and photography, and other violations of sexual taboos and gender norms. These practices occur in police stations, jails, prisons, and military bases, on public streets and in "undisclosed locations." The victims include men, women, and children; suspects, convicts, political enemies, and people who are manifestly innocent of any offense. The perpetrators are cops, guards, soldiers, mercenaries, paramilitary troops, intelligence officers, secret police, and sometimes other inmates. This catalog of atrocities is remarkable for its diversity, certainly, but more so for what it seems to have in common.[37]

The most endemic allegations of police-perpetrated torture have come from Chicago's Area 2, in the south of the city. For nearly two decades the part of the city's jails known as Area 2 was the center of what has been called the "systematic torture of dozens of African-American males by Chicago police officers." In 1990, the Chicago Police Department's Office of Professional Standards conducted a study of police torture in Area 2. Michael Goldston, the city investigator, identified 50 cases between 1973 and 1986 involving over 30 officers. Goldston identified a number of different torture techniques, including electrotorture, suspension, and bagging. Other reports indicate detectives were extracting confessions of guilt by means of torture as early as 1968. In total, more than 135 people say they were subjected to abuse by police, including having guns forced into their mouths, bags places over their heads, and electric shocks inflicted to their genitals. Most of the alleged incidents in Area 2 implicated Commander Jon Burge and the detectives he supervised. Burge was dismissed in the early 1990s. At the time of his dismissal, Burge was the commander of the Area 3 detective division, "outranking 99 percent of all policemen in the city."[38]

In 2003, Governor George Ryan commuted the sentence of all 167 prisoners on Illinois's death row. Four men have been released from death row after government investigators concluded torture led to their wrongful convictions. Yet the case around Area 2 is nowhere near resolution—to date, not one Chicago police officer has been charged with any crime. Since his dismissal, Burge retired to Florida, where he continues to collect a pension.

David Bates is one of the men who was tortured in Area 2. In October 1993, several officers knocked on his mom's door and told her he was going to be taken away but would be coming home shortly. Allegedly, they had some questions regarding a case. When Bates got to the station, he let the officers or detectives know that he had nothing to do with the case and knew nothing about it. The questioning went on for two days. He endured five sessions of torture each day, starting with slaps and kicks and threats. Two particular sessions of torture he described as "very devastating." These times, a plastic bag was placed over his head while he was punched and kicked.[39]

Governor Ryan not only commuted the sentences of all of those on death row, but he looked specifically at four cases of torture by Burge and others. He found that the victims in those cases were innocent, that they had been tortured into giving false confessions, and he gave full innocence pardons to those four individuals. Those individuals are Aaron Patterson, Stanley Howard, Madison Hobley, and Leroy Orange. Those four men have now brought lawsuits in federal court.

Ryan, however, bears some responsibility for the failure to hold Burge and the others accountable. Richard Daley was previously the State's Attorney of Cook County. In 1982, when the Andrew Wilson case broke, the superintendent of police was informed by the head of the prison hospital where Wilson was being held that there was serious evidence of torture. He said that Andrew Wilson had physical evidence that supported his statements that he had been tortured by electric shock and beating. Wilson had 15 different injuries, including burns, lacerations, and bruises. The head of the hospital was so shocked he brought it straight to the superintendent of police. The superintendent of police then brought it straight to Richard Daley. Daley knew that Andrew Wilson had been charged with very serious offenses—shooting two police officers and killing them. So Daley decided that he would not investigate the torture allegations, and no one was prosecuted.[40]

For the next eight years, Daley was head of the State's Attorney's office, which took more than 55 confessions from 55 different victims of Burge and police torture. Daley again ignored the allegations of abuse and put all the accused behind bars, many of them on death row. Again, he did not even investigate the continuing allegations that were coming out of Burge's police headquarters. Daley then became the mayor of the city of Chicago. In the early 1990s, another investigation was conducted that found evidence of systemic torture. The superintendent of police suppressed that report, and he and the mayor went on to denounce the findings as mere rumor and innuendo.[41]

According to Attorney Flint Taylor, the city has paid over $5 million to a set of private lawyers to represent the police officers, including Burge, in all the cases against them. Burge and the more than 50 detectives that are named in one or more of the 192 cases are all getting free lawyers, who are generally advising them to take the Fifth Amendment. "So you now have the spectacle of, in these federal cases and in front of the special prosecutor, that former and present law enforcement officers, rather than to answer questions about whether they tortured and abused people like David Bates and the men on death row, they have all lined up and taken the Fifth Amendment as to each and every allegation of police torture." Taylor, an attorney with the People's Law Office in Chicago, the group that has represented many of the men who have voiced torture allegations, explained that the lack of real resolution has been tremendously detrimental, not only to the individuals involved but as a blight on the entire judicial process.

Part of the difficulty in prosecuting the officers has been that the men involved were career policemen,

men who appeared to comply with professional rules, who were evaluated regularly by their supervisors, and who were even commended by the city for their conduct. By contrast, the prisoners who made allegations were hard to believe. Andrew Wilson, the most important victim, had spent most of his life in institutions, having been on the street for a total of four months in twenty-five years. He was impulsive, emotional and adolescent; in short, "his ability to function in the community" was "severely limited."[42]

Unfortunately, in Chicago, many feel "there is no community outrage. People don't care. As in every society in which people are tortured, there's a torture book class in Chicago. It's African American men, most of them with criminal records. And they're just beyond the pale of our compassion. We just don't care."[43]

Given that violence by law enforcement officers is quite pervasive, it is shocking yet not surprising that discussions of police brutality so frequently focus on the behavior of individual officers. The explanation offered most frequently to explain police misconduct, and the one favored by police commanders and their ideological allies, is often called the "rotten apples" theory. The theory suggests that police abuse is exceptional, and that the officer who misuses his or her power is part of a tiny minority. Along these lines, it is unfair to judge other officers or departments by the misbehavior of a few. Similar to the Bush administration's approach, another response to allegations against police or corrections officials has been to deny that torture is actually occurring. In the case of Abner Louima, then–New York Mayor Rudy Giuliani and the New York City Police Department both decried the attack as depraved, but claimed it was the work of a handful of rogue cops.[44] Jorge Martinez, a spokesman for the Justice Department, said, "None of these cases rise to the level of being torture."[45] Yet these are all clearly acts perpetrated by a public official, and the actual allegations most certainly are covered by the torture definitions described by various international agreements and court precedents. The rotten apples explanation "is a handy tool for diverting attention away from the institution, its structures, practices, and social role, pushing the blame, instead, onto some few of its agents. It is, in other words, a means of protecting the organization from scrutiny, and of avoiding change."[46]

The opposite argument focuses on police culture and addresses the violence as institutional. Rather than seeing torturers as exceptionally sadistic or mentally ill, this explanation suggests that any one of us, in the right (or wrong) culture, might commit disgraceful acts. John Conroy, author of *Unspeakable Acts, Ordinary People*, explained that he titled his book that because "we want our torturers to be monsters, but it turns out that they're just ordinary people like you and me."[47] Both the formal and informal aspects of an organization can help create a climate in which unnecessary force is accepted, and sometimes encouraged.

Among the formal aspects contributing to violence are the organization's official policies, its identified priorities, the training it offers its personnel, its allocation of resources, and its system of promotion, awards, and other incentives. When these aspects of an organization encourage violence—whether or not they do so intentionally, or even consciously—we can speak of brutality being promoted "from above." This understanding has been well applied to the regimes of certain openly thuggish leaders—Bull Connor, Richard Daley, Frank Rizzo, Daryl Gates, Rudolph Giuliani (to name just a few)—but it needn't be so overt to have the same effect. On the other hand, when police culture and occupational norms support the use of unnecessary violence, we can describe brutality as being supported "from below." Such informal conditions are a bit harder to pin down, but they certainly have their consequences. We may count among their elements insularity, indifference to the problem of brutality, generalized suspicion, and the intense demand for personal respect.[48]

ABUSE IN DETENTION

Abuse may continue or even escalate once a person is convicted and sentenced to some form of detention. Allegations of abuse in the United States began with the very first prison. The first prison was built at Elmira, New York, in 1876. In theory, prisoners there were provided treatment, not punishment. Warden Zebulon Brockway implemented a system much like today's parole, whereby an inmate who complied with regulations and did well in school could be released into the care of a parole officer. "Inmates who did not comply with Brockway's strict regimen were taken to the prison's notorious 'Bathroom #4.' Here they were made to lower their pants and then grab hold of a rail while they were beaten with rubber hoses or leather straps." Brockway himself often administered these beatings, which he called "spankings." In the course of just one year, he delivered 19,497 blows, which is an average of 53 lashes per day, seven days a week. Inmates feared the beatings so much that, upon entering Bathroom #4, many soiled themselves. The terror did not stop at Bathroom #4, however. After the beating, inmates were frequently chained in dungeons, sometimes for months. There they were given nothing but bread and water.[49]

As noted in the introduction to this chapter, Texas prisons are notorious for their abuse. In 1948, O. B. Ellis inherited a system of prisons in Texas that were in terrible shape. Inmates had only enough soap to bathe every three weeks. Since there were no laundry facilities, inmates lived and worked in the same clothing day after day until the garments literally rotted off their bodies. Ellis completely revamped the system, modeling it after an Israeli kibbutz. Inmates made and grew everything they needed, from harvesting cash crops like cotton to slaughtering their own meat. The system was, however, undeniably brutal. Field bosses routinely beat the men while they worked. They forced other convicts to strip the offending inmate naked and hold him down for a lashing with a leather strap known as a "bat" because it was so wide. "Rather than face abuse like this, some inmates crippled themselves. A favorite form of mutilation was known as heel-stringing. Inmates would sever their own Achilles tendons with razor blades, an excruciating act that sent the muscle lapping up into the calf like a window shade snapped up by its spring. Painful as it was, heel-stringing kept them from the fields—and from the bat."[50]

Texas prisons also used inmates to oversee field work. These armed inmates were called trusty shooters and, until 1974, were authorized to fire at any inmate who tried to escape. The prison system also used inmate-workers called building tenders. Although they were not officially allowed to be armed, in many cases they were as deadly as the trusty shooters. "The use of building tenders, trusty shooters, and their like created a savage underworld in prisons. The strong ruled and the weak acquiesced; at the end of the day what mattered was power. In Texas, the building tenders functioned as enforcers for the administration, meting out beatings and other forms of punishment to inmates who got out of line." Tenders were allowed to keep ax handles, blackjacks, brass knuckles, and knives in their cells. Many had keys to secure parts of the prison and access to confidential inmate files. They also enjoyed close ties to the officials for whom they worked. When a warden moved to a new prison, his favorite tenders often went with him. The tenders were typically the toughest, most sadistic men in the prison. One of the more notorious was

Butch Ainsworth, an inmate at the maximum-security Eastham Unit near Huntsville. A former warden at the prison once described Ainsworth as the most violent inmate he had ever known. Ainsworth once cut off several of his own fingers and delivered them to a guard as a means of protesting the transfer of a friend to another facility. On another occasion, when a fellow inmate resisted his sexual overtures, Ainsworth forced the man to stand with his feet in the water of a cell toilet. Then he applied the bare ends of an electrical cord to the man's body, shocking him senseless. After Ainsworth finished raping the man, he took his commissary goods.[51]

In 1972, an inmate named David Ruiz filed a handwritten petition in federal court, accusing the Texas Department of Corrections (as it was then known) of violating a variety of his civil rights. Ruiz claimed that building tenders beat and intimidated inmates, all with the blessings of the prison administration. These charges were certainly not new. Inmates had long complained about the abuses they suffered in the state's prisons, but the federal bench in Texas, like those in the rest of the country, generally preferred to allow states to run their own prisons with little interference. Until the 1960s, American courts pretty much ignored the legal claims filed by prisoners. Inmates were considered legal nonentities, devoid of most constitutional rights. They were, as one court put it, "slaves of the state."[52]

The first signs of change emerged in the early 1960s. A new and powerful group of inmates, the Black Muslims, was unlike any group American prisons had ever held. They were organized, disciplined, and highly political. Muslims converts quickly appeared through the nation's prisons. Leaders organized inmates in big cities like Washington and New York but also in small towns like Terra Haute, Indiana. At first, wardens responded by isolating Muslim inmates from one another, but still the Muslims' influence spread. By 1962, their stature was such that the convention of the American Correctional Association passed a resolution denouncing them as a "race hatred group" and called them unworthy of the recognition granted bona fide religious groups.

The Muslims' breakthrough success came at the Stateville Correctional Center, located about 40 miles southwest of Chicago. For a quarter century, from 1936 to 1961, Stateville was ruled by the legendary Joseph E. Ragen, a former small-town sheriff with a ninth-grade education. Like his friend O. B. Ellis, Ragen was a tough man and an exacting disciplinarian. Inmates were not allowed to talk in the dining hall. They could speak to guards only in response to questions. And they were permitted to write just one letter a week, on Sundays. Those who broke the rules could expect a beating by guards, followed by years of segregation. Ragen's reign was harsh, but many called it effective. During his 25-year tenure there were no riots and not a single escape. But the calm was deceiving. The racial unrest that would sweep America in the 1960s was already under way in prison. Like many institutions in the free world, prisons were segregated. Black inmates typically ate, slept, and worked apart from whites, and nearly always under inferior conditions. But while blacks were a minority in the free world, they were quickly becoming a majority behind bars. This was especially true in prisons like Stateville that were built close to big cities.

In 1960, there were only 58 documented Muslims at Stateville, but Ragen considered them to be a special threat to order in the prison. He kept a "Muslim file" and meticulously documented their activities. He even ordered guards to eavesdrop on "secret" conversations Muslims held by speaking to each other through the empty toilet bowls in their cells.[53]

Ragen was quick to assign solitary confinement to the Muslims for any infraction, real or perceived. Although Muslims accounted for less than 2 percent of the prison's population, they comprised between one-third and one-half of all the inmates Ragen placed in solitary confinement. One of them was 22-year-old Thomas Cooper, a former foundry worker serving a 200-year sentence for murder. In 1957, after Cooper slugged a guard, Ragen locked him in segregation (isolation). For the next decade, that is where he would remain. But instead of neutralizing Cooper, isolation radicalized him. When Cooper entered Stateville in 1953 he was listed as a Catholic. In 1957 he wrote to Elijah Muhammad and asked permission to become a member of the Black Muslims. Muhammad consented, and Thomas Cooper became Thomas X. Cooper. In 1962, from his solitary cell, Cooper sued Ragen, who by then had been promoted from warden to director of public safety, and Ragen's successor, warden Frank Pate. Muslim inmates, Cooper complained in his lawsuit, were not allowed to purchase or read the Koran. Nor were they allowed to attend religious services, or to communicate with ministers of their faith. Christian inmates, on the other hand, were allowed and even encouraged to read the Bible and to attend regular services. Illinois even had a law requiring the admission of clergymen to the state's prisons. But the law, Cooper complained, apparently did not apply to Muslims. Initially, Cooper's case seemed doomed. The District Court and the Court of Appeals both dismissed his claim. But in 1964 the Supreme Court, to the surprise of many, accepted his appeal. This so alarmed Joe Ragen that he wrote a letter to Assistant U.S. Attorney General Ramsey Clark, begging him to do whatever he could to stop Cooper's suit. "There is absolutely no question but that the Black Muslims are dedicated to destroying the discipline and authority in the prison system," Ragen wrote. "Any concession is a step toward chaos." In *Cooper v. Pate* (1964), the Supreme Court ruled that state inmates could sue prison administration under Section 1983 for violation of their constitutional rights. Plaintiffs were required to demonstrate that prison administration exercised deliberate indifference to or gross negligence of the inmates' risk of injury.[54]

Despite Ragen's efforts the power of the Black Muslims grew, and the chaos he predicted came to pass. In 1964, six of the Muslims in segregation presented Stateville officials with the first written demands ever tendered by the prison's inmates. When the demands were ignored, the inmates rioted. They burned their cells, broke up their sinks and toilets, and pelted guards with food and other debris. It was the first collective violence at Stateville in more than 30 years, and the harbinger of much more to come.

Cooper's victory marked a turning point for inmates, not only in Illinois but around the country. The hands-off policy that had kept them out of court was now dead. So, too, was the iron reign of men like Ragen. This was a tremendous shift. Before *Cooper,* all power in prisons had flowed from the wardens. Now, it flowed from the courts. Almost overnight, the formerly hostile federal bench turned friendly. Inmates filed suits by the thousands in response. In many cases, federal judges were shocked by the conditions their petitions revealed. Many prisons, especially those in the South, were barbaric places. In Alabama, as many as six inmates would be packed into a cell that measured just four feet by eight. In these cells there were no beds, no lights, and no running water. The toilet was a hole in the floor. In Arkansas, as in Texas, convicts were allowed to do the work of free-world employees. At the state penitentiary in Cummins, there were only 35 free-world employees in charge of a thousand inmates. Of those 35, only 8 were available for guard duty. And of those 8, only 2 worked at night. Because individual cells were expensive, the state built open barracks at Cummins where the inmates slept. But with no guards to protect them, sleeping inmates were tremendously vulnerable. Predatory convicts called "creepers" or "crawlers" stalked their victims at night, climbing over beds to pounce on their sleeping victims. Rape and murder were common.[55]

Other court cases soon followed. *Holt v. Sarver* (1970) set a precedent in establishing minimum standards for prison conditions. In *Estelle v. Gamble* (1976), the court specifically addressed medical care for inmates. The court determined that a person's right to be protected against cruel and unusual punishment was violated when his or her basic medical needs were neglected purposefully. *Jackson v. Bishop* (1968) marked the first time a court ruled that corporal punishment violated the Eighth Amendment's prohibition on cruel and unusual punishment. In this case, inmates in Kentucky were beaten with an 18-inch-long, two-inch-wide leather strap that had been soaked in water and dragged through sand. State prisoners could also seek protection and relief from abusive or neglectful treatment under the Fourteenth Amendment.[56]

Yet prison abuse did not end when these decisions took effect. On December 14, 1981, a bloody siege in Hawaii's Oahu Prison, termed the "'81 Shakedown," called attention to horrific conditions of confinement there. According to Michael Hess, a former unit manager at the prison, guards refused to enter dorm areas, inmates moved freely to and from the recreation yard, and staff often called in sick when assigned to dangerous posts. In the summer of 1980, the prison experienced three days of rioting, and the following spring the inmates forced the guards out of the cell block and held for 10 hours. In September 1981, the inmates again forced the guards out, injuring a lieutenant in the process. On December 14, the authorities undertook a programmatic effort to establish their control. National Guard troops, officers with the Honolulu Police Department, and guards from the Halawa High Security Facility (HHSF) were brought in as reinforcements. At first, the inmates just taunted the new guards. But on the morning of December 15, the warden of HHSF asked his Oahu counterpart to "allow HHSF to conduct the strip search of the cellblock inmates" and "discipline" those who behaved disrespectfully. The request was granted, and HHSF staff stripped the inmates as they returned to the cell block.[57]

Clearly, they did more than just search. The prison's medical personnel reported numerous injuries immediately after. Seventeen prisoners received medical treatment and an unknown number were prevented from seeking care. One man was so badly beaten that he had to be sent to an outside hospital. On December 16, the Oahu guards continued the process their HHSF colleagues had begun. Some guards beat inmates during the mandatory strip search; others fought their colleagues to protect the prisoners. One guard described the scene as "chaos...guys went berserk." Michael Hess said he heard "a fear and pain type of screaming" and "saw two guards holding an inmate while a third beat him with a baton." The next day peace was restored, and news of the incident reached the media. Several investigations were initiated, but with little result. The ombudsman's office interviewed 398 people and found 44 separate cases of excessive force. It identified 22 guards and 12 supervisors (including both wardens) who should be disciplined, but the director of the department dismissed all charges. This sequence of events set the pattern for the next several years. While inmate violence practically disappeared, complaints of staff violence continued to escalate.[58]

Sometimes abuse is less overt. Rather, the conditions of confinement in many prisons can be said to be inherently abusive. Author Joseph Hallinan described his visit to Capshaw, Alabama. Capshaw is a tiny town near the Tennessee line, so tiny it has no official population except for the 1,700 inmates who occupy the Limestone Correctional Center. Each morning, just after dawn, more than 100 of them are dragged out of bed and shuffled off to the prison rock pile to begin the state's latest experiment in rehabilitation. Wearing iron shackles around their ankles and safety goggles to protect their eyes, the men in the chain gang spread out as far as their iron links allow. They grab the yellow-handled sledgehammers, draw them up high, and begin pounding on boulders of limestone, sending stone chips flying through the air. This is their job all day long, five days a week, smashing boulders into rocks. It is an unnecessary task. The state does not need the rocks, and has had to import more than 100 tons of boulders just to make the work. The rock will be used, among other things, to pave the road to the cemetery nearby. But in Alabama, this is what passes for penal innovation.

Imprisonment is itself degrading. It is marked by a pronounced lack of power over even the most basic elements of life. It is a regiment of imposition and deprivation, isolation and overcrowding. Food, fresh air, sunlight, social contact, showers, information and entertainment, meaningful work, medical care—all these are restricted, rationed, doled out as privileges, or prohibited altogether. Privacy and free movement can hardly be said to exist. Rote labor, isolation and pain can be readily imposed. To be a prisoner is to be subject to control. It is also, as a means to such control, to be subject to violence. The threat is ever present. One cannot maintain these conditions without also creating opportunities for abuse.[59]

By 1980, two-thirds of all inmates in the United States lived in cells or dormitories that provided less than 60 square feet of living space per person, which is the minimum standard deemed acceptable by the American Public Health Association, the Justice Department, and other authorities. Many lived in cells measuring half that amount. In 1975, at what was then Ohio's only maximum-security prison, more than a thousand inmates shared cells that provided them, on average, with just 31½ square feet of cell space. In other words, each man lived in an area almost exactly the size of a queen-size bed. Yet, in 1979, the Supreme Court determined there was no constitutional right to being alone in a prison cell. Two years later, the court ruled there was no right to a "comfortable prison." These decisions prompted a spiral of overcrowding, which makes the environment ripe for abuse.

The case of Luis Palacio is instructive. Palacio was sent to Stateville Correctional Center in Illinois in 1990. Because of a wound to his leg, he was given the rare opportunity to have a cell to himself. Because of this, many other inmates presumed him to be a gang member. He woke up in the middle of one night to find a wire around his neck and a knee in his back. An inmate named Sky King raped him for approximately 30 minutes, although Palacio blacked out at some point. Another inmate found him, lying in a pool of blood, after breakfast. After the rape, Palacio was transferred to another prison. He contracted the very painful condition herpes of the anus.[60]

Another way inmates are abused is through the use of cruel restraints. Restraint chairs, a relatively new piece of technology, have been used across the country. These devices have straps across the legs, arms, and torso that restrict the subject's movements. Allegedly used to restrain violent inmates who pose an immediate threat, they have not always been used in this way. At least 12 people have died in incidents involving restraint chairs. Utah authorities kept one inmate in a four-point restraint—strapped in a chair with arms and legs spread wide apart—for 12 weeks in 1995. He was removed from the restraint and allowed to shower only four times per week, but was forced to urinate and defecate where he was restrained.[61] In 1996, Scott Norberg died when officers confined him in a restraint chair in Maricopa County Jail in Arizona. Guards had strapped a towel over his mouth and shocked him multiple times. Although guards admitted shocking Norburg between two and six times, according to the inmates, it was more like eight to twenty times. The medical examiner hired by Norberg's family found evidence of up to twenty-one shocks. Yet the coroner still ruled the death was accidental asphyxiation.[62] In August 1999, a judge in a Tennessee case ruled that confessions extracted while suspects were strapped in a restraint chair were invalid. In November 1999, a judge in Ventura County, California, issued a preliminary injunction banning their use in the county jail after a lawsuit alleged widespread abuse.[63]

Although reports of abuse occurred before the disaster, accounts worsened at the Orleans Parish Prison in New Orleans after Hurricane Katrina devastated the region. As water rose into the prison buildings, deputies evacuated, leaving the prisoners in locked cells for days without power, food, or water, and with many standing in sewage and rainwater up to their chests and necks. Rather than merely an oversight from a chaotic time, testimonials obtained by the ACLU from more than 1,000 prisoners make it clear the evacuation plan went precisely as intended. Prisoners had been forced into their cells prior to the evacuation, with deputies shooting them with bean bags, smacking them, and Tasing them. They were then handcuffed to the cell doors. As the flooding began, some prisoners tried to hang signs from broken windows seeking help, and others jumped into the water below. Deputies and members of the Special Investigation division shot at the backs of these prisoners many times.[64]

Many times, "the institutional setting, with its depersonalized regulation of nearly every aspect if the inmates' lives, can reduce the prisoners, in the eyes of the guards, to mere bodies rather than persons. Such a perception is, on its own, dangerous for the prospects of human rights. But it takes on a particularly egregious character when combined with the ideology of male dominance."[65] Female prisoners are not only reduced to bodies, but to sexualized bodies. Worse, despite the obvious potential for abuse when males guard females, prison authorities make only minimal efforts to control such high-risk situations, offering little in the way of training, supervision, or enforcement of the existing regulations.[66]

The use of sex and sexual humiliation as torture in Abu Ghraib and the other American prisons in Iraq is endemic to the American prison. Psychological and physical sexual torture is exacerbated by the underlying policy of denying prisoners any volitional sex, making the only two forms of sexual activity that are physically possible—homosexuality and masturbation—both offenses subject to punishment. Strip searches, including invasive and often intentionally painful examination of the mouth, anus, testicles, and vagina, frequently accompanied by verbal or physical sexual abuse, are part of the daily routine in most prisons. A 1999 Amnesty International report documented the commonplace rape of prisoners by guards in women's prisons.[67]

Women in custody have been subjected to all the terrible methods of inflicting pain that torturers have devised. They have been beaten and subjected to electric shocks, mock executions, death threats, sleep deprivation, and sensory deprivation. They have been suspended by their hands and feet, suffocated, and submerged in water.[68] In Nevada, a court ruled that males could conduct searches of women even when the search involved touching breasts and genitals. In New York men can pat down female prisoners. In 1994, a court found that female prisoners in three facilities in Washington, D.C., were frequently subjected to violent sexual assault and harassment. That same year, the Justice Department found evidence of widespread sexual abuse, including rape, in facilities for females in Michigan. And in 1997, a similar investigation concluded that authorities in Arizona failed to protect women from systemic rape, sexual touching, and fondling at the hands of correctional officers. In many cases, no one is ever arrested, let alone punished. In other cases, perpetrators have been held accountable. In 1997, the sheriff of Grant County, West Virginia, was sentenced to seven years in prison for forcing female inmates to engage in sex acts with law enforcement officials. In 1998, the Federal Bureau of Prisons was forced to settle a lawsuit that reported, among other things, that guards had taken money from male inmates in exchange for allowing them to enter women's cells so they could sexually abuse them. In that same year alone, one or more correctional officers were found guilty of rape or sexual assault of incarcerated women in Florida, Idaho, Illinois, Maryland, Michigan, New Hampshire, Texas, Virginia, Washington, and Wyoming.[69] One report from a Texas prison found female prisoners being held for hours in tiny cells (eight by four feet) in temperatures exceeding 100 degrees Fahrenheit. They were made to stand and were not allowed to use the bathroom, so many had to defecate in the cell.[70]

Private prisons have also been the subjects of numerous allegations of abuse. In February 1998, authorities at a facility owned by the Corrections Corporation of America (CCA) in Youngstown, Ohio, responded to the murder of an inmate by conducting cell raids in riot gear, forcing inmates to kneel or lie naked on the floor while they were strip-searched and handcuffed. Guards admitted to spraying pepper spray on their sleeves and purposely wiping it in inmates' eyes. Similar abuse was documented months later at a CCA-run facility in Tennessee.[71]

Supermax prisons are particularly troublesome. Everett Hoffman, executive director of the American Civil Liberties Union of Kentucky, described standards in Super Maximum (supermax) prisons this way:

Typically, inmates are confined in 8 x 10 foot cells for 23 hours a day in enforced idleness. The cells are windowless and have solid doors, so that the inmate cannot see or hear anything going on outside the cell. Inmates are "cell fed"—their meals are delivered through slots in the cell doors, with no verbal or visual contact with the guards delivering the meals. No furniture or other amenities are allowed beyond the concrete and steel furniture in the cell—not television, no radio, no tobacco. Inmates in Super Max units are allowed one hour a day of solitary "recreation" in a concrete enclosure, their movements monitored by video cameras. Inmates are within close proximity of staff only when they are being visually searched as they stand naked before a control booth window before their one hour of "recreation." Typically, they remain shackled in front of their families during non-contact visits conducted behind clear partitions. There is always a physical barrier between the inmate and other human beings. They are deprived of human contact or touch for years on end.[72]

Although many talk of "country club" prisons, the truth is they are very violent and uncomfortable places. It is difficult to say exactly how violent they are because of incomplete reporting. In 1990, the nation's corrections departments reported an average of 239 attacks per year on their guards. By 1997, that figure had risen to 311. In 1996, 65 inmates were reported to have been killed behind bars. But that number probably understates the actual total, according to the Bureau of Justice Statistics, because many states—and the federal government—do not report inmate homicides as a separate offense. Instead, they lump all inmate deaths under one category: "unspecified cause." In 1996, the deaths of 295 inmates were attributed to "unspecified cause."[73]

When it comes to other forms of violence, the statistics are even sketchier. There are no reliable reports, for instance, on the number of rapes behind bars, even though, as many prison administrators admit, rape is a common experience. In Texas, no attempt is made to monitor the total number of reported sexual assaults inside its prisons, so the frequency is a matter of guesswork. In 1999, though, several of the state's inmates testified before Judge William Wayne Justice during a trial in the U.S. District Court in Houston. Of 32 male inmates who testified before the court, at least 9 had been sexually assaulted. One inmate testified that after complaining to officers about threats to his safety, he was attacked in the showers by four inmates, three who beat him while one inserted his fingers into the man's rectum. Another inmate testified that he was beaten up by a new cell mate who was "checking him" to see if he would "be a girl." A psychiatrist testified that after another inmate was sexually assaulted, he sought to have his anus sewn shut by a prison doctor.[74]

Some assert that prison abuse is an inevitable result of the get-tough mentality that has permeated American jurisprudence for the last three decades. In 1996, a bloody melee broke out at the Forest Hays, Jr. State Prison in northwestern Georgia. It occurred during an unannounced "sweep" of the prison by a roving squad of riot officers. The officers were led by their commander in chief, a former mortician and state senator named J. Wayne Garner. In 1995, Garner was appointed as the state's commissioner of corrections and soon became one of the nation's most outspoken advocates of getting tough on inmates. Under Garner, Georgia's penal facilities were no longer to be called correctional institutions. With one exception, they were officially renamed state prisons. Shortly after taking office, Garner made headlines when he said that a third of the inmates in his care "ain't fit to kill." One of his favorite techniques for showing these inmates who was boss involved sweeps, or shakedown raids, conducted by the department's riot unit. The sweep of Hays was needed, according to Garner's spokesman, because the inmates were not subservient enough. "We had," he said, "to take them down a notch." According to sworn accounts filed in federal court by guards who were present during the raid, violence erupted after A. G. Thomas, an aide to Garner, grabbed an unresisting inmate by the hair and dragged him across the floor. "When Mr. Thomas did that," said Ray McWhorter, the lieutenant in charge of the tactical squad, "we were all under the impression it was O.K. to do it. If Mr. Thomas can slam one, then we can slam one, too. That is just the dad-gum way it was." What followed, Lieutenant McWhorter said, was a bloody free-for-all.[75] More than a dozen inmates were beaten that day. Garner denied playing any role in abuse, but in 1998 the state of Georgia agreed to pay $283,000 to settle suits from 14 inmates.

Between 1990 and 1995, inmates at Clinton Correctional Facility in New York filed seven federal claims alleging excessive force by correctional officers, and the state of New York settled 10 brutality lawsuits in the same time period. In 1999, California agreed to pay $2.2 million to an inmate who had been shot in the neck and paralyzed by a guard at the California State Prison at Corcoran. Corcoran opened in 1988 in the San Joaquin Valley and within a few years was holding more than 5,000 inmates, despite being designed to hold just 2,400. Corcoran was the nation's most violent prison in the 1990s. The prison has been the site of some brutal abuse. Between 1989 and 1995, guards shot 50 prisoners in the Secure Housing Unit, seven of them fatally. In the prison as a whole, there were 185 shooting incidents in 1990 alone, and 38 inmates were wounded. Another 205 shootings occurred in 1991, wounding 17. The event that finally brought scrutiny to this pattern, however, was the April 1994 death of Preston Tate. Security cameras recorded Tate, a black man serving time for robbery, entering a small recreation area. A few minutes later he was joined by two Latino members of a rival gang. Immediately, the three men began to fight. Guards fired less-lethal wooden bullets, followed by a single round from an assault rifle, which killed Tate. Soon thereafter, three guards went to the FBI telling of prearranged "cockfights" between gang members. Guards in Corcoran set these fights up, bet on them, and then ended them with gunfire.[76]

Other allegations quickly surfaced, many of them centering around a gang of guards, calling themselves "the Sharks," who greeted new inmates by beating them when they arrived. Such institutionalized, but extra-legal, violence seems to have been the norm at Corcoran.[77] A former guard, Roscoe Poindexter, explained that he strangled prisoners while other guards crushed their testicles. They called this move the "Deep Six," and Poindexter admitted that although the move was not presented through official training, it was passed along from sergeant to sergeant. Another favorite technique of the guards was to place inmates in a cell with Wayne Robertson, known as the Booty Bandit, who would rape them repeatedly. Guards knew this and arranged to reward Robertson with extra food and tennis shoes. Eddie Dillard was raped multiple times over a two-day period, with guards mocking his cries for help much of the time.[78] Similar abuse occurred at California's Pelican Bay State Prison, where guards used live ammunition to break up fights, regularly hog-tied prisoners, and left prisoners naked in cages during harsh weather.[79]

Among the inmates tortured at Corcoran was Reginald Cooke, who had spit on an officer and exposed himself to a female guard. In November 1989, guards wanted to inspect his cell. But Cooke would not budge until an "extraction" team of guards came to forcibly remove him. After a brief fight, guards carried Cooke, his arms and legs shackled, to the unit's rotunda. As more than 20 officers watched, a lieutenant ordered Cooke's pants lowered and delivered a jolt to his genitals with an electronic stun gun.[80]

Similar to Corcoran, a sign at California's Folsom Prison used to read, "There will be no warning shots fired." Former warden James H. Bruton commented, "It was an appalling way to communicate. First of all, this type of violence control completely disregards the safety of those involved. Second, it creates an environment of hostility, which in turn creates the need for this type of brutal control. In terms of creating a hostile atmosphere, the California prison system used to be one of the worst offenders."[81]

Another group particularly vulnerable to abuse is the mentally ill. Mental illness impairs prisoners' ability to cope with the extraordinary stresses of prison and to follow the rules of a regimented life predicated on obedience and punishment for infractions. These prisoners are less likely to be able to follow correctional rules. Their misconduct is punished—regardless of whether it results from their mental illness. Even acts of self-mutilation and suicide attempts are too often seen as "malingering" and are punished as rule violations. As a result, mentally ill prisoners can accumulate extensive disciplinary histories.[82]

International human-rights laws and standards specifically address conditions of confinement, including the treatment of mentally ill prisoners. If, for example, U.S. officials honored in practice the International Covenant on Civil and Political Rights, to which the United States is a party, and the United Nation's Standard Minimum Rules for the Treatment of Prisoners, which sets out detailed guidelines on how prisoners should be treated, practices in U.S. prisons would improve dramatically. These human-rights documents affirm the right of prisoners not to be subjected to cruel, inhuman, or degrading conditions of confinement and the right to mental health treatment consistent with community standards of care.[83]

Lance Tarpley, reporter for the *Portland Phoenix,* interviewed inmates at several facilities. He heard about one especially troubling incident involving a mentally ill man. Five guards barged into the man's cell, all decked out in full body armor. After spraying the man in the face with mace, the guards twisted the man's hands behind his back and handcuffed him. Then they chained the handcuffs to leg irons, stripped him naked, and carried the screaming man down the hallway while they continued to spray him with mace.[84] One prisoner from Nevada described his situation in an interview with Human Rights Watch in 2002: "At one point and time in my life here in prison I wanted to just take my own life away. Why? Everything in prison that's wrong is right, and everything that's right is wrong. I've been jump[ed], beat[en], kick[ed][and punch[ed] in full restraint four times....Two times I've been put into nude four point as punishment and personal harassment..."[85] A mentally ill female inmate housed in a facility in Illinois described her treatment: "I was placed in a situation where I've lost a peace of mind within fear frustration depression, the feeling of being helpless. I've picked up a self harm behavior of cutting myself to where I need 5 to 14 stitchies [*sic*] at a time. Or smearing feces over my body to keep officers not wonting [*sic*] to touch me as they always cause me harm, stumping [*sic*] my feet or bending my hand...."[86]

Human Rights Watch reported in 2003 that a number of mentally ill prisoners had died in recent years as a result of being placed in restraint chairs. Michael Valent died from blood clots in a Utah jail in 1997 after being held nude for 16 hours in a restraint chair. Another mentally ill man in an Osceola, Florida, prison died the same year when he was placed in a restraint chair and his head was snapped back so violently he fatally injured his brain stem. In February 2001, lawyers from the Southern Center for Human Rights representing inmates at Phillips State Prison in Georgia filed a class action suit alleging widespread abuse and "a culture of guard brutality at the prison." Three hundred seriously mentally ill prisoners had been segregated, and whenever they made any form of complaint, guards beat them up, and then wrote them up and placed them in solitary confinement.[87]

Juveniles, too, are vulnerable to abuse in detention. This was particularly true when common practice was to house juvenile offenders with adults. Although federal legislation has been enacted to end that practice, in some rural areas, where there are not enough facilities to separate inmates, juveniles and adults may still be housed together for short times. Journalists were the first to expose the widespread abuse against detained juveniles in the 1970s. For instance, interviews with youth from the Audy Home in Chicago revealed stories of youth being hit, kicked, slapped, forced to endure harsh elements, made to drink from the toilet, and sodomized with broomsticks.[88] In the fall of 2000, several lawsuits were filed against the state of Louisiana. The suits maintained that youth detained in several facilities, but especially the Tallulah Correctional Center for Youth, were being held in dangerous restraints, had been denied food, medical care, and other necessities, and in some cases had been sexually abused. Paul Choy died in 1992 under restraints. An autopsy revealed Choy had been anally raped as well.[89] More than 20 charges against the Greenville Hills Academy in Florida also cite use of painful restraints.[90] In 2005, the General Accounting Office (GAO), the investigative arm of Congress, found widespread abuse at juvenile boot camps. Abuse included youth being forced to eat their own vomit and to lie in urine and feces.[91]

Detained immigrants are also subject to a vast array of abuses by their jailers. Eric Mensah, an immigrant from Ghana who worked at the Union County Jail, made this comment about abuse of prisoners: "When you abuse people, that's when the adrenaline gets high. To be part of the clique, you have to abuse inmates.... The institution is built up paramilitary style. Your first 101 is that you don't report anything to the director." Another guard from the same facility commented, "It's a prison mentality. When you're sitting around, when you're hanging around with a lot of tough guys and there's a lot of things going on, you certainly do become a tough guy. I mean that's part of the business, there's no doubt about that." He also commented on hiring practices for correctional officers, saying, "You're getting the bottom of the barrel. You're getting guys who can't fuckin' spell their name. You're getting guys who are cheating on the test."[92]

Felix Oviawe was a state assemblyman in Nigeria. A democratically elected local politician, he fled his country after the 1993 coup d'etat and sought political asylum in the United States. He acknowledged to Kennedy Airport immigration officials his passport was not legitimate but asked to apply for asylum. Instead, he was taken to the Esmor Detention Center, then transferred to the Union County Jail. He described the transfer: "We are coming out from the van, about thirteen of us. As we are coming out, your hands are tied. A guard would grab you, throw you on the floor. You understand me? And someone else grab you, throw you back to the van. Somebody push you out again, then they throw you on the floor, another one would pick you up, just continuous like that. They started beating us. Started beating us. Even while they were taking us to the cell, [a guard] said he feel like killing somebody. One of the guards, he said he feel like killing somebody. So he grabbed me by my shirt. Beated my head on the wall. You understand me?" The inmates were then taken to their cells, forced to strip naked, kneel down, and pull on the ear of another inmate kneeling next to them. This lasted for hours, while guards came in to berate them and one spat on them.[93]

Prejudice against Africans is widespread inside INS facilities across the nation. Mark Dow, author of *American Gulag,* offers the following example.

The "nigger roast" took place in the office parking lot. An INS supervisor was frustrated by the number of Somalis applying for asylum in his district. These were "affirmative" applicants, meaning that they were not being detained but were presenting themselves voluntarily at the INS office to apply for asylum. The supervisor decided to "make an example" of one Somali to discourage others from applying. He handcuffed the applicant and forced him to sit for about half an hour in a locked car, with the windows shut, in the midday heat. The car was parked in front of the main entrance to the building. Judith Marty, another supervisory asylum officer, complained to the director of the office. She found out that he knew what was going on, and he justified the supervisor's actions by saying, "I'm not trying to prosecute them. I just want them to quit coming here." Marty, who is forty-seven, told me the incident made her think of Alabama in the 1950s, but this was Los Angeles in the 1990s.[94]

Tony Ebibillo, a Nigerian, was detained at Krome Detention Center in Miami. He described abuse at the hands of guards. On December 6, 1991, after he had spent one year at Krome, guards removed him from his cell, claiming he looked sick. They tied his hands, legs, waist, and arms to the bed face down, and told him they were going to "make him sleep" and he would wake up in Nigeria. Ebibillo knew a return to Nigeria would be certain death, since his father, his uncle, and he had openly criticized the country's military rulers. The guards gave him multiple injections and capsules to swallow. The medicines were Thorazine, Benadryl, and Ativan, and Ebibillo received them every 4 hours for 12½ hours, then again at the start of the next day. Some time the next morning he briefly regained consciousness only to find himself in the INS van, handcuffed, shackled, in a straightjacket, and with his mouth taped shut. He was taken to Miami International Airport, where American Airlines staff saw the bound Ebibillo. One remembered seeing an immigration official continuously elbow Ebibillo. The airline refused to transport Ebibillo in that condition. In all, three attempts were made to unlawfully deport Ebibillo. At one point, immigration officials claimed Ebibillo, despite being bound in every way imaginable, had forcibly assaulted an officer. Human Rights Watch has documented that this type of "countercharge" is commonly used by INS officials, as it conceals the abuses perpetrated by those in charge.[95]

Positional forms of torture, found in the Abu Ghraib pictures, are common in detention facilities. Edward Calejo, a prison guard in Miami's Krome Detention Center, described how he treated detainees in the early 1990s. "I mean, we make guys stand in line—they just stand there, just to stand there. Don't move, you know. And we'd make them stand there all day long." In addition to forced standing, Calejo described a regimen at Krome that included slapping, beating, pointless exercises, and humiliation. In 1998, inmates at Florida's Jackson County Jail described a large concrete slab to which individuals were tied in a crucifix position. The slab had iron rings in the corners and leather straps for the arms and legs. As one prisoner stated, "Concrete. Cold, cold, cold. And they'll turn the AC up high, high, high, and you'll be butt-naked.... You're on your belly.... And when time to eat, they loose one hand. So you eat, and they strap you back. It's torture, man." Other prisoners described how guards shocked them with stun guns and electric shields while they were in prison.[96]

Yet as appalling as abuse of immigrant detainees is, minorities who are citizens also face abusive conditions and treatment in U.S. prisons. "The Iraq abuse scandal shows how America keeps forgetting its mistakes at home. Rumsfeld says the abuse was un-American. African-American men remain the proof that abuse is an American pastime."[97] A recent investigation lead by Earl Devaney, Interior Department Inspector General, revealed horrific conditions at Bureau of Indian Affairs (BIA) prisons in the United States. Devaney and his team visited 27 BIA prisons and spoke to 150 tribal and BIA leaders. They concluded that BIA prisons were comparable to "the third world." The investigation prompted Devaney to testify to the Senate seeking change and additional funding.[98]

There are 74 Bureau of Indian Affairs prisons in the United States. Less than $1 million annually is devoted to running all 74 of them.[99] Native Americans are often housed in overcrowded facilities with no running water and no heat. In many cases, the plumbing is perpetually broken.[100] At one facility in north central Montana, raw sewage floods the men's cell block whenever a toilet in the women's section is flushed.[101] The facilities are overcrowded; in June 2001, BIA prisons were operating at 126 percent capacity, with nearly half of the inmate population in 2001 being held in 10 facilities. For instance, Pine Ridge Correctional Facility held 168 inmates in 2001, over seven times greater than its capacity.[102] Frustrated by the lack of attention to these atrocities, retired guard Ed Naranjo videotaped several facilities. While the tapes did not reveal absolute torture of inmates, they did demonstrate the horrible conditions under which Native American prisoners are held. These conditions are in violation of international guidelines prohibiting cruel, inhuman, and degrading treatment. In many cases, the facilities had received no maintenance in 25 years.[103]

Juveniles are frequently held with adults in Indian country jails and prisons. Reports indicate rape and assaults are commonplace when juveniles and adults are housed together.[104] Catherine (Cedar Woman) described the seven rapes she endured from jailers during her three-and-a-half-month incarceration. After the rape, one jailer laughed, cleaned up, then forced her to perform oral sex. She was told she better not tell. Besides, no one would believe her if she did tell.[105]

Access to and quality of medical treatment for incarcerated Native Americans is a significant problem. One 16-year-old, Cindy Gilbert Sohappy of Warm Springs, Oregon, was sent to a BIA jail for underage drinking. She died of alcohol poisoning when no one checked on her. Catherine (Cedar Woman) says she witnessed an excessive amount of hysterectomies performed on women between 1988 and 1992, a problem also documented by Ross in 1996.[106]

Misty Ford, a 27-year-old, was less than two months into a six-month sentence in the BIA's Spokane Jail for DUI and eluding an officer when she died of hypertension. Ford had complained of chest pains the day before, and relatives had begged jail personnel to give her medical attention, but none was provided.[107] A wheelchair-bound inmate in a Montana prison was moved to an inaccessible block. The inmate was also diabetic, but because of his difficulty accessing meals at regular times, his sugar was dangerously erratic. For two years, another Montana inmate was denied treatment despite a potentially fatal brain disorder. In addition, facilities housing Native

Americans have woefully inadequate suicide prevention. An inmate at one New Mexico facility attempted suicide seven times with clothes and towels left in his cell.[108]

There have been more than 12 suspicious deaths in BIA prisons in recent years. The BIA was forced to investigate the suicide of a Yakama Tribal Detention Center inmate in 2004. Ricky Owens Sampson was left hanging for at least five hours because only one guard was on staff the night he hung himself.[109] In addition, since President Bush took office in 2001, 1,236 Native American inmates have attempted suicide and 632 have tried to escape.[110] Tina Newman, a member of the Tonawanda Band of the Seneca/Cherokee from Tuscaloosa, Alabama, sums it up: "Americans can't believe the deplorable conditions in Third World countries. Well, wake up! You have Third World reservations all over the USA."[111]

Others claim prisons should be more restrictive and prisoners should not have it too easy, though prisons should not be needlessly punitive. Tough conditions, they say, will reform criminals. For instance, conservative writers Michael Lockwood and Rachel Alexander applauded Arizona Sheriff Joe Arpaio for his more punitive approach to corrections. They claimed Arpaio is strict but not abusive, as his critics contend. In response to critics, Arpaio installed webcams in the jail, and no abuse or mistreatment was recorded. In addition, they lauded Arpaio for his efforts to cut costs, stating that his 3,200-member volunteer posse is the largest in the nation and saves the country the cost of hundreds of deputies. Arpaio has also cut costs on inmate meals, which average $4–5 at other facilities. He spends $0.22 per meal.[112]

What is certain is that, in recent years, it has become more difficult for inmates to file lawsuits, even in cases where they have been abused. In 1995, Congress passed the Prison Litigation Reform Act, which took effect the next year. This legislation made it more difficult for federal courts to provide relief in cases alleging inhumane prison conditions.[113] In November 2007, a House Judiciary Committee subcommittee on Crime, Terrorism, and Homeland Security met to address the Prison Litigation Reform Act (PLRA). The intent of PLRA was to curtail frivolous lawsuits, but instead it has made it almost impossible for prisoners to report any types of abuse or constitutional violations occurring in detention. Under PLRA, prisoners have to demonstrate they suffered physical injury in order to make a claim. The PLRA also requires prisoners to submit a series of grievance forms in order to file a suit, regardless of age, mental illness, or capacity to physically complete the forms. These requirements also open the door for retaliatory violence, as many times inmates are required to submit the paperwork first to guards. "There are two kinds of walls in American prisons: One that keeps prisoners from escaping, and another that keeps the abuse that happens inside from ever reaching the light of day," said Jesselyn McCurdy, Legislative Counsel for the ACLU. "The Prison Litigation Reform Act creates prisons within prisons, except with paperwork instead of locks and administrative hurdles instead of bars. The PLRA gave a blank check to guards and corrections officers, and it's time for the prison system to pay the piper."[114]

The failure at the policy level to track mistreatment at BIA and the other prisons described above is in clear violation of Article 11 of the CAT. There does not seem to be any formal training on human rights for officers or medical professionals working in these prisons, which could be in violation of Article 2 of the CAT, which requires preventive efforts, as well as Article 4 and Article 10, which require that human-rights training and information be provided to relevant personnel. The use of restraints might also constitute torture, especially when combined with the other forms of mistreatment. Since the mistreatment described in prisons is clearly being conducted by or with the knowledge of prison officials, and in many cases statements made by guards indicate the *intent* to do harm, these behaviors would seem to violate U.S. law as well.[115]

In the same way that Bush administration and military officials have trivialized the abuse of foreign prisoners and detainees, and in the same way that police deny they torture during interrogations, denial and dismissal are the common responses. For instance, the head of the Bureau of Indian Affairs prisons responded to Devaney's findings by saying, "In any prison environment you are going to have a certain amount of improprieties."[116]

Prison abuse is integrally tied to the abuse occurring in the war on terror. One overt connection is that, prior to their work in prisons overseas, many military guards worked in domestic prisons. Prior to his assignment to Abu Ghraib, Charles Graner worked as a guard at the State Correctional Institution—Greene in Greene County, Pennsylvania. The prison was notorious for a situation that occurred several years ago in which a dozen guards were fired for, among other things, sodomizing a prisoner with a nightstick and writing "KKK" on a cell floor, in blood, following a particularly brutal beating. The authorities deny that Graner was involved in that scandal, but his employment record was not exemplary. His reputation among inmates and guards alike was that of a sadistic thug. Colleagues tell of Graner wearing black gloves with padded knuckles, and numerous witnesses remember him beating and mocking prisoners.[117] He was reprimanded three times and suspended four times, although these were allegedly for absenteeism and lateness.

"The trap is almost perfect: A general panic over terrorism is used to justify a broad sweep of targeted immigrant communities" who are then denied basic constitutional protections based on their status as noncitizens. After September 11, the familiar strategy of racial profiling and then denial of basic rights was applied to those at least perceived to come from the Middle East.

But the institutions responsible for arrests and detention, and the practices they employ, predate the War on Terror. Official policy has become more aggressive, and the authorities have focused somewhat more of their attention against Arabs and Muslims, but none of this required a radical shift in the direction of government activity. Instead, it brought the existing patterns into sharper focus and signaled to functionaries at every level of government that they need not be concerned, even in principle, with the rights or dignity of those they have been ordered to control.[118]

Detainees in the United States after 9/11 have complained of being slammed into walls, having their fingers and hands twisted painfully, sleep deprivation, unnecessary strip searches, and being forced to wear painful restraints. Many of these accusations have come from New York's Metropolitan Detention Center (MDC), although similar accusations, mostly by Arabs or Muslims, have been made about facilities in Charlotte, North Carolina, San Diego's Metropolitan Correctional Center, and other locations.[119]

The Department of Justice's Inspector General recently reported on the abuse Muslim men who were picked up after September 11 endured while detained at the federal Metropolitan Detention Center in Brooklyn. For example, officers slammed unresisting, shackled inmates into walls and mocked them during body-cavity searches. A lawsuit by one of the detainees alleges that one of the officers maliciously pushed a pencil into his anus.[120]

Abuses against inmates, whether committed by other prisoners or by guards, are rarely effectively prosecuted. Because police do not patrol prisons to monitor crime there, prison abuses are only prosecuted when they are reported. Although inmates do have the right to file complaints to local police and prosecutors regarding prison crimes, Human Rights Watch's research suggests that local officials generally ignore complaints made by prisoners. Nor do prison employees often report crimes that occur in their facilities. Although overall figures are lacking, it is evident that criminal charges are brought only in the most egregious cases—or in instances of prisoner violence against guards—and that many instances of violence, extortion, and harassment do not even result in administrative sanctions against the responsible party. The rule of impunity holds true both for inter-prisoner abuses and abuses committed by guards against inmates. In California, for example, not a single local prosecutor has ever prosecuted a guard for prison shootings that have killed 39 inmates and wounded more than 200 over the past decade.[121]

The prison system institutionalizes isolation and secrecy. The prison's walls are designed not only to keep the prisoners in but to keep the public out, thus preventing observation or knowledge of what is going on inside. Unknowable to all but prisoners and guards, the prison thus becomes a physical site where the most unspeakable torture can continue without any restraint.[122]

THE DEATH PENALTY

According to Robert Johnson, author of *Death Work: A Study of the Modern Execution Process,* the death-row process bears striking similarity to the definitions of torturous confinement. Inmates are isolated, the institution has total control of their basic life activities, they must deal with uncertainty regarding when precisely they will die, and they are personally humiliated. In at least one case, a court ruled that the conditions in death row were inhumane. Mr. Harries had lived on Tennessee's death row for many years before he filed suit in the mid-1980s. He was confined to his cell, a six-foot by eight-foot box, for 23 hours each day, with 45 minutes of recreation and a 15-minute shower allowed daily. The temperature in the cell was between 80 and 85 degrees. As a result of the finding, Tennessee revamped their death row.[123] As noted in an earlier chapter, the Supreme Court is currently debating the constitutionality of lethal injection as an execution method.

Perhaps the dominant image, promulgated by the very forces that have instituted the prison-building frenzy, envisions prison as a kind of summer camp for vicious criminals, where convicts comfortably loll around watching TV and lifting weights. Just as false images of the slave plantations strewn across the South encouraged denial of their reality, false images of the Abu Ghraibs strewn across America not only legitimize denial of their reality but also allow their replication at Guantanamo, Baghdad, Afghan desert sites, or wherever our government, and culture, may build new citadels of torture in the future.[124]

NOTES

1. Lomax, A. (2005, June 16). The *real* American gulag. *Counterpunch.* Retrieved January 21, 2006, from http://www.counterpunch.org/lomax06162005.html.

2. Conroy, J. (2000). *Unspeakable acts, ordinary people: The dynamics of torture.* New York: Alfred A. Knopf.

3. Fellner, J. (2004, May 22/23). *Prison abuse: How different are U.S. prisoners?* Human Rights Watch. Retrieved April 18, 2007, from http://www.hrw.org/english/docs/2004/05/14/usdom8583.html.

4. Ibid.

5. Ibid.

6. Franklin, B. (n.d.). *The American prison and the normalization of torture.* Historians Against the War. Retrieved October 9, 2007, from http://www.historiansagainstwar.org/resources/torture/brucefranklin.html.

7. Fellner (2004).

8. Conroy (2000), p. 33.

9. Fellner (2004).

10. Franklin (n.d.).

11. Ibid.

12. Amnesty International. (2000, May). *United States of America: A briefing for the UN Committee against torture.* New York: Amnesty International.

13. Ibid.

14. Hornblum, A. (1998). *Acres of skin.* New York: Routledge.

15. Gillespie, W. (2004). Prisoners' rights and states' responsibilities. In Stanko, S., Gillespie, W., & Crews, G. (Eds.), *Living in prison: A history of the correctional system with an insider's view* (pp. 111–127). Westport, CT: Greenwood, p. 114.

16. Ibid.

17. Finley, L. (2007). Our own Abu Ghraib? Torture of the "other" in the U.S. *War Crimes, Genocide, and Crimes Against Humanity*, *2*(2).

18. Ibid.

19. Williams, K. (2006). *American torture and the logic of domination.* Cambridge, MA: South End Press.

20. Amnesty International. (2001). *Broken bodies, shattered minds: Torture and ill treatment of women.* New York: Amnesty International, p. 9.

21. Rathbone, C. (2005). *A world apart: Women, prison, and life behind bars.* New York: Random House.

22. Williams (2006).

23. Ibid.

24. Ibid., p. 115.

25. Ibid.

26. Ibid.

27. Rejali (2007).

28. Ibid.

29. Williams (2006).

30. Ibid.

31. Rejali (2007).

32. Williams (2006).

33. Ibid.

34. Ibid.

35. Rejali (2007).

36. Ibid.

37. Ibid.

38. Ibid.

39. Goodman, A. (2006, May 9). Chicago's Abu Ghraib. *Democracy Now.* Retrieved January 15, 2008, from http://www.democracynow.org/206/5/9/chicagos_abu_ghraib_un_committee_against.html.

40. Ibid.

41. Ibid.

42. Ibid.

43. Ibid.

44. Vann, B. (2000, March 9). The Abner Louima case: Three New York cops guilty in cover-up of torture. *World Socialist Web Site.* Retrieved May 21, 2005, from http://www.wsws.org/articles/2000/mar2000/loui-m09_prn.shtml.

45. Chinyelu, M. (2003, July 17). Defining torture: At home and abroad. *New York Amsterdam News, 5–7,* p. 6.

46. Williams (2006).

47. Goodman (2006).

48. Williams (2006).

49. Ibid.

50. Hallinan, J. (2003). *Going up the river: Travels in a prison nation.* New York: Random House, p. 23.

51. Ibid.

52. Ibid.

53. Ibid.

54. Ibid.

55. Ibid.

56. Ibid.

57. Williams (2006).

58. Ibid., pp. 184–185.

59. Hallinan, J. (2005). Prisons are cruel and needlessly punitive. In Bailey, K. (Ed.), *How should prisons treat inmates?* (pp. 9–21). Farmington Hills, MI: Greenhaven Press.

60. Hallinan (2003).

61. Amnesty International (2000).

62. Rejali (2007).

63. Amnesty International (2000).

64. American Civil Liberties Union. (2005, December 14). *Prison conditions and prisoner abuse after Katrina.* Retrieved November 17, 2007, from http://www.aclu.org/racialjustice/gen/23007res20051214.html.

65. Smith, B. (2006, January 1). Sexual abuse of women in United States prisons: A modern corollary of slavery. *Fordham Urban Law Journal.*

66. Ibid., pp. 216–217.

67. Rathbone (2005).

68. Franklin (n.d.).

69. Rathbone (2005).

70. Amnesty International. (2001). *Broken bodies, shattered minds: Torture and ill treatment of women.* New York: Amnesty International.

71. Hallinan (2003).

72. Human Rights Watch. (1997). *Cold storage: Super-maximum security confinement in Indiana.* New York: Human Rights Watch.

73. Hallinan (2003).

74. Ibid.

75. Ibid.

76. Ibid.

77. Ibid., p. 177.

78. Ibid.

79. Ibid.

80. Bruton, J. (2004). *The big house.* Stillwater, MN: Voyageur Press.

81. Abramsky, S., & Fellner, J. (2003). *Ill-equipped: U.S. prisons and offenders with mental illness.* New York: Human Rights Watch.

82. Ibid.

83. Tarpley, L. (n.d.). Torture in Maine's prisons [Electronic version]. *Portland Phoenix.* Retrieved January 11, 2008, from http://www.portlandphoenix.co/features/top/ts_multi/documents/05081722.asp.

84. Abramsky & Fellner (2003).

85. Ibid.

86. Ibid.

87. Wooden, K. (2000). *Weeping in the playtime of others* (2nd ed.). Columbus, OH: Ohio State University Press.

88. Riok, J. (2006, April). *Deadly restraint.* Project NoSpank. Retrieved February 11, 2007, from http://www.nospank.net/camps.

89. Miller, C., & Caputo, M. (2006, October 14). New claims of abuse at boys camp. *Miami Herald,* pp. 1–2A.

90. Reid, T. (2007, October 12). Torture, starvation, and death: How American boot camps abuse boys [Electronic version]. *London Times.* Retrieved January 12, 2008, from http://www.timesonline.co.uk/tol/news/world/us_and_americas/article2641635.ece.

91. Dow, M. (2004). *American gulag: Inside U.S. immigration prisons.* Berkeley, CA: University of California Press, pp. 153–154.

92. Ibid., p. 142.

93. Ibid., p. 68.

94. Ibid.

95. Ibid.

96. Ibid.

97. Martin, J. (2004, August 6). Suicide triggers probe of tribal detention center. *The Seattle Times,* p. B1.

98. Newman, T. (2004, May 27). Prisons aren't Indians' only problem. *USA Today,* p. 12A.

99. Finley (2007).

100. Johnson, K. (2004, May 20). Former BIA official urged prison fixes [Electronic version]. *USA Today.* Retrieved from http://www.usatoday.com/news/nation/2004–05–20-indian-prisons-usat_x.html.

101. Minton, T. (2002, May). *Jails in Indian country, 2001.* Bureau of Justice Statistics.

102. Johnson (2004).

103. Heilpin, J. (2004, September 22). *Indian jails likened to Iraq.* Tribal Court Clearinghouse. Retrieved March 15, 2005, from http://www.tribal-institute.org/message/00000052.htm.

104. Ross, L. (2001). Punishing institutions. In Lobo, S., & Talbot, S. (Eds.), *Native American voices* (2nd ed., pp. 455–465). Upper Saddle River, NJ: Prentice Hall.

105. Ross, L. (1996). Resistance and survivance: Cultural genocide and imprisoned Native American women. *Race, Gender, and Class, 3*(2), pp. 143–164.

106. Tirado, M. (2005, February). Help for the forgotten. *American Indian Report, 21.*

107. Newhouse, E. (2003, January 13). *Watchdog group says prison fails to give proper treatment.* Prison Activist. Retrieved June 10, 2005, from http://www.prison activist.org/pipermail.prisonact-list/2003-January/006443.html.

108. Martin (2004).

109. Heilpin (2004).

110. Ibid.

111. Newman (2004).

112. Lockwood, M., & Alexander, R. (2005). Prisoners should not have it easy. In Bailey, K. (Ed.), *Race, Gender, and Class, 3*(2), pp. 143–164.

113. American Civil Liberties Union. (2007, November 8). *Disparate advocates tell Congress to fix law that silences prisoner abuse.* Retrieved November 17, 2007, from http://www.aclu.org/prison/gen/32771prs20071108.html.

114. Ibid.

115. Finley (2007).

116. Newhouse (2003).

117. Williams (2006).

118. Ibid., p. 179.

119. Dow (2004).

120. Ibid.

121. Franklin (n.d.).

122. Ibid.

123. Johnson, R. (1998). *Death work: A study of the modern execution process* (2nd ed.). Belmont, CA: West/Wadsworth.

124. Rajiva (2005).

6

Abuse in Guantanamo Bay, Afghanistan, and Iraq

This chapter focuses on the allegations of abuse occurring at prisons and detention centers overseas. It begins with a review of the Bush administration's directives after the terrorist attacks of September 11, which authorized the use of "harsh" interrogation techniques that were said to be essential in this "new" war, the war on terror. The chapter then presents evidence that torture and cruel, inhuman, and degrading treatment occurred first at Guantanamo Bay, Cuba, then in Afghanistan, and finally, in Iraq. The most notorious incident, the Abu Ghraib abuse, is well documented. Also presented in the chapter are overviews of major reports in which various officials investigated the conditions at detention centers and prisons overseas and the recommendations they made.

In addition to the abuses at Guantanamo and in Afghanistan and Iraq, the chapter discusses the CIA's rendition program. It concludes with a brief examination of the fallout from Abu Ghraib, which is taken up in greater detail in the discussion of the pros and cons of torture provided in the final chapter.

It wasn't until the 1970s that any form of comprehensive public auditing of torture began. Amnesty International (AI) issued its *Report on Torture* in 1973. Before this report, no specific group monitored the use of torture, and the International Committee of the Red Cross (ICRC) was the only international organization that performed audits of prison conditions, but they did so under limited conditions. Until 1955, ICRC reports were limited to camps for prisoners of war and only pertained to specific countries.[1] Even into the 1990s, none of the reports on torture focused on the United States, although

AI did cite U.S. domestic prisons and the death penalty as problematic (this is discussed in chapter 4).

The public was not really prepared, then, to discover that abuse was indeed a staple in our prisons and detention centers. It took some careful crafting by politicians to convince at least a good portion of the populace that harsh interrogations were needed. The first goal was to convince people the war on terror was a "new" form of warfare. Second, Bush administration officials had to convince us that new, tougher approaches were required in the war on terror in order to maintain the nation's safety and security. What was not happening, according to the Bush administration, was torture. Anything that had been authorized, the argument went, fell short of the actual definition of torture.

The Convention against Torture and Other Cruel, Inhuman, or Degrading Treatment or Punishment defines torture as

any act by which severe pain or suffering, whether physical or mental, is intentionally inflicted on a person for such purposes as obtaining from him or a third person information or a confession, punishing him for an act he or a third person has committed or is suspected of having committed, or intimidating or coercing him or a third person, or for any reason based on discrimination of any kind, when such pain or suffering is inflicted by or at the instigation of or with the consent or acquiescence of a public official or other person acting in an official capacity. It does not include pain or suffering arising only from, inherent in or incidental to lawful sanctions.[2]

U.S. federal law defines torture as any act committed by an official with the intent to inflict severe physical or mental pain or suffering on a person within his or her custody or care. Mental pain and suffering includes prolonged pain from the following: the infliction of or threatened infliction of severe physical pain; the administration or threatened administration of mind-altering substances or procedures designed to profoundly disrupt the senses or personality; the threat of imminent death; and the threat to imminently torture, either mentally or physically, or kill, another person.[3]

Court decisions have offered further clarity on what, specifically, constitutes torture. They include: being beaten, shocked, and then forced to stand, hooded, for long hours, where the victim then fell, broke his leg, and was denied medical treatment for a period of time; being given electric shocks, having one's hooded head put into foul water, having objects forced into one's anus, and being forced to remain standing, hooded and handcuffed, for several days; and enduring a fractured jaw while being kept handcuffed for hours by the arms, subjected to electric shocks, thrown on the floor, covered in chains connected to electric current, and kept naked and wet.[4]

Another critical component of the Bush administration's denial that torture has occurred involves the status of the person being interrogated or detained. The Geneva Conventions ban the use of torture or other forms of coercion on prisoners of war. A similar protection extends to civilians during times of hostility or foreign occupation. The Conventions do not apply to illegal combatants, however. Although the less specific protections of the Convention against Torture remain in force in cases involving legal combatants, the Bush administration had found their opening—if they were to dub those detained at Guantanamo Bay, in Afghanistan, and in Iraq as "illegal combatants," they could say there was no obligation to follow the Geneva Conventions or other international agreements regarding torture and prison abuse.[5]

Violations of the Geneva Conventions by any member of the U.S. armed forces or any national of the United States are punishable by lengthy jail sentences or even death under the War Crimes Act (WCA) of 1996.[6] The United States has even gone further than other countries in denouncing the use of torture, passing the Torture Victim Protection Act in 1991, which holds those perpetrating torture on others civilly liable.[7]

The WCA was amended in 2006, and until that time, its language was very close to that found in the Geneva Conventions. According to the Act, war crimes are "grave breaches" of the Geneva Conventions. These grave breaches of Geneva include: "willful killing, torture or inhuman treatment, including biological, experiments, willfully causing great suffering or serious injury to body or health...willfully depriving a protected person of the rights of fair and regular trial prescribed in the present Convention, taking of hostages and extensive destruction and appropriation of property, not justified by military necessity and carried out unlawfully and wantonly."[8] Documentation supports the fact that White House Counsel Alberto Gonzalez was concerned about possible prosecutions based on the WCA. This was one reason he cited for the reinterpretation of whether the Geneva Conventions applied to the war in Afghanistan. Attorney General John Ashcroft sent a similar memo to President Bush.[9]

Many believe that the evidence clearly shows U.S forces did indeed violate the Geneva Conventions. First came a series of reports of abuse at facilities overseas that are documented herein. In addition, in 2006, physician Steven Miles reported that there were 19 prisoners known to have died due to beatings, asphyxiation, or other torture by American soldiers or intelligence officers. That figure does not include all prisoners who died due to torture. It does not include homicides by torture committed by British soldiers, nor homicides of "ghost prisoners." Also excluded are suspicious deaths that were not investigated or that were barely investigated, or when the cause of death was misattributed to natural causes. Nor does it include deaths of prisoners who had been moved to other countries so that they could be tortured.[10]

BUSH ADMINISTRATION ARGUMENTS

After September 11, 2001, powerful Bush administration policymakers immediately promoted war against Iraq. When concerns about the legitimacy of the war and the suggested tactics arose, Bush reportedly responded: "I don't care what the international lawyers say, we are going to kick some ass." On January 25, 2002, White House Counsel Alberto Gonzalez advised President Bush that the Geneva Conventions did not apply to detainees in the "war on terrorism" at Guantanamo. Gonzalez described provisions of the Geneva Conventions as "quaint" and "obsolete."[11]

On August 1, 2002, Alberto Gonzalez requested a Justice Department memo (referred to as "The Torture Memo") that narrowly defined "torture" under U.S. law and offered a different interpretation of the Geneva Conventions. Under this definition, torture is limited to practices causing physical pain "equivalent in intensity to the pain accompanying serious physical injury, such as organ failure, impairment of bodily function, or even death." The memo also offers approval for specific controversial practices, including waterboarding. The author, Attorney General Jay Bybee, has subsequently been appointed to a lifetime position as a federal appellate judge.[12] Bybee also offered the following statement, which suggests the White House intended to support any number of interrogation tactics if they would allegedly help prevent another attack.

On September 11, 2001, al Qaeda launched a surprise covert attack on civilian targets in the United States that led to the deaths of thousands and losses of millions of dollars. According to public and government reports, al Qaeda has sleeper cells within the United States that may be planning similar attacks. Indeed, al Qaeda plans apparently include efforts to develop and deploy chemical, biological, and nuclear weapons of mass destruction. Under these circumstances, a detainee may possess information that would enable the United States to prevent attacks that potentially could equal or surpass the September 11 attacks in their magnitude. Clearly, any harm that might occur during an interrogation would pale to insignificance compared to the harm avoided by preventing such an attack, which could take hundred or thousands of lives.[13]

In the weeks after 9/11, advisors to President Bush offered the argument that, in a time of war, the president was authorized to make any final decisions. This argument was first offered via a memo from John Yoo, then deputy assistant attorney. Yoo described the president's broad constitutional powers as allowing him to determine the appropriate response to terrorist threats. Yoo defended this perspective, many times stating that it was obvious that there are certain categories of behavior that were simply not addressed by our legal system. Yoo further argued that these powers were also applicable to the methods of interrogation used to elicit information to fight the war on terror, and that Congress should not limit what the President was able to authorize. Hence, the Bush administration authorized a number of tactics that were unquestionably harsh. Further, officials at the highest levels looked away while military police and military intelligence committed brutal acts against prisoners overseas.

GUANTANAMO BAY

The United States has occupied Guantanamo Bay Naval Base in Cuba since the Spanish-American war. The 1903 treaty that ended that conflict provides the United States complete jurisdiction and control over Guantanamo. At the same time, the United States has argued no court has authority over the island. "All of this, from the state's perspective, makes Guantanamo a perfect place for exercising maximum authority while extending literally no rights—a fine place for imprisoning refugees without having to consider their pleas for asylum, as it was used in the 1990s. Or for operating an extra-legal prison camp where suspected terrorists are dealt with in whatever way the government sees fit."[14] The Supreme Court has rejected the idea that Guantanamo is beyond the reach of the courts, however. In *Rasul v. Bush,* the court ruled that detainees do indeed have the right to challenge their detention and can do so in federal courts.

As early as 2002, there were claims of abuse at Guantanamo. These took many forms, from overt physical torture to psychological abuse to denial of medical attention. Without a doubt, the conditions at Guantanamo were brutal. A Russian detainee who was arrested in Pakistan and then sent to Guantanamo commented, "Every country has its own way of torturing people. In Russia, they beat you up; they break you straight away. But the Americans had their own way, which is to make you go mad over a period of time. Every day they thought of new ways to make you feel worse."[15]

On October 11, 2002, interrogators in Guantanamo requested approval to use a list of tactics in questioning suspected 9/11 conspirator Mohammed al-Kahtani. This list included hooding, stress positions, sensory deprivation, and dogs. They also sought permission to use scenarios that would convince a detainee being questioned that severe pain or death, to himself or his family, was imminent. The memo specifically described interrogation sessions of 20 hours, light and sound assaults, stress positions, "exposure to cold weather," and the "use of a wet towel and dripping water to induce the misperception of suffocation" (waterboarding).[16]

Two months later, Rumsfeld approved the use of these techniques, not just for the interrogation of al-Kahtani but for wider application. A military investigation later confirmed that at least some of these techniques were used with al-Kahtani. He had been forced to wear a leash and "perform a series of dog tricks," foreshadowing what would emerge with the publication of the Abu Ghraib photos. Al-Kahtani had also been forced to wear women's underwear, and interrogators threatened to spread rumors he was gay. Six weeks later, Rumsfeld was forced to rescind that order under pressure from the Department of Defense General Counsel.[17]

Rumsfeld then established a Working Group that was supposed to delineate the tactics approved for interrogations. The Group listed 35 techniques, 26 of which were approved for use with noncombatants and the remaining for specific purposes or at specific locales. The latter included isolation, interrogation for as long as 20 hours per day, forced grooming (forcing a detainee to shave hair or beard), prolonged standing, sleep deprivation (although this still must be under 4 days), physical training such as jumping jacks and running, facial or stomach slapping, removing of clothing, and "increasing anxiety by use of aversions," such as the presence of dogs. On April 16, 2003, Rumsfeld approved 24 of the techniques, arguing the others would be reserved in case they were needed for specific situations.

One way inmates were abused was by denying them medical attention, which was authorized by Defense Secretary Donald Rumsfeld in December 2002. This is in violation of the Geneva Conventions. Under pressure, Rumsfeld revoked the order a month later. The practice continued, however. Inmates who had been shot and were in terrible pain were denied painkillers. There is even some suggestion that inmates may have been given mind-altering drugs to facilitate interrogation. Four Guantanamo and Afghanistan detainees and prisoners filed a lawsuit in which they claimed they had been denied a prosthetic limb, antibiotics for festering wounds, and treatment for constipation.[18]

The first detention center in the Guantanamo complex was called Camp X-Ray. Prisoners there were kept in small wire cages, which were many times infested with mice, rats, frogs, snakes, and scorpions. Detainees were exposed to hot sun, cold nights, wind, and rain. Floodlights illuminated the camp at night, making sleep difficult. They were not allowed to talk. Many reported they were beaten if they prayed.[19]

Between August 18 and August 26, 2003, nearly two dozen prisoners at Guantanamo Bay, or "Gitmo," tried to hang or strangle themselves. This included 10 simultaneous attempts in a single day. All of the attempts were to protest conditions at Gitmo, and they were among the 350 "self-harm" incidents recorded in 2003. All of these suicide attempts occurred after Major General Geoffrey Miller took command, charged with getting more information from the prisoners.[20]

Camp commandant Major General Miller merged the Joint Detention Group, the guards, with the Joint Interrogation Group, the people responsible for interrogations. This gave the interrogators greater authority over the guards, and consequently, over the prisoners. "At the bottom of Miller's scale ranking privileges and deprivations, is violence. The threat of pain—of torture—provides the grounding for the entire system of coercion and reward; the chief benefit of 'cooperation'—of compliance, submission—is the promise that one will not be so mistreated. A prisoner's privileges are measured by his distance from intolerable suffering."[21]

The worst abuses at Guantanamo came from the Internal Reaction Force, nicknamed the "Extreme Reaction Force," or ERF. The ERF was charged with responding to disturbances and conducting "cell extractions." Tarek Dergoul described his encounter with ERF:

They'd already searched me and my cell twice that day, gone through my stuff, touched my Koran, felt my body, around my private parts....And now they wanted to do it again, just to provoke me, but I said no, because if you submit to everything, you turn into a zombie. I heard a guard talking into his radio, "ERF, ERF, ERF," and I knew what was coming. The five cowards, I called them, five guys running in with riot gear. They pepper sprayed me in the face, and I started vomiting....They pinned me down and attacked me, poking their fingers in my eyes, and forced my head into the toilet pan and flushed. They tied me up like a beast and then they were kneeling on me, kicking and punching. Finally, they dragged me out of the cell in chains, into the rec yard, and shaved my beard, my hair, my eyebrows.[22]

Lest someone think this is just a prisoner seeking attention or revenge, reports of similar treatment have come from ERF members themselves. Specialist Sean Baker was ordered to put on an orange jumpsuit and crawl under a bunk for a practice cell extraction. He reported,

They grabbed my arms, my legs, twisted me up and unfortunately one of the individuals got up on my back from behind and put pressure down on me while I was face-down. Then he—the same individual—reached around and began to choke me and press my head down against the steel floor. After several seconds, 20–30 seconds, it seemed like an eternity because I couldn't breathe, I began to panic and I gave the code word I was supposed to give to stop the exercise, which was "red."...That individual slammed my head against the floor and continued to choke me. Somehow I got enough air. I muttered out, "I'm a U.S. soldier. I'm a U.S. soldier."

Not long after, Baker was examined by an Army Physical Evaluation Board, which determined he suffered from a traumatic brain injury as a result of playing a noncooperative detainee. He was discharged in April 2004.[23]

In addition to the Extreme Reaction Force's brutal methods, U.S. military authorities at Guantanamo utilized more sophisticated methods of torture. One of these was to identify, and then exploit, the sexual norms of prisoners so as to humiliate them. Female interrogators wore skimpy clothing, made provocative remarks, rubbed their bodies against those of the captives, and sometimes smeared them with dye resembling menstrual blood.[24] An interrogation tactic used with at least one detainee was documented in Erik Saar's *Inside the Wire*. "Brooke" unbuttoned her shirt and asked the detainee, Fareek, "What's the matter, Fareek? Don't you like women?" and "Do you like these big American tits, Fareek? I can see you are starting to get hard. How do you think Allah feels about that?"[25]

In 2004, a U.S. military official confirmed that a regular procedure at the main prison facility, Camp Delta, was to make prisoners who were not cooperating with interrogators strip to their underwear, sit in a chair with hands and feet shackled to a bolt in the floor, and endure strobe lights and loud rock and rap music played through two close loudspeakers. The air conditioning was also turned up to maximum levels. One prisoner recalled being left in a room with a strobe light flashing and Eminem playing repeatedly. A similar tactic was reported in Iraq, where interrogators exposed detainees to Metallica and Barney the Dinosaur.[26]

AFGHANISTAN

In August 2003, Amnesty International reported abuse at Bagram in Afghanistan, including two deaths. The Bush administration stonewalled that investigation, although on May 4 they acknowledged that as many as 20 investigations of abuse were ongoing. Although they deny it is cruel, degrading, or inhuman, some U.S. officials admitted to using "a little bit of smacky-face" to "soften up" Afghan prisoners.[27] Many people minimized this type of conduct, even asserting it was necessary to win the war on terrorism. A national security official said it was true officers might "kick them around a little bit in the adrenaline of the immediate aftermath." Another person contended, "If you don't violate someone's human rights some of the time, you probably aren't doing your job."[28]

Williams reported in 2006 that there had been more then 400 allegations of prisoner abuse since the start of the Afghan war, and more than 230 soldiers and officers faced court-martials or other administrative discipline for them. In November 2005, five officers were indicted for beating Iraqi prisoners.

All five pleaded guilty to dereliction of duty, and four pleaded guilty to assault and battery. Two pleaded guilty to maltreatment. Their sentences ranged from 30 days to six months in prison, as well as dishonorable discharges in two of the cases and reductions in rank of the others. As of May 2004, the Army Criminal Investigations Division was conducting 33 investigations concerning deaths in custody. The Defense Department released the death certificates for 23 of the cases. Three were from Afghanistan and the other 20 from Iraq. Three had occurred outside of detention facilities, and eight were considered homicides. At the time, the army was prosecuting 36 soldiers and investigating 21 others for their involvement in suspicious deaths.[29]

Like the abuse at Guantanamo, inmates in Afghanistan were often subject to highly sexual forms of torture as well as inadequate medical attention. During a medical exam of an inmate at a prison in Kandahar, Afghanistan, a large military police officer (MP), who was not the clinician, lubricated two of his fingers and performed an intrusive rectal exam. "Without warning the EPW [enemy prisoners of war], and in a cruel way, he pushed both of his finger's into the EPW's anus. This caused the EPW to scream and fall to the ground violently." A quarter of the medical personnel told military surveyors that they had seen prisoners who had reported being abused, although few said they saw signs of injuries. The Surgeon General's researchers found that 34 of 463 clinic records noted either suspected abuse or an allegation of abuse, but only 10 of those charts recorded any action taken to address the abuse. However, the researchers ignored records describing traumatic injuries that were simply diagnosed and treated without any comment on how the injury was acquired.[30]

Mr. Dilawar's case is one of the most extreme. He was tortured at Bagram Collection Point for five days in December 2002 before he died. Soldiers pulled a sandbag over his head and Dilawar complained that he could not breathe. He was then shackled and suspended from his arms for hours, denied water, and beaten so severely that his legs would have had to been amputated had he survived. He cried "Allah! Allah!" while guards were beating him with their batons. The guards found this so amusing that they beat him some more, evidently just to hear him cry. Although he was promised medical attention after the beating, he was returned to a cell and chained to the ceiling. Several hours later, a physician found him dead. "By then, the interrogators had concluded that Dilawar was innocent and had simply been picked up after driving his new taxi by the wrong place at the wrong time."[31]

One problem with this and other interrogations at Bagram was the inexperience of the interrogators—only 2 of the 13 soldiers charged with doing that job had ever conducted interrogations before arriving in Afghanistan. The officers were also aware that President Bush and Secretary Rumsfeld had ruled that the Geneva Conventions did not apply to Afghanistan, and the interrogation policies for the facility were unclear. This makes it easier to take an "anything goes" attitude toward the treatment of detainees. Army and intelligence officers who knew of the ongoing pattern of abuses at the Bagram facility did not intervene to stop them. In fact, just six days before Dilawar died another prisoner, Habibullah, died at the same facility under similar circumstances. In addition, the Pentagon covered up the real cause of death. An autopsy on December 13 found that Dilawar's death was a homicide. It had been caused by extensive and severe "blunt force injuries to lower extremities complicating coronary artery disease." The Pentagon, however, reported that the prisoner died of natural causes. Later, a coroner testified that Dilawar's legs were "pulpified" and his body looked as if it had been "run over by a truck." Twenty-seven soldiers were charged with various roles in causing and concealing Dilawar's death, but none were charged with murder. Five of those charged pleaded guilty, and the lengthiest sentence received was five months in a military prison. One soldier, who was convicted of maiming, assault, maltreatment, and making a false statement, received only a demotion and was given an honorable discharge.[32]

It is not just the army that has suffered from allegations of abuse. Records show 10 unsubstantiated allegations involving 24 marines from the First Marine Division. Eleven of the accused were court-martialed. In one of the incidents occurring in April 2003, three marines shocked a prisoner with an electronic transformer. In another incident a month later, marines in Karbala took turns holding a pistol to the head of a bound prisoner while posing for photos. In a horrific Independence Day tribute, marines ordered teenagers to kneel beside holes dug in the ground while they fired pistols in a mock execution. In August of the same year, a marine used alcohol-based cleaning fluid to light a prisoner's hands on fire. He was court-martialed for assault and was convicted, demoted, and jailed for 90 days.

In 2004, Brigadier General Charles H. Jacoby Jr. identified tremendous potential for abuse in the two dozen facilities he visited. He cited minimal training and inadequate supervision as primary factors. "Prisoners would have told him there was much more than potential—actual abuse was occurring, in the form of sleep deprivation, exposure to freezing temperatures, severe beatings, and, in a preview of Abu Ghraib, photographs of prisoners in embarrassing and obscene positions. Several suspicious deaths occurred in Afghan prisons as well."[33]

Many of the intelligence officers suspected to be involved in abusive behavior were part of the 519th Military Intelligence Battalion. Some of these troops were transferred to Abu Ghraib, where their job was to establish interrogation procedures. Specialist Damien Corsetti, nicknamed "Monster" by his peers and "King of Torture" by his superiors, was one of them. At Bagram, army investigators said Corsetti placed his penis on the face of a prisoner, simulated anally sodomizing another detainee, and was known to threaten inmates with rape.[34]

IRAQ AND ABU GHRAIB

Although the abuse occurring at Abu Ghraib has received the most attention because of the pictures, there have been many allegations of abuse at other facilities in Iraq. According to Human Rights Watch, some of the most serious abuse allegations have come from a special military and CIA task force based at Camp Nama in Baghdad. It has been known at times as Task Force 20, Task Force 121, Task Force 6–26, and Task Force 145. It has been charged with capturing or killing high-level combatants, including Saddam Hussein and Abu Musab al-Zarqawi. "Jeff" was a sergeant with the task force who described the "black room" where interrogations occurred. He described speakers in all four corners that were used to patch in horrifying noises as well as loud music and strobe lights. According to Jeff, detainees were generally forced to stand in stress positions in the black room. He also knew some interrogators beat detainees there. Detainees might be moved to other rooms, the blue and red, in which they were treated with far more kindness. The shift between rooms was much like the "good cop, bad cop" routine law enforcement uses to obtain information from suspects. In the case of an alleged financier of Abu Musab al-Zarqawi, Jeff described more abusive detention. The man was stripped naked, placed in the mud, and hosed down with very cold water in February. He was taken out of the mud and placed naked next to a very cold air conditioner. This was repeated throughout the night, and, according to Jeff, everyone knew about it, including the sergeant major. Jeff said that written authorization was required for some of the harsher techniques, but that this was easy to obtain. There was a template saved on their computers in the form of a checklist. Once someone selected the tactics they wished to use, they simply printed it, signed it, and sent it up the chain of command for a signature. Jeff said he never saw one returned unsigned. In addition, Jeff said the colonel in charge at the center often observed these abusive interrogations.

After a few weeks of witnessing abusive interrogations, Jeff and some others complained to the colonel, who told them he would get back to them. Within a few hours, some Judge Advocate General (JAG) officers and lawyers gave them a presentation explaining why those behaviors were both legal and necessary. The presentation was in PowerPoint, previously prepared and saved on a laptop computer. Jeff said that Camp Nama was completely closed off and that there was no Criminal Investigative Command (CID) there to whom they could register further complaints. Jeff felt the only way he could have reported the abuse was to leave his command at Camp Nama. He never saw any representatives from Human Rights Watch or the International Red Cross at Camp Nama, and said that he overheard someone saying they would never allow the Red Cross or CID investigators to access the facility. According to Human Rights Watch, Jeff's story was corroborated through numerous documents and accounts.[35]

"Nick" was a sergeant with the 82nd Airborne Division stationed at Forward Operating Base (FOB) Tiger in western Iraq from May to September 2003. Nick was ordered to serve as MP at the interrogation and detention center for most of his time in Iraq, where he was responsible for guarding detainees and for transporting them to be interrogated. He said he and other guards were under orders to subject detainees to severe sleep deprivation and expose them to temperatures reaching 135 and 145 degrees Fahrenheit. In the interrogation rooms music was played very loudly to disturb the detainees' senses. Nick described seeing interrogators punch detainees, often in the back of the elbow, kneecaps, or in other areas where they were less likely to leave visible marks. Although Nick said interrogations were conducted by many people at FOB Tiger, the civilian and CIA interrogators tended to be the roughest. It was difficult for soldiers at FOB Tiger to register complaints about what they saw. Once Nick tried, only to be dismissed. Nick said he looked up the Geneva Conventions on a laptop and found that what he was witnessing was in violation. When he reported to a superior, he was told to drop it and that they were following the directives they had been given. Nick also said he heard a lot of racist slurs, and felt that racism against Arabs played a large role in the abuses. Nick's account was corroborated by multiple other sources upon an investigation by Human Rights Watch.[36]

First held at Baghdad International Airport, Ahmed Shehab Ahmed, an Iraqi citizen, was transferred for interrogation at Rehidwaniya, an old property belonging to Saddam Hussein. There Ahmed endured multiple forms of brutal torture, including food and sleep deprivation, beatings, threatened rape (both of him and his family), sexual assaults with unidentified substances, and many others. He has become impotent as a result of the sexual abuse.[37]

Abuse was also widespread at Mosul, in northern Iraq. Human Rights Watch investigated the Brigade Holding Area (BHA) for the 2nd Brigade Combat Team and a special detention compound used by a select Navy Seals group, Naval Special Warfare Squadron 7, also known as Navy Seal Team 7. Tony Lagouranis was an army interrogator working at Mosul from February to April 2004. He was charged with conducting interrogations, and he told Human Rights Watch he witnessed abuse of detainees from his first moments there. He saw sleep deprivation, exposure to severe temperatures, forced exercise and use of painful stress positions, use of dogs to intimidate blindfolded detainees, and continual exposure to loud music and strobe lights. Lagouranis said he also saw bruises and injuries on detainees who had been transferred to the Navy Seals detention areas, suggestive of more physical abuse. Although he was charged with interrogating detainees, Lagouranis claimed there was no training regarding what and what was not appropriate. Nor did he receive much guidance or oversight from his superiors. Again, Lagouranis's accounts were corroborated by other sources.[38]

The most notorious incidents—those at Abu Ghraib prison—although no more horrifying than other examples cited here, gained notoriety with the very public airing of photographs depicting the abuse. Prior to the events at Abu Ghraib, both journalists and lawmakers expressed concerns about abuses in Iraqi prisons. The International Committee of the Red Cross (ICRC) reviewed the prisons in Iraq. Well before the Abu Ghraib scandal, they identified many abusive practices, including: insults and threats, sleep deprivation, and very tight handcuffing leading to lesions and wounds, as well as inappropriate punishments such as forcing inmates to walk around naked or wearing women's underwear on their heads.[39] Various reports described the leadership at the prisons as weak, and critiqued them for not providing adequate training and supervision in regards to conducting interrogations. "In the absence of effective formal authority, informal authority exercised disproportionate influence—specifically, the expertise of soldiers who worked as prison guards stateside."[40] Several of the soldiers who were later found guilty for their role in the abuse depicted in the pictures had worked as prison guards in the United States.

In another report prior to the Abu Ghraib scandal, Christian Peacemaker Teams (CPT), a faith-related group, described how GIs allowed a military dog to attack civilians during a raid on Ramadi, 30 miles west of Fallujah, in November 2003. Thirty people were arrested, including Saad al-Khashab, an attorney with Organization for Human Rights in Iraq. Al-Khasab told CPT that 30 detainees were handcuffed, laid on the ground, and then pushed into a house where the soldiers let the dog loose to bite several people.[41]

A major part of the problem was that facilities across the country were overcrowded and, consequently, sanitation and other proper conditions were lacking. For instance, the Mosul Collection Center in Iraq was designed to hold two or three prisoners. Yet the army put as many as 27 prisons in two small pens, making it impossible to meet sanitation standards. Each pen had a 6-by-12-foot roof to provide shelter from the Iraqi sun and one exposed plastic tank that served as a toilet. The prisoners were not given enough water to wash themselves or their clothes. Some wore the same clothes for more than two months.[42]

Senators Patrick Leahy and Arlen Specter wrote about rumors of unlawful interrogation techniques to then–National Security Adviser Condoleeza
Rice in June 2003, and two months later, Lieutenant Paul Bremer expressed
concerns that were forwarded to Rice, Defense Secretary Rumsfeld, and President Bush. Amnesty International reported abuse of prisoners as early as
April 2002 and again just 10 months before the scandal broke. They reported
hooding, sleep deprivation, and forced standing.[43]

Many have argued that the transfer of practices from Guantanamo Bay
to Abu Ghraib was not an accident, but a deliberate shift in strategy. The
Schlesinger Commission's investigation of abuse found that the migration
of interrogation techniques from Guantanamo Bay to Afghanistan, then to
Abu Ghraib, came largely from the 519th Military Intelligence Battalion.[44]
In July 2003, less than four months before the photos were taken in cell
block 1, the operations officer who had been in charge at Bagram took charge of
detainee interrogations at Abu Ghraib and began using "remarkably similar"
techniques, according to a high-level army inquiry quoted by the *Times*.[45]

When Major General Geoffrey D. Miller took over running the prison
he did so without this type of background experience. He immediately instituted the use of hoods, forced nudity, dogs, shackling in painful positions,
and extreme temperatures. It was Miller who argued, successfully, that the
primary purpose of army prisons was interrogations. Now, in addition to
military intelligence, military police serving as guards would also be perform-
ing interrogations. This undermined one of the most important safeguards
against abuse, which was the separation of guard duties from interrogation
practices.[46] Miller was asked to take a group to Iraq and share that philosophy.
His ideas were implemented quickly and horrified the Red Cross investigators who visited Abu Ghraib in October 2003. They documented persons
left completely naked in totally empty concrete cells and in total darkness
for several consecutive days. The military intelligence officer in charge of the
interrogation explained that this practice was normal and simply part of the
process.[47]

On October 16, 2003, Captain Carolyn A. Wood of the 519th Military
Intelligence Battalion posted "Interrogation Rules of Engagement" on the
wall of the Joint Interrogation and Debriefing Center at Abu Ghraib prison.
Authorized for use in interrogation were changes to an inmate's diet, sleep or
sensory deprivation for as long as 72 hours, up to 30 days of isolation, and the
use of stress positions for as long as 45 minutes at a time. Rather than alter
what the 519th was doing, this document merely verified the procedures that
had already been in use.[48]

Another specialized group that has faced numerous charges of abuse is an
elite CIA task force called Task Force 6–26, formerly known as Task Force 121.

In June 2004, Vice Admiral Lowell E. Jacoby headed an investigation of abuse by Task Force 6–26. They had received 10 reprimands for abuse and two court-martials were in process at the time. Four members had been reassigned after they tortured prisoners with Tasers. The creation of clandestine special forces like Task Force 6–26 emerged after President Bush authorized a top-secret Special Access Program (SAP) in late 2001 or early 2002, authorizing the Defense Department to establish a clandestine team of special forces to capture or kill al Qaeda operatives. Journalist Seymour Hersch reported about the SAPs:

In theory, the operation enabled the Bush Administration to respond immediately to time-sensitive intelligence: commandos crossed borders without visas and could interrogate terrorism suspects deemed too important for transfer to the military's facilities at Guantanamo. They carried out instant interrogations, often with the help of foreign intelligence services—at secret CIA detention centers scattered around the world.[49]

Seven Special Forces interrogators faced charges by the end of 2004, including at least six SEALs from 6–26. One of their victims died in CIA custody and was depicted in the notorious photograph of the body packed on ice at Abu Ghraib.[50]

Navy SEALs were involved in the abuse as well. In the early morning of November 4, 2003, SEAL Team 7 arrested Monadel al-Jamadi at his home near Baghdad. Al-Jamadi was a suspect in attacks against U.S. forces. He fought the soldiers while his family watched. The SEALs shackled him and threw him into the back of their Humvee, where they proceeded to beat and kick him, then sit on him during the short ride to an army base. An hour later, he was taken to a SEALs base, Camp Jenny Pozzi. There, he was threatened and interrogated in the "romper room" as a medic, Jerrod Holferty, watched. Al-Jamadi groaned, "I'm dying, I'm dying," to which the interrogator responded, "You will be wishing you were dying." Al-Jamadi was not given any medical evaluation or care. He was again thrown into a Humvee and this time taken to Abu Ghraib. Despite being beaten, kicked, and struck in the head with barrel of a rifle, al-Jamadi walked into the prison. His head was enclosed in a sandbag, he was naked below the waist, and he was shaking from the cold, fright, and fatigue. He was having difficulty breathing.

Al-Jamadi was not admitted to Abu Ghraib as a normal military prisoner. Instead, the CIA imprisoned him as a "ghost" prisoner. This meant that his name was not registered and that, despite his injuries and complaints, he did not receive the customary medical examination that is supposed to be given to new prisoners. The SEALs turned him over to the CIA at five A.M. Under

CIA supervision, al-Jamadi's arms were bound together behind his back and he was shackled to a barred shower-room window in such a way that if he fell down, his arms would be wrenched backward and upward in the shoulder sockets. This technique is called Palestinian hanging because it has reportedly been used by the Israelis. It has been used by Turkey and other nations as well. Another allegation was that a water-soaked cloth was placed over his face to constrict breathing, although the CIA did not respond to this claim, calling it classified. After a short interrogation, al-Jamadi fell down. A CIA interrogator called guards, telling them, "This guy does not want to cooperate." Guards came and tried to lift the wrist shackles behind al-Jamadi's back higher. The prisoner's arms were bulging backwards out of the shoulder sockets and blood was dripping from his mouth. The guards took the sandbag from his head and realized al-Jamadi was dead. An Iraqi physicians working with the CIA pronounced the death.

Military intelligence and CIA personnel were upset that al-Jamadi had died before giving information. Captain Donald Reese, commander of the Abu Ghraib guards, came to the shower room to hear Colonel Thomas Pappas, commander of military intelligence, say, "I am not going down for this alone." CIA personnel ordered that the corpse be kept overnight in a shower room, and Lieutenant Colonel Steve Jordan was sent to get ice. Sergeant Ivan "Chip" Frederick described the incident in an e-mail, "They stressed him out so bad that the man passed away. They put his body in a body bag and packed him in ice for about 24 hours."

Sabrina Harman and other members of the military police posed for photographs with the body packed in the melting ice. The next day, a medic inserted an IV in al-Jamadi's lifeless arm and guards rolled the body out of the prison on a gurney, so as to "not upset the other detainees." The Army Surgeon General's investigation accepts Colonel Pappas's word that this was not an attempt to conceal the manner or time of death. Vice Admiral Albert Church, however, concluded that medical personnel might have been attempting to conceal the homicide. Interrogators at Abu Ghraib were told that al-Jamadi died of a heart attack. The Armed Forces Institute of Pathology helped conceal the homicide. Five days after the death, institute pathologists conducted an autopsy and concluded that al-Jamadi had died of 'blunt force injuries complicated by compromised respiration." The autopsy and death certificate were not released to the Red Cross to give to the family even though the navy had taken al-Jamadi from his home.[51]

Just after midnight on November 7, 2003, a group of Abu Ghraib guards put sandbags on seven prisoners' heads, ordered them to strip, and forced them into a "dog pile." Over the next 20 minutes, one or two soldiers jumped on the pile multiple times and stomped on the prisoners' fingers, toes, and feet. They also passed around cameras and took pictures of the abuse, then sent them via computer where many other soldiers saw them.[52]

Specialist Sivits, in a sworn statement, described Specialist Graner punching a naked detainee who had an empty sandbag covering his head. The punch, done with a closed fist, hit the man so hard in the temple that he lost consciousness. Still, some argued this was not torture, as it was not "excessive." Mr. Womack, lawyer for Specialist Graner, maintained, "Striking doesn't mean a lot.... Breaking a rib or bone—that would be excessive." Mr. Bergin, lawyer for Sergeant Davis, who stomped on a prisoner's fingers, said, "He may have stepped on the hands, but there was no stomping, no broken bones." Graner described the directions he received from Military Intelligence (MI):

I was instructed to start sleep-management programs by [a civilian contractor] on three high-profile prisoners....The prisoners were known to me as Taxi Driver, an Iraqi; Smiley, a prisoner from Yemen; and Piggy...also a third-country national. Yell and scream at the prisoners. In Taxi Driver's case, have him wear female underclothing on his head. Cuff them in different standing positions when they would not remain standing on their own. And utilize loud music in the middle of the night. With Piggy, I was to use the isolation cell....In a word, I was to manhandle them and treat them rough...if a prisoner was not following your instructions, smack them around a little or use cold water, such as throwing a 1.5 liter bottle of water on them. Use sandbags as hoods always.[53]

The horror of the Abu Ghraib pictures may not capture all the heinous "interrogations" taking place there. Kasim Mahaddi Hilas and Mustafa Jassim Mustafa described witnessing Graner sodomize a prisoner with a chemical light while another soldier watched and a female soldier took pictures. One female prisoner, described only as Hilkas, was stripped naked, forced to wear underwear on her head, and hung, handcuffed, for hours. Other detainees told stories of rape and sodomization at the hands of interrogators.[54]

Although the MPs called him "Jihad Jerry" or "Gus," his real name remains unknown. He is the prisoner pictured in the infamous photograph being lead on a leash by MP Lynndie England. England, who was a clerk, not a guard or interrogator, was not supposed to be involved in handling prisoners. Major David Ausch, MD, the commander of Abu Ghraib's medical unit, had authorized guards to use a restraint around the abdomen of this prisoner, who was psychotic and who threw his feces and engaged in self-mutilation. Dr. Ausch did not know how to use psychiatric medications and says that he could not transfer mentally ill persons to a special psychiatric facility in Iraq. Abu Ghraib's psychiatrist worked for the BSCT (Behavior Science Consultation Team) and did not have clinical duties for the prison. Sergeant Neil

Wallin, a medic, testified that Gus was often restrained and sometimes given intravenous fluids when he refused to drink.[55]

Severely mentally ill prisoners often suffered the most degrading and abusive treatment in prisons in Iraq, just like at Guantanamo. Abu Ghraib guards took still and video photographs of prisoners who smeared themselves with feces, consumed or threw feces or urine, or inserted objects—for example, a banana—in their rectums. A videotape of an Abu Ghraib prisoner known as "Shitboy" shows the prisoner repeatedly slamming his head against the wall. Lieutenant Colonel Steven Jordan, who was responsible for the Interrogation and Debriefing Center at Abu Ghraib, says that a Dr. Anderson, a military physician, knew that this man was in the cell block and needed psychiatric care. He also says that he and Dr. Anderson asked Colonel Jerry Phillabaum, commander of Abu Ghraib's military police, to move "mentally unstable" prisoners out of the cell block, to no avail. Some guards would compel inmates who smeared feces on themselves to roll in the dirt before hosing them off with cold water. At Camp Bucca in Iraq, the Army Surgeon General confirmed a report that psychotic prisoners were left to lay in their feces and urine in metal storage containers where the air temperature reached 130 degrees.[56]

Inadequate training to conduct interrogations was surely a factor that encouraged abuse. Lieutenant Colonel West had never received any form of interrogation training, nor had he ever witnessed an interrogation. In August 2003, an Iraqi informant said that Mr. Yehiya Hamoodi, a Shiite police officer working with West's unit, was plotting to ambush West and some of his soldiers. West promptly sent his soldiers to arrest Mr. Hamoodi. They beat and shackled him and loaded him into their vehicle. When they arrived at the base in Taji, Iraq, they threw him off the Humvee. A medic cleared Mr. Hamoodi for questioning, despite the fact that his ribs had been hurt by the beating. Soldiers then took Hamoodi to an interrogation room, and Colonel West told the interrogators that they had one hour to obtain information or he would come down and "do it himself." For 40 minutes, four soldiers kicked and beat Hamoodi. Colonel West arrived during the later part of the interrogation and sat facing the prisoner with a cocked pistol on his lap, which he would occasionally point at Mr. Hamoodi. Colonel West tells how he became increasingly angry and threatened Mr. Hamoodi's life. In a sworn statement, a soldier reported that West told the prisoner, "I have come here for one of two reasons: one, to get the information I need or two, to kill you." A soldier displayed a knife and the translator told Mr. Hamoodi that his toes or fingernails would be cut off if he did not tell the truth. Another appalled soldier left the room after reminding West of the Geneva Conventions, an appeal that West apparently rejected. Finally, Colonel West had his soldiers blindfold Hamoodi and escort him outside, where six soldiers surrounded him with guns as the interrogation continued for another 15 minutes. A translator told

Hamoodi, "If you don't talk, they will kill you." West counted down from 10 and shot into the air. Two soldiers forced Hamoodi's head into a barrel. West did another countdown and, angling his gun close to the prisoner's head, fired into the barrel.[57]

As described earlier in this chapter, others were complicit in the abuse. Medical personnel, too, were involved in varying degrees. In November 2003, an Iraqi guard smuggled a pistol into Abu Ghraib and gave it to a prisoner, Armeen Sa'eed al-Sheikh. An informant promptly told the MPs, and they locked down the cell block and began a cell-to-cell search. When they got to his cell, al-Sheikh went for the pistol hidden in his bedding and gunfire was exchanged. Sergeant William Cathcart was hit by a ricochet, but was not injured. The soldiers wrestled al-Sheikh to the floor and sent him to the hospital with a dislocated shoulder and shotgun wounds to his legs. When al-Sheikh returned to the cell block after several days in the hospital, Specialist MP Charles Graner beat his wounded leg with a baton, all the time demanding that the prisoner renounce Islam. He then suspended al-Sheikh by his injured shoulder, even though the prisoner's wounded legs would not bear weight. Staff Sergeant-Medic Layton Reuben and another medic saw the beating while providing health care in the cell block. On three occasions, Medic Layton found al-Sheikh handcuffed with his arms over his head, putting stress on his injured shoulder and leg. Each time, he says that he told Graner to remove the handcuffs. Layton considered that to be adequate action. It is definitely not, according to the many guidelines on ethical medical behavior with prisoners and detained persons.[58]

In late 2004, an air force medical team claimed they investigated every Abu Ghraib detainee before and after interrogation. Yet a 2005 investigation by the army's Surgeon General found less than 50 percent of prisoners in Iraq, Afghanistan, and Guantanamo Bay were examined for injuries after being questioned. "Silence about abuse has two general forms: failing to see abuse for what it is, and failing to act when abuse is seen."[59] There is much evidence to suggest medical clinicians failed to "see" abuse. Officers watched prisoners get beaten but did not report it because they felt it was reasonable or warranted. Others walked away from abuse that they witnessed because they saw military intelligence involved and assumed the actions must have been authorized. Medical staff was also involved in falsifying records. Injuries were recorded as being present at capture, and medical personnel sometimes took great liberties in documenting the cause of injuries. In other cases, medical records were conveniently lost.[60]

According to Dr. Steven Miles, "U.S. medical societies were unprepared for the possibility that American military medical personnel might be complicit with prisoner abuse and neglect." Miles argued that, because the American Medical Association's (AMA) 250,000 members included a large group of physicians with military background, the group expressed little concern over medical complicity, even while allegations of prisoner abuse escalated. The 120,000 internists of the American College of Physicians (ACP) were much more active. In October 2003, six months before the Abu Ghraib photographs surfaced, the ACP president wrote President Bush, expressing deep concern about reported abuses of prisoners. The ACP did not receive a reply. They sent another letter to President Bush in May 2004, after the Abu Ghraib photos became public. That summer, the ACP failed to persuade the AMA to support a call for independent investigations of prisoner abuse. The AMA did endorse and offered to assist the Department of Defense in their own investigations. During the summer of 2004, the *New England Journal of Medicine* and the British medical journal the *Lancet* published articles claiming that American military medical personnel were complicit with prisoner abuse. The British Medical Association, the British Medical Foundation for the Care of Victims of Torture, and the American Medical Student Association (which is not part of the AMA) called on the AMA to investigate and discipline physicians who abetted the abuses. Dr. Matthew Wynia, director of the AMA Institute for Ethics, affirmed the organization's pre–Abu Ghraib position on physicians and torture, which was that physicians were to have absolutely no role in torture, nor were they to condone its use. Even AMA medical publications, which are editorially independent from the organization, did not publish articles on prison human-rights abuses until late 2005.[61]

The 82nd Airborne reported to Human Rights Watch that they regularly denied prisoners food and water, forced them to perform strenuous exercises in extreme temperatures, deprived them of sleep, and beat them, sometimes with bats. One soldier explained,

It was like a game. You know, how far could you make this guy go before he passes out or just collapses on you. From stress positions to keeping them up ___ing two days straight, whatever. Deprived them of food, water, whatever. . . . We would give them blows to the head, chest, legs, and stomach, pull them down, kick dirt on them. This happened every day. . . . Some days we would just get bored so we would have everyone sit in a corner then make them get in a pyramid. This was before Abu Ghraib but just like it. We did that for amusement.[62]

At Abu Ghraib, the various agencies competed to gather information. "Torture is a zero-sum game, and organizations have incentives to interrogate the prisoner before others do."[63] Abu Ghraib MPs staged contests "to see how quickly a prisoner could be brought to tears." Interrogators competed for information, then bragged about their successes, despite the fact that officials acknowledge most of the useful battle intelligence came before prisoners got to Abu Ghraib.[64] The Abu Ghraib photos circulated among select groups of colleagues and friends. One of the computers in Abu Ghraib's office of military intelligence even used the now-famous image of naked detainees arranged in a pyramid as a screen saver.[65]

In the Abu Ghraib photos, Americans are the kings while prisoners are stripped and posed so that every part of their bodies is available to handling by their tormenters and inspection by the camera's eye. But the prisoners are hooded, physically prevented from returning their captors' gaze; hooding literally makes the prisoners faceless, preventing guards and interrogators from seeing them as people.[66]

Although most of the attention about the abuses at Abu Ghraib has focused on male victims, females too are subject to abuse in prison and detention. During the first few months of the U.S. occupation of Iraq, 42 women were held at Abu Ghraib. They describe being strip searched repeatedly and held for no discernible reason in solitary confinement. Military officials claim this protects them from male inmates, but it also makes them more vulnerable to abuse by male guards. Khadeja Yassem described her interrogation at Abu Ghraib: "They took me to a room with a dog. It was on a leash, and it was standing two metres from me. I was terrified—I felt as if I would go mad. My legs buckled and I collapsed."[67] General Antonio Taguba had reported an MP "having sex" with a female, although that the interaction was consensual seems unlikely. One article made a brief reference to the rape of an Iraqi boy by American soldiers. Reports on activist websites and in foreign papers tell of far more abuse of females. One former Abu Ghraib detainee told of being forced to sleep in a tiny, insect-infested cell where, because she vomited so often, she was given fluid through a dirty IV. Reportedly, Iraqi women were forced at gunpoint to bear their breasts and were videotaped naked. In December, an anonymous woman calling herself "Noor" described being stripped, raped, and impregnated by American soldiers. A lawyer investigated and found her claims to be credible and representative of abuse across all of Iraq.

Many [of the] Abu Ghraib images also are pornographic in the conventional sense. Their subjects are naked and lewdly posed, some with clothed American women playing dominatrix roles. These photos—some depicting corpses and brutal interrogation practices—are like stills from snuff films, statements of the utter worthlessness of the prisoners and the life-and-death power over them exercised by their captors.[68]

THE INVESTIGATIONS

In the fall of 2003, army investigators began a criminal inquiry into abuse allegations at Abu Ghraib, although the public did not learn what they had found until after the pictures surfaced in April 2004.[69] After the army found troubling evidence of abuse in their first investigations, in January 2004 Lieutenant General Ricardo S. Sanchez, the overall military commander in Iraq, appointed Major General Antonio M. Taguba to expand the investigation. Taguba widened the scope of inquiry to include the entire 800th Military Police Brigade, commanded by Brigadier. General Janis Karpinski, and the 372nd MP Company of the brigade's 320th MP Battalion, which was the guard unit in charge at Abu Ghraib. Taguba found the entire brigade to be poorly trained. Most of the soldiers in the brigade had very low morale, as they had expected to go home in spring of 2003, after the United States occupied Baghdad. Taguba also found inadequate procedures for identifying and handling detainees and confusion about the duties of the brigade, the Military Intelligence soldiers, and the CIA civilians who were interrogating the prisoners. Taguba found evidence of abuse by military police, including holding prisoners naked for several days, forcing them to masturbate while being photographed and videotaped, placing a dog chain around a prisoner's neck and photographing him next to a female guard, and using dogs without muzzles to frighten detainees. He recommended disciplinary action against 12 officers and civilians, although the highest in rank was General Karpinski.[70]

Another investigation by Major General George R. Fay focused on the role of intelligence soldiers. Fay also found part of the problem was low soldier morale, exacerbated by the frequent mortar attacks that followed the occupation of Baghdad. He concluded that only a small group of "morally corrupt and unsupervised soldiers and civilians" were responsible for the physical and sexual abuse, but noted that "the climate created at Abu Ghraib provided the opportunity for such abuse to occur and to continue undiscovered by higher authority for a long period of time." He recommended administrative action but not court-martials for Lieutenant Colonel Steven L. Jordan, who was in charge of the interrogation center at the prison, and for Colonel Thomas M. Pappas, 205th Military Intelligence Brigade commander. Later, Lieutenant General Anthony R. Jones took over Fay's investigation. He reached the same conclusions, but emphasized that the climate for abuse was set by the Bush administration when they confused the issue of how to interrogate prisoners in late 2001 and early 2002. For instance, in December 2002, Defense Secretary Donald Rumsfeld authorized the use of dogs and the removal of detainees' clothing to induce stress during questioning of "unlawful combatants" held in Afghanistan and at Guantanamo Bay. General Jones acknowledged that these techniques were not meant to apply to the prisoners in Iraq, but found that some of the same military personnel involved in interrogations in Iraq had served as interrogators in other locations and did not have a clear understanding of what was expected there. Consequently, "the existence of confusing and inconsistent interrogation technique policies contributed to the belief that additional interrogation techniques were condoned in order to gain intelligence."[71]

In addition, the presence of the CIA and perhaps other secret government interrogators operating under their own rules at Abu Ghraib caused tremendous confusion, according to General Fay's report. Their more lax procedures "eroded the necessity in the minds of soldiers and civilians for them to follow Army rules." None of the techniques approved by President Bush or Secretary Rumsfeld had ever authorized sexual abuse or physical violence against prisoners, according to Fay, but the confusion regarding what precisely was approved had "led indirectly to some of the non-violent and non-sexual abuses," concluded General Jones when he finished the investigation Fay started.[72]

"In such a morally ambiguous climate, under stress, rotten apples among the guards on the night shift at Abu Ghraib went further. If all the normal rules no longer apply, those inclined to brutality may feel that anything goes." Rather than holding those at the highest levels responsible, the weight of military justice fell on Private England, Specialist Graner, and the other low-ranking soldiers who had clearly committed illegal acts in Abu Ghraib. Junior officers and enlisted men in Navy SEAL and other Special Forces units were charged with similar offenses in Afghanistan. Those charged with conducting interrogations at Abu Ghraib claim they did not realize they were breaking any rules, since no rules were posted. Specialist Sabrina Harman stated, "The Geneva Convention was never posted, and none of us remember taking a class to review it.... [My] first time reading it was two months after being charged. I read the entire thing highlighting everything the prison is in violation of. There's a lot."[73]

In all, 11 soldiers—those depicted in the photographs—were found guilty of various charges. Some supervisors received reprimands, but only one, Brigadier General Janis L. Karpinski, was demoted (to Colonel). Lynndie England was convicted on six of seven counts, including one conspiracy, four counts of maltreatment of detainees, and one count of committing an indecent act.[74]

In his court-martial, Graner offered a "Nuremberg defense." That is, he argued that any abuse he committed or authorized was on orders from his commanders. This was unsuccessful, as Graner was found guilty of committing abuses in the first full-scale court-martial. He was convicted on five counts of assault, maltreatment, and conspiracy. He received a 10-year sentence.[75] But his defense, although not accepted, pointed out an important concept. The role of higher leadership in condoning and ignoring the abuse was clear. Contrary to Bush administration claims, the abuses at Abu Ghraib did not just involve a "few bad apples." Rather, official reports, including the Defense Department's investigative committee, found the chain of command knew about and ignored allegations of abuse in at least 10 percent of cases.[76] As attorney Scott Horton, Chair of the International Law Committee of the Association of the Bar of the City of New York commented, "Those who craft immoral policy deserve the harshest punishment."[77]

Soldiers' personal accounts, accumulated by Human Rights Watch, detail the role of Military Intelligence (MI) in abuse of detainees. Many of the tactics they note were authorized by people at or near the top of the chain of command, but as of 2006 no MI officers who served in Iraq had been charged with criminal acts. In fact, General Barbara Frost, Chief of Military Intelligence in late 2003 and 2004, was promoted to commander of the Army Intelligence Center at Fort Huachuca, Arizona. Of the relatively few court-martials that have occurred, most have involved military police. Similarly, several homicide cases involving CIA agents who abused detainees until they died were referred to the Department of Justice for prosecution in 2004 and 2005, yet not one CIA operative has been tried. As of June 2006, only one civilian contractor had been indicted.[78]

The role of multiple players higher up the chain of command was documented in an Independent Panel to Review Department of Defense Detention Operations, headed by former Secretary of Defense James R. Schlesinger. Rumsfeld commissioned the report in the spring of 2004 to determine "the cause of the problems and what should be done to fix them," not only in Abu Ghraib but elsewhere. The Independent Panel issued its report and recommendations in August, finding 66 cases substantiated by that time, 8 in Guantanamo, 3 in Afghanistan, and 55 in Iraq, one-third of them (including five detainee deaths) during interrogations. The shocking abuses in the photographs, the forced masturbation, and the gratuitous violence committed "just for the fun of it," the panel found, had not occurred during intelligence questioning but "would have been avoided with proper training, leadership and oversight."[79]

The Independent Panel acknowledged that the techniques used at Gitmo had not "accidentally" migrated to Afghanistan and Iraq. "Although specifically limited by the Secretary of Defense to Guantanamo, and requiring his personal approval (given in only two cases), the augmented techniques for Guantanamo migrated to Afghanistan and Iraq, where they were neither limited or safeguarded," the Independent Panel found. When Major General Geoffrey Miller was sent from Guantanamo to Iraq in August 2003, he, "brought the Secretary of Defense's April 16, 2003 policy guidelines for Guantanamo with him and gave this to [General Sanchez] as a possible model for the command-wide policy that he recommended be established," the panel reported, although General Miller noted that it applied only to unlawful combatants at Guantanamo and not in Iraq. Nevertheless, in the panel's findings, General Sanchez did authorize a dozen interrogation techniques beyond those permitted by standard army doctrine, and though he later rescinded that authorization, in the ensuing confusion some soldiers in the field came to believe that harsher techniques were condoned. And a few apparently concluded that all the wraps on torture were off.[80]

The Independent Panel explained that "there is no evidence of a policy of abuse promulgated by senior officials or military authorities. Still the abuses were not just the failure of some individuals to follow known standards, and they are more than the failure of a few leaders to enforce proper discipline. There is both institutional and personal responsibility at higher levels."[81]

The Fay report acknowledged the following abuses at Abu Ghraib: (1) physical, including slapping, kicking, various inappropriate restraints, restricting a detainee's breathing by covering the mouth, and poking at existing injuries; (2) use of dogs to intimidate and in some cases physically attack detainees, including one documented contest in which two Army dog handlers tried to see who could make a detainee urinate or defecate from fear first; (3) humiliating and degrading treatment, including inappropriate nakedness and taking photographs of detainees in various stages of undress and in humiliating positions, and forcing detainees to pose in simulated sexual positions; (4) improper use of isolation; (5) failure to safeguard detainees from threats and acts of violence; and (6) failure to report abuse of detainees.[82]

Other sources were even more likely to recognize that responsibility for the abuses went to the highest levels. Amnesty International, the Red Cross, and Human Rights Watch all made this case. For instance, Reed Brody, an HRW lawyer, pointed out that the bold poses of the soldiers with the prisoners "suggests they had nothing to hide from their superiors."[83]

On May 7, 2004, the Senate Armed Forces Committee heard testimony from Donald Rumsfeld, Richard Myers, Les Brownlee, Peter Shoomaker, Lance Smith, and Steve Cambone. Republican John Warner of Virginia chaired the committee, which focused on who knew what about the abuses and when they knew it. The testimony reflected many contradictions—for instance, Rumsfeld claimed he heard about the abuse after a January 16, 2004, briefing while Myers said he knew before the briefing. Yet these two admitted they spoke to one another every day, typically multiple times. Another contradiction that emerged in the testimony was the impact of Miller's "gitmoization." Miller was criticized for his use of military intelligence in the week of March 3–9, after General Taguba submitted his report in late February. Then, in late March, after Karpinski was suspended, Miller was brought from Guantanamo to head Abu Ghraib, at least one month before the Taguba report was approved. Some have suggested the Taguba report was hastily approved in order to make it appear that army was ready to conduct a fair investigation.[84]

It is obviously illogical to believe that those at the highest levels of the government did not know about the allegations. Long before the ICRC report of February 2004, Human Rights Watch had written to Bush on December 27, 2002; the directors of several rights groups had written to Deputy Secretary of the Department of Defense Paul Wolfowitz on January 14, 2003, to Bush on January 31, and to White House counsel Haynes on February 5; to Rumsfeld on January 12 and February 10; and to Rice again on May 3. The HRW report on Abu Ghraib had come out on March 8, 2004. Before 2003, the Coalition Provisional Authority (CPA) had also heard complaints from Iraqi officials and reporters and a case of abuse in May 2003 at Bucca had been investigated and disposed on December 29, 2003. It is simply not credible that Bush administration leaders were ignorant of a matter that attracted such extensive attention.[85]

Janet Karpinski is the highest-ranking official to be held responsible for the abuse. Depictions of Janis Karpinski often represent her as completely incompetent. Yet there were no allegations of abuse at the other two camps she ran. There was certainly overcrowding at Abu Ghraib, and the chaos that ensues from overcrowding supports Karpinski's claim that it had been turned into an all-purpose pen for every type of detainee, convenient to Baghdad but also somewhat outside the scrutiny of international observers in the capital city. Although some claim Karpinski was present during the abuse of some of the prisoners, others doubt the credibility of these allegations given her background. She is fluent in Arabic and has demonstrated in other ways that she is more fair to Iraqis than other prison leaders.[86] Some have argued "the torture and humiliation taking place at Abu Ghraib as nothing more than what might have been expected from putting a woman in charge of a group of impressionable young men." Conservative pundit Ann Coulter offered this view:

I think the other point that no one is making about the abuse photos is just the disproportionate number of women involved including a girl general running the entire operation. I mean, this is lesson, you know, one million and 47 on why women shouldn't be in the military. In addition to not being able to carry even a medium-sized backpack, women are too vicious.[87]

In her book, *One Woman's Army*, Janet Karpinski described the first time she was told about the abuse allegations. She received an email from Colonel Mark Marcello, commander of the Criminal Investigation Division (CID) units, which said that he was on his way to provide a brief to General Sanchez about allegations of prisoner abuse depicted in photos. She said the color went out of her face and she thought she would pass out. "It wasn't just Marcello's words that shocked me. It was the fact that I had no idea what he was talking about."[88] Karpinski also described the horror she felt when she saw the first picture of Specialist Graner and Private First Class Lynndie England grinning and flashing their thumbs up in front of a pyramid of naked prisoners. She commented,

The next picture was even more heartbreaking. It showed a female MP with a nineteen-year-old Iraqi woman, a detainee whom she had befriended. I had spoken to the young Iraqi woman after she was arrested for prostitution. She said through her sobs that her husband forced her to into the profession. If we had released her, her father or brothers might have killed her to uphold the family honor. So we held her in our section for women and juveniles on what amounted to humanitarian grounds. One of our female MS had taken her under her wing, tried to boost her spirits, taught her a bit of English. But while the MP was escorting the Iraqi woman in another part of the prison one day, somebody had told the MP to lift up the teenager's shirt and expose her breasts to the camera, and the MP had complied, humiliating and betraying her friend. I will never understand why.[89]

Karpinski reported to her commander, Sanchez, shortly after seeing the photos. She described the interaction: "The commander said not a word. He sat at a small conference table, and I sat opposite him. He put his hand on a piece of paper, turned it toward me, and pushed it at me. It was an admonishment directed at me, dated January 17, almost a week before our meeting. The date would indicate for the record he had acted promptly, yet he had kept it in the drawer for a week before deciding to actually spring it on me." It derided her for her poor leadership and required Karpinski to suspend the platoon leader, company commander, and battalion commander and assess their "leadership positions."[90]

Conditions at Abu Ghraib were appalling well before the abuses. Karpinski was told not to release anybody, and the result was a surge in prisoners. She commented that not all of these prisoners were involved in terrorist acts or in the insurgency—rather, many were ordinary street thugs. "The rule around Iraq seemed to be, If in doubt, send'em out to Abu Ghraib." The population grew to 8,000 at one point. "As the population at Abu Ghraib grew, the mortar attacks become more frequent, and more accurate."[91]

Karpinski described her first interaction with Major General Geoffrey Miller. Miller, upset at some challenging questions presented by Military Intelligence officers, commented, "Look, the first thing you have to do is treat these prisoners like dogs. If they ever get the idea that they're more than dogs, you've lost control of your interrogation." She said Miller later denied using those words.[92]

One positive aspect of the Abu Ghraib scandals was the initiative demonstrated by Sergeant Joseph Darby, a 24-year-old army reservist. Darby saw what his fellow soldiers were doing, was appalled, and he acted to stop it.[93] Another soldier had given Darby a CD that had the disturbing photos on them. Darby was upset at what he saw and decided to turn the CD in to a superior. Although the subsequent investigation did not identify Darby, he lived in fear for the next six weeks that someone would know he was the whistle blower. Since then, Darby's mother and wife have been threatened and he now lives in hiding in protective custody. Other officers had previously expressed horror at abuse they witnessed, despite great danger to themselves. "I pulled the guy out [an E6 interrogator, and said]: 'I looked—I looked this stuff up and this is not the way it is supposed to be,' you know? He was like, 'This is the directive we had. You need to go ahead and drop this, sergeant.' You know, and he outranked me." These were the words of a U.S. Military Police Sergeant who was stationed at Forward Operating Base Tiger in al Qaim, Iraq, in 2003. In writing about torture in Iraq and Afghanistan, Miles received a number of nasty emails. One read, "Who gives a dam [sic] about these sub human animals. You so called educated asses need to worry more about us americans and america which is your country yes. so smarten up and care about us before you go off worrying so much about terrorists. Who by the way may or may not have been abused."[94]

In describing why there was little coverage in the mainstream media of the abuses that many groups had identified far early than those at Abu Ghraib, Katrina van den Heuvel of the Nation argued that journalists are intimidated and are too afraid not to be patriotic in a war atmosphere. There is some evidence to support this. A reporter who videotaped a marine shooting a wounded Iraqi in the head was the target of death threats. There have been charges, although the government denies them, that reporters have been targeted on the battlefield. Author and activist Lila Rajiva maintained that there were many other disturbing stories of abuse that received little or no attention. She cites the ICRC report that there were more than 100 children in U.S. custody and that interrogators molested a 15-year-old girl and physically abused a 16-year-old boy. Rajiva commented,

Compare the attention given to the torture photos with the complete silence shrouding these two explosive pieces. Was the overexposure of some crimes meant to distract from the existence of others? Was the tripping and humiliating of adult males seen as more publicly defensible than the abuse of children? Male rape, after all, can be used manageably in a partisan attack, but child abuse might be ammunition strong enough to blow up both sides. Or were the torture photos leaked intentionally in a calculated damage-control effort as some have suggested? There is a documented history of ties between the CIA and the major media—from CBS to Newsweek and the New York Times. Reaching far back to the Cold War, this record makes it impossible to discount the possibility of a damage-control campaign.[95]

What is clear is that Abu Ghraib was not an isolated incident. Rather, it was part of a long history of torture and abusive interrogations. As documented in earlier chapters,

The water tortures that American forces used in the Spanish-American war come home to American police stations. The electric torture used in Vietnam reappears in Arkansas prisons in the 1960s and in Chicago squad rooms in the 1970s and 1980s. Torture continues today in American prisons where guards wear and use electric stun guns routinely. Reiterating these meanings not differently but only more completely, Abu Ghraib is the externalized heart of an American gulag no different in kind if not in degree from that of the Soviets, no different from the carceral system of any empire.[96]

Given the history of torture and abuse perpetrated by the United States, the photos of abuse at Abu Ghraib "no longer seem aberrant or exceptional but completely in line with practices that were being used or planned in classified research. The prisons merely provided the experimental lab, with prisoners the guinea pigs, for a practical experiment in the forms of mental subjugation."[97]

THE CIA'S RENDITION PROGRAM

"After the attacks on September 11, 2001, the White House made torture its secret weapon in the war on terror." Publicly, Washington sent its regular military forces for conventional combat in Afghanistan and Iraq. Yet this alone was not deemed adequate to address the ad hoc, mobile nature of terrorist units. "With its countless Cold War victories, overthrowing enemies on four continents with coups and covert operations, the CIA had an aura of invincibility and soon became Washington's chosen instrument for the fight against Al Qaeda."[98]

As documented in chapter 3, the CIA had previously resorted to torture in attempting to amass intelligence, and had been unsuccessful in their attempt to topple the underground movements in Vietnam. In the years between the last known dissemination of the CIA's torture manuals and the declaration of war against terror after the September 11th attacks, the agency worked to outsource torture to U.S. allies. Starting in the mid-1990s, the agency sent detainees to third world allies known to torture. In 1995, CIA agents kidnapped terror suspects in the Balkans, some of them Egyptian nationals, and shipped them to Cairo for brutal interrogation. At first the agency specifically targeted people named in foreign arrest warrants. Former CIA Director George Tenet later testified that, in the years before 9/11, the CIA was involved in the transport of approximately 70 individuals to foreign countries without formal extradition. Recently, the rendition program has been expanded to include anyone the United States designates as an illegal combatant—"in other words, anyone the Bush administration wants to push outside the protection of the law."[99] This process has been called "extraordinary rendition" or just "rendition." When the extraordinary rendition program began, all the prisoners sent to other countries were put under the authority of the government in those countries. The United States maintained a hands-off approach. "When questioning was about to begin in a host country, CIA agents would hand lists of questions to the interrogators, then leave the room—thereby removing direct culpability for any torture that was used."[100]

But that changed after 9/11, with the United States taking a more direct role in their treatment. The United States is now taking prisoners into their own control in third world countries, which significantly jeopardizes the detainees' due process rights. Robert Baer, who spent 21 years working in the Middle East for the CIA until he left in the mid-1990s, argued renditions were always about making prisoners talk, and different countries had different values. He remarked, "If you send a prisoner to Jordan, you get a better interrogation. If you send a prisoner, for instance, to Egypt, you will probably never see him again; the same with Syria."[101]

According to a former senior officer in the directorate of operations at the CIA, "Before 9/11, these renditions were much simpler. They looked at people who were wanted in these countries and brought them back there. But that's quite a different scale to what happened after 9/11." For CIA case officers, the program had one important point. Every decision was signed off on at the highest level, ultimately by President Bush himself. They were aware President Bush had signed a specific "finding" (an authorization for covert action) in the days following 9/11 that gave clear approval for the CIA to capture terrorist suspects and transfer them to foreign countries at will. As one former CIA official, who was directly involved in renditions, told me, "Everything we did, down to the tiniest detail, every rendition and every technique of interrogation used against prisoners in our hands, was scrutinized and approved by headquarters. And nothing was done without approval from the White House—from [National Security Adviser Condoleeza] Rice herself, and with a signature from [Attorney General] Ashcroft."

Rendition is clearly illegal, both internationally and domestically. It has been specifically banned under several international conventions as described in chapter 3. In 1998, Congress passed legislation making it illegal to expel, extradite, or otherwise affect the involuntary return of any person to a country in which there are substantiated grounds for believing that person would be in danger of being tortured. This legislation was to apply regardless of whether the person was ever physically present in the United States.[102]

The case of Maher Arar illustrates the rendition process. In 2002, Arar, a Syrian-born Canadian citizen, was arrested at New York's JFK airport on his way home from vacation. Despite repeatedly acknowledging Syria as a country that employs torture, U.S. officials shipped Arar there. He was kept for 10 months in a windowless cell resembling a grave. He was repeatedly whipped with electric cables and threatened with shocks until he confessed to whatever accusations were made. "You just give up. You become like an animal," he said.[103]

German citizen Khaled El-Masri was detained at the border of Macedonia on New Year's Eve 2003 because his name resembled that of a wanted terrorist. The Macedonian police notified the CIA, and the Director of the CIA Counterterrorism Unit's al Qaeda Unit ordered him rendered. El-Masri described what happened to the *Los Angeles Times:*

I was handcuffed, blindfolded, and taken to a building where I was severely beaten. My clothes were sliced from my body with a knife or scissors, and my underwear was forcibly removed. I was thrown to the floor, my hands pulled behind me, a boot placed on my back. I was humiliated.

Eventually my blindfold was removed, and I saw men dressed in black, wearing black ski masks. I did not know their nationality. I was put in a diaper, a belt with chains to my wrists and ankles, earmuffs, eye pads, a blindfold and a hood. I was thrown into a plane, and my legs and arms were spread-eagled and secured to the floor. I felt two injections and became nearly unconscious. I felt the plane take off, land and take off. I learned later that I had been taken to Afghanistan.

There, I was beaten again and left in a small, dirty, cold concrete cell. I was extremely thirsty, but there was only a bottle of putrid water in the cell. I was refused fresh water.

That first night I was taken to an interrogation room where I saw men dressed in the same black clothing and ski masks as before. They stripped and photographed me, and took blood and urine samples. I was returned to the cell, where I would remain in solitary confinement for more than four months.[104]

As documented in chapter 3, "The US does not just take advantage of the harsh methods, low standards, and torture-chamber infrastructure common in authoritarian societies. It helps to build and maintain these systems of brutality by providing the necessary money, weapons, training, and diplomatic cover."[105] Israel is the single largest recipient of U.S. foreign aid. The country also has a well-documented history of torture and abuse. "So long as Israel struggles for control of the Occupied Territories, its recourse to torture is likely to persist. And so long as Israel continues to serve our government's agent in the region, the US will support it both in its territorial claims and in its general abuse of the Palestinian population, including the use of torture."[106]

Egypt is another recipient of U.S aid, as well as a "partner" in the CIA's rendition program. Egypt has a notorious record of human-rights abuses, in particular its repression of Islamic militants.

Michael Scheuer is a former CIA counterterrorism expert who helped establish the rendition program. Since leaving the agency in 2004, he has written several critiques of the war on terror using a pseudonym, including the best seller *Imperial Hubris.* At the time the rendition program was started in the 1990s, Scheuer claims the agency was desperate for information and feared using traditional methods to obtain information from terror suspects. Even if they could find the people they needed to question to obtain critical information, Scheuer claimed they had nowhere to put them because of U.S. legal prohibitions. "We had to come up with a third party," Scheuer said. The clear choice was Egypt, as it is the largest recipient of U.S. aid after Israel and its secret police force, the Mukjabarat, had a reputation for brutality.[107]

The case of Ibn al-Shaykh al-Libi was a turning point in the use of Egypt as a torture clearinghouse. The initial interrogations of Ibn al-Shaykh al-Libi, number 17 on the State Department's most wanted list, were conducted by the FBI in Afghanistan. Agents were directed to be respectful and to build rapport in order to obtain the maximum amount of useful information. But the CIA grew restless with the pace of the interrogation and the results attained, and they arranged for al-Libi to be sent to Cairo, Egypt, to be interrogated. "Al-Libi's rendition marked a turning point in interrogation operations in the war on terror. From that point forward, interrogations were handled primarily by the CIA, while the FBI—and rapport-building—were sidelined. Following the al-Libi episode, the CIA began sending other suspects to Cairo, and to other Middle Eastern states known to torture.... Today more than 100 suspects have been rendered to states known to employ torture. High-value suspects like al-Libi weren't the only suspects sent abroad. Countless others have been transferred as well in a process now known as 'extraordinary rendition.'"[108] Other countries, like Syria, might have been publicly classified as enemies of the United States, but they were allies in the secret torture program.

Mamdouh Habib was arrested in Pakistan and transferred, at the request of the United States, to Egyptian custody. No warrant had been issued for his arrest, no charges were filed, and he was not allowed to appear before any court. In Egypt, Habib was kept in a bare six-by-eight-foot cell, where he slept on the concrete floor with only a single blanket. He also spent time in three other cells—one with water up to his chin, forcing him to stand for hours on tiptoes; one with a low ceiling and water up to his knees, forcing him to stoop uncomfortably; and one with ankle-deep water and a generator within sight, where he was told he would be electrocuted if he did not confess. Habib was repeatedly kicked, punched, hit with sticks, burned with cigarettes, shocked with a cattle prod, doused with cold water, and deprived of sleep. Many other forms of torture were used.[109]

23-year-old Ethiopian Binyam Mohamed recalled his torture in a Moroccan prison. After being denied food, water, and use of a bathroom, "a circle of torture began....They'd ask me a question. I'd say one thing. They'd say it was a lie. I'd say another. They'd say it was a lie. I could not work out what they wanted to hear. They'd say there's this guy who says you're the big man in Al Qaida. I'd say it's a lie. They'd torture me. I'd say, okay, it's true. They'd say, okay, tell us more. I'd say, I don't know more. Then they'd torture me again." The worst torture came in late August 2002. One interrogator, Marwan, ordered that he be stripped. Then they cut his chest with a scalpel. They made a series of little cuts on his penis. According to Binyam, they did this 20 to 30 times over a two-hour period. Much of Binyam's account can be verified. His description of the Moroccan interrogation center matched the description of a prison used for interrogations called Temara. It had previously been identified as a site for torture by Amnesty International. When AI investigated the center in 2003, they found inmates had been beaten with metal rulers, electrocuted, and that interrogators had threaten to rape wives or relatives of suspects as well as simulated drowning. Additionally, Stephen Grey traced the flight log of a CIA Gulfstream V jet used for renditions to the exact dates and locales Binyam described.[110]

The Bush administration has both denied and defended the CIA's actions. The most frequently used defense against rumors of CIA-perpetrated tortures and renditions was to keep everything as secret as possible. As details emerged about the CIA's "black sites," the agency went to enormous lengths to have all employees, former and current, remain silent. "Porter Goss, then director of the CIA, railed against those who damaged national security by leaking secrets, and the agency's office of security started putting pressure on many of those who had recently retired. Anyone with a security clearance, including the thousands of contractors who worked alongside the agency, were told that all public comments and contacts with journalists needed to be vetted in advance."[111]

For a long time, the Bush administration denied that they outsourced the torture of prisoners. In response to allegations in March 2005 that the United States was rendering prisoners elsewhere to be tortured, the administration claimed it had investigated the claims and that compliance with domestic and international law was very high. In an announcement to the press on April 28, 2005, President Bush was asked whether the United States took terror suspects to other countries for interrogation. He first chuckled and called it "a hypothetical." Then he explained, "We operate within the law, and we send people to countries where they say they're not going to torture the people." This was in contrast to his remarks four months earlier, when he announced, "Torture is never acceptable, nor do we hand over people to countries that do torture."

The difference between Bush's remarks in January and April masked a real weakness with the rendition system: the fear that it could be in violation of both domestic and international law, and of a clearly stated policy to abhor all forms of torture. The suggestion made by President Bush in January that a country like Egypt did not torture was clearly unsustainable. So, with the help of his advisers, Bush had inserted a new clause. And his use of the reference to places "where they say" they would not torture was a reference to one of his administration's crucial legal arguments in its efforts to defend renditions. Egypt, as recoded by the State Department, might indeed torture, and torture frequently. But, for prisoners sent by America, they had promised not to follow their normal practices. So rendition just might be legal.[112]

The CIA utilized several different tactics to conceal or defend their use of renditions. At first, they attempted to keep U.S. involvement minimal "so they would function, in effect, as a travel agency."[113] The next defense, crafted by John Yoo, who was deputy assistant attorney general between 2001 and 2003, was based on the exceptions the United States had made when they ratified the Convention Against Torture described earlier in the chapter. "And so, while the full Convention might in theory protect everyone from transfer to torture, a sort of 'Convention Lite,' was not so sweeping."[114]

POST-ABU GHRAIB

In August 2004, Yemeni citizen Salim Hamdan, an alleged chauffeur for Osama bin Laden, was the first to be tried in front of a military tribunal following several Supreme Court cases requiring the state to provide enemy combatants notice of their status and the opportunity to rebut that classification before a neutral party (*Hamdi v. Rumsfeld, Rasul v. Bush,* and *Odah v. United States*). Challenges emerged regarding whether this tribunal satisfied the conditions set forth by the Geneva Conventions, and the Supreme Court agreed to hear Hamdan's appeal in November 2005. One month later, the Detainee Treatment Act (DTA) was enacted. It implemented revised procedures for the questioning and treatment of detainees. It mandated specific procedures for tribunals as well as set forth procedural protections for Americans accused of improprieties in the treatment of detainees. On June 29, 2006, the Supreme Court ruled in favor of Hamdan, holding that a foreign detainee's rights were protected by the Geneva Conventions and enforceable through federal courts. After the Hamdan ruling, the Bush administration claimed vast changes had been made to ensure that the handling of terror suspects by the military or CIA was in accordance with the Geneva Conventions. In September 2006, the army published a revised field manual that prohibited such practices as lengthy solitary confinement, aggressive use of dogs, and simulated drowning. On October 17, 2006, President Bush signed into law the Military Commissions Act (MCA). The MCA was a compromise bill that provided some limits on interrogation of and trials for detainees, but still allowed the government to introduce hearsay evidence and coerced statements in trials of suspected al Qaeda detainees. The MCA still allowed those classified as unlawful enemy combatants to be detained indefinitely. The MCA also established defense for government employees who engaged in unlawful interrogation practices between 2001 and 2005.[115]

On the morning of September 6, 2006, top officials gathered at the Pentagon to announce the release of a new army field manual on interrogation. Across the Potomac River, President Bush readied himself for a national televised address from the White House's East Wing. The Pentagon press conference started first. "The Army has taken pretty dramatic steps over the last two and a half years to improve our human intelligence capabilities and capacity, to include interrogation.... And by interrogation, I really mean getting truthful answers to time-sensitive questions on the battlefield," began Lieutenant General John Kimmons, army deputy chief of staff for intelligence. He then unveiled the *Human Intelligence Collector Operations* field manual, which replaced the 1992 version of *Intelligence Interrogation*.[116]

The Torture Victim Protection Act of 1991 (TVPA) allows civil suits against foreign perpetrators of torture who enter American soil, and U.S. Statute prohibits torture perpetrated by an American anywhere outside U.S. jurisdiction. The definition of torture used in the TVPA is similar to that crafted by Bush's Office of Legal Council, which requires demonstration of prolonged mental harm. No U.S. court has heard a case involving a violation of TVPA. In one case, *Hilao v Estate of Marcos* (1996), the court ruled that a plaintiff who spent eight years in solitary confinement, seven months of which he was shackled to a cot in a hot, unlit cell that measured two and a half square meters, was not tortured. In *Eastman Kodak v Kavlin* (1997), the plaintiff had been held in a dirty cell in Bolivia for eight days without food. The court found he had not been tortured as the term is defined by the TVPA.[117]

In the fall of 2005, Senator John McCain, who had been tortured as a prisoner of war in Vietnam, attached an amendment to a defense-spending bill that limited the military to standard techniques authorized in the Army Field Manual. The Senate voted 90 to 9 to include McCain's provisions in the bill. The administration proposed exempting the CIA from any restrictions.

Ultimately, Bush signed the bill but issued a signing statement that reserved his right, as Commander in Chief, to override the bill's provisions. Although this drew a lot of attention, it really did little but assert that officers must follow the law.[118]

As this book went through the editorial process, new evidence emerged about Bush administration knowledge of and support for torture in Iraq. In April 2008, the Associated Press reported that Vice President Dick Cheney approved the use of harsh interrogation techniques and had asked the Justice Department to endorse them as legal. They also reported that efforts were made to insulate President Bush from meetings in which CIA use of waterboarding and other illegal methods of torture were discussed and approved.[119]

NOTES

1. Rejali, D. (2007). *Torture and democracy.* Princeton, NJ: Princeton University Press.

2. United Nations General Assembly. (1984, December 10). Convention against torture and other cruel, inhuman, or degrading treatment or punishment. Adopted as Resolution 39146. Retrieved in full from the Office of the High Commissioner for Human Rights from http://www.unhchr.udhr/index.html

3. Harbury, J. (2005). *Truth, torture, and the American way.* Boston: Beacon.

4. Conroy, J. (2000). *Unspeakable acts, ordinary people: The dynamics of torture.* New York: Alfred A. Knopf.

5. Danner, M. (2004). *Torture and truth: America, Abu Ghraib, and the war on terror.* New York: New York Review of Books.

6. Ratner, M. (2005). The Guantanamo prisoners. In Meeropol, R. (Ed.), *America's disappeared* (pp. 31–59). New York: Seven Stories Press.

7. Watt, S. (2005). Torture, "stress and duress," and rendition as counterterrorism tools. In Meeropol, R. (Ed.), *America's disappeared* (pp. 72–112). New York: Seven Stories Press.

8. Harbury (2005).

9. Holtzman, E. (2005). Watergate and Abu Ghraib: Holding war criminals accountable in the U.S. courts and Congress. In Brecher, J., Cutler, J., and Smith, B. (Eds.), *In the name of democracy: American war crimes in Iraq and beyond* (pp. 260–271). New York: Metropolitan Books.

10. Miles, S. (2006). *Oath betrayed: Torture, medical complicity, and the war on terror.* New York: Random House.

11. Stephens, T. (2005, May 13). A chronology of U.S. war crimes & torture, 1975–2005. *Counterpunch.* Retrieved November 17, 2007, from http://www.counterpunch.org/stephens05132005.html.

12. Ibid.

13. The Bybee Torture Memo. (n.d.). Retrieved May 13, 2008, from www.tomjoad.org/bybeememo.htm.

14. Brody, R. (2005). The road to Abu Ghraib. In Meeropol, R. (Ed.), *America's disappeared* (pp. 113–129). New York: Seven Stories Press.

15. Otterman, M. (2006). *American torture.* London: Pluto.

16. Stephens (2005).

17. Ibid.

18. Ibid.

19. Rose, D. (2004). *Guantanamo: The war on human rights.* New York: The New Press.

20. Ibid.

21. Hersch, S. (2004). *Chain of command: The road from 9/11 to Abu Ghraib.* New York: HarperCollins, p. 59.

22. Ibid.

23. Ibid., p. 73.

24. Williams, K. (2006). *American torture and the logic of domination.* Cambridge, MA: South End Press.

25. Saar, E., & Novack, V. (2005). *Inside the wire: A military intelligence soldier's eyewitness account of life at Guantanamo.* New York: Penguin, p. 134.

26. Ibid.

27. Bravin, J., & Fields, G. (2003, March 4). How do U.S. interrogators make a captured terrorist talk? *Wall Street Journal,* p. B1.

28. Priest, D., & Gellman, B. (2002, December 26). U.S. decries abuse but defends interrogations. *Washington Post,* p. A1.

29. Williams (2006).

30. Ibid.

31. Ibid.

32. Ibid.

33. Ibid.

34. Hersch (2004).

35. Human Rights Watch. (2006, July). "No blood, no foul": Soldiers' accounts of detainee abuse in Iraq. *Human Rights Watch, 18*(3), 1–55.

36. Ibid.

37. Center for Constitutional Rights. (2005). Individual accounts of torture. In Brecher, J., Cutler, J., and Smith, B. (Eds.), *In the name of democracy: American war crimes in Iraq and beyond* (pp. 79–81). New York: Metropolitan Books.

38. Human Rights Watch (2006).

39. Williams (2006).

40. Ibid., p. 31.

41. Danner (2004).

42. Hersch (2004).

43. Ibid.

44. Ibid.

45. Ibid.

46. Ibid., p. 70.

47. Williams (2006).

48. Ibid.

49. Hersch (2004), p. 50.

50. Williams (2006).

51. Ibid., pp. 43–45.

52. Strasser, S. (2004). *The Abu Ghraib investigations.* New York: Public Affairs Books.

53. Danner (2004).

54. Ibid.

55. Ibid.

56. Human Rights Watch (2006).

57. Ibid., p. 9–10.

58. Miles (2006).

59. Ibid.

60. Ibid.

61. Ibid.

62. Human Rights Watch (2006).

63. Rejali (2006).

64. Ibid., p. 509.

65. Fay, G. (2004). AR 15–6 investigation of the Abu Ghraib Detention Facility and 205th Military Intelligence Brigade (U). In Danner, M. (Ed.), *Torture and truth: America, Abu Ghraib, and the war on terror* (pp. 437–579). New York: New York Review Books.

66. Tetreault, M. (2006, fall). The sexual politics of Abu Ghraib: Hegemony, spectacle, and the war on terror. *NWSA Journal, 18*(3), 33–51.

67. Ibid.

68. Ibid.

69. Strasser (2004).

70. Ibid.

71. Ibid.

72. Ibid.

73. Spinner, J. (2004, May 8). Unit's role was to break down prisoners: Reservist tells of orders from intelligence officers. *Washington Post.*

74. Gutierrez, T. (2005, September 26). England convicted. *USA Today.* Retrieved January 12, 2008, from http://www.usatoday.com/news/nation/2005_09_26-england_x.html.

75. Reid, T. (2005, January 15). Graner convicted in the first trial from Abu Ghraib. *Washington Post,* p. A01.

76. Ibid.

77. Horton, S. (2005, January 20). A Nuremberg lesson: Torture scandal began far above "rotten apples." In Brecher, J., Cutler, J., and Smith, B. (Eds.), *In the name of democracy: American war crimes in Iraq and beyond* (pp. 112–114). New York: Metropolitan Books, p. 113.

78. Human Rights Watch (2006).

79. Ibid.

80. Ibid.

81. Schlesinger, J. (2004, August). Final report of the independent panel to review Department of Defense operations. In Strasser, S. (Ed.), *The Abu Ghraib investigations* (pp. 1–101). New York: Public Affairs Press.

82. Fay (2004).

83. Brody (2005).

84. Hersch (2004).

85. Ibid.

86. Ibid.

87. Tetreault (2006).

88. Karpinski, J. (2005). *One woman's army.* New York: Miramax books, p. 12.

89. Ibid., p. 18.

90. Ibid., p. 19.

91. Ibid., pp. 190–191.

92. Ibid.

93. Marsh, J. (2006–7, Fall/Winter). The prison guard's dilemma. *Greater Good,* p. 35.

94. Rajiva (2006).

95. Ibid.

96. Rejali (2007).

97. Hersch (2004).

98. Otterman (2006).

99. Ibid.

100. Ibid.

101. Ibid.

102. Ibid.

103. Mayer, J. (2005, February 14). Outsourcing torture: The secret history of America's "extraordinary rendition" program. *The New Yorker,* p. 106.

104. Masri, K. (2005, December 18). America kidnapped me. *Los Angeles Times.*

105. Williams (2006).

106. Ibid.

107. Otterman (2007).

108. Ibid.

109. Grey, S. (2006). *Ghost plane.* New York: St. Martin's Press.

110. Ibid.

111. Ibid.

112. Ibid.

113. Ibid.

114. Ibid.

115. Levin, B. (2007, May). Trials for terrorists: The shifting legal landscape of the post 9–11 era. *Journal of Contemporary Criminal Justice, 23*(2), 195–218.

116. Harbury (2004).

117. Ibid.

118. Otterman (2007).

119. Miami Herald Staff and Wire Reports. (2008, April 11). Torture methods got Cheney's OK. *Miami Herald,* p. 3A.

7

Summing Up the Torture Debate

This chapter concludes the historical examination of torture and prison abuse by examining the arguments in favor of their use. These are contrasted with the arguments made by torture opponents. In addition, it offers recommendations for the future, drawing on official governmental investigations as well as the ideas provided by human-rights organizations.

ARGUMENTS IN FAVOR OF USING TORTURE

As noted throughout this book, one of the key modern arguments in favor of harsh interrogation methods is that they are required in order to gain needed information for prosecutions and to prevent terrorist attacks. Allegedly, the war on terror is a new kind of war that requires new methods. Heather Mac-Donald offers this perspective when she describes the interrogation systems in Afghanistan, Cuba, and later, Iraq. She describes "planeloads" of al Qaeda and Taliban prisoners being dumped into overcrowded, ramshackle facilities. Interrogations were then intended to debrief each prisoner and determine which ones were of enough importance to be sent to Guantanamo for higher-level interrogation. Army interrogators then had 16 approaches they could use to extract the information. "Applied in the right combination, they will work on nearly everyone, as the intelligence soldiers had learned in their training. But the Kandahar prisoners were not playing by the army rule book. They divulged nothing."[1] Some of the al Qaeda fighters had received resistance training, which instructed that Americans were limited in how they could question

prisoners. Al Qaeda manuals stated that failure to cooperate with U.S. interrogators "carried no penalties and certainly no risk of torture—a sign, gloated
the manuals, of American weakness."[2] Others who had not studied American
detention policies allegedly learned quickly there were significant barriers in
what the interrogators could do.

MacDonald goes on to explain that interrogators were forced to fall back
on harsher techniques when they encountered an enemy who did not respond to their traditional forms of psychological torture. These tactics, she
argues, were no more severe than those used against U.S. forces, however.
"Even more challenging was that these detainees bore little resemblance to
traditional prisoners of war. The army's interrogation manual presumed adversaries who were essentially the mirror image of their captors, motivated
by emotions that all soldiers share." The soldiers found, however, that tactics like playing on the prisoners' desire to return to home and to reunite
with family were ineffective, as many of these prisoners "cared little about
life itself." Thus, interrogators developed a "hybrid and fluid set of detention
practices. As interrogators tried to overcome the prisoners' resistance, their
reference point remained Geneva and other humanitarian treaties. But the
interrogators pushed into the outer limits of what they thought the law allowed, undoubtedly recognizing that the prisoners in their control violated
everything the pacts stood for."[3] Interrogators at Kandahar reached the following guidelines:

If a type of behavior towards a prisoner was no worse than the way the army treated
its own members, it could not be considered torture or a violation of the conventions.
Thus, questioning a detainee past his bedtime was lawful as long as his interrogator
stayed up with him. If the interrogator was missing exactly the same amount of sleep
as the detainee—and no tag-teaming of interrogators would be allowed, the soldiers
decided—then sleep deprivation could not be deemed torture.[4]

The most common argument made by torture proponents is the "ticking
time bomb" scenario. The concept is that, in the event that interrogators
know a suspect—the ticking time bomb—has information that can save lives
but will not divulge it after using normal interrogation strategies, the interrogator should be permitted to use whatever tactics are needed to elicit that
information.

Another argument made by torture proponents parallels arguments made
by defenders of severe prison conditions; that is, that the environment is not
too harsh but instead too accommodating when balanced against the offenses committed. McDonald argued, "Consistent with the president's call
for humane treatment, prisoners received expert medical care, three culturally

appropriate meals each day, and daily opportunities for prayer, showers, and exercise. They had mail privileges and reading materials. Their biggest annoyance was boredom, recalls one interrogator."[5]

Macdonald suggested that the cruel and degrading practices that Rumsfeld allegedly authorized for use at Guantanamo were not so bad, and that the restrictions placed on interrogators were laughable. They made it virtually impossible for interrogators to gain information.

Providing a detainee an incentive for cooperation—such as a cigarette or, especially favored in Cuba, a McDonald's Filet-O-Fish sandwich or a Twinkie [was forbidden] unless specifically approved by the secretary of defense. In other words, if an interrogator had learned that Usama bin Laden's accountant loved Cadbury chocolate, and intended to enter the interrogation booth armed with a Dairy Milk Wafer to extract the name of a Saudi financier, he needed to "specifically determine that military necessity requires" the use of the Dairy Milk Wafer and send an alert to Secretary Rumsfeld that chocolate was to be deployed against an al Qaeda operative.[6]

As noted several places in this text, another key argument of proponents of harsh methods is that they do not qualify as exceptionally cruel, abusive, or as torture. "None of the treatments shown in the Abu Ghraib photos, such as nudity or the use of dogs, was included in the techniques certified for the unlawful combatants held in Cuba. And those mild techniques that were certified could only be used with extensive bureaucratic oversight."[7] Indeed, some maintain that the United States already permits far worse, such as application of the death penalty or infliction of "smart" weapons of war that efficiently kill, mutilate, and maim.[8]

In fact, some have argued that, because of hyper concern about torture and abuse, the United States has shut down usage of many tactics that are needed to elicit important information. "The experiment is over. Reeling under the public relations disaster of Abu Ghraib, the Pentagon shut down every stress technique but one—isolation—and that can be used only after extensive review. An interrogator who so much as asks for permission to question a detainee into the night could be putting his career in jeopardy."[9] Interrogators have become far too timid, the argument goes, and have lost the ability to obtain vital information. Legal scholar and attorney Alan Dershowitz has argued that a complete ban on torture will always be merely lip service, and that this can have a disastrous impact on our image and credibility internationally. Former attorney Andrew McCarthy sums up this perspective, saying, "By imposing an absolute ban on something we know is occurring, we promote disrespect for the rule of law in general and abdicate our duty to enact tailored and meaningful regulations."[10] Dershowitz and others have supported the idea of limited torture, which would be facilitated through torture warrants. The government would apply to a federal court for permission to use torture in a specific case, and the methods would be predetermined. Only upon reasonable cause to believe that a catastrophe would be prevented would the warrant be issued.

Some invoke religious beliefs to support torture. Although many religious groups have been outspoken critics of the war on terror and of the abuse that occurs in prisons and detention centers, many argue torture is not a moral or religious concern. Some Christians see torture as part of original sin. Other Christians see torture as the influence of the devil. Muslims do not have a concept of original sin. They see each person as morally innocent in nature. Torture is seen as an example of a free choice made by persons who elect to live in sin. Buddhists explain conflict as being rooted in greed, desire, hatred, and delusion. "Throughout history, religion has had an intimate relationship with torture. And within a variety of religious traditions, one can find practices and beliefs that justify the use of torture in particular situations including self-torture to express spirituality, torture to save souls, and torture to preserve the greater good."[11] Self-torture of some degree is a feature of some religious traditions, including Christianity, Taoism, Buddhism, Hinduism, and some Shia Muslims. "The Inquisition is a clear, well-known example of how members of one religious community came to support the use of torture for what it believed were rightful ends. The Inquisition's tortures were intended as instruments of salvation targeting Muslims and Jews, and were used to identify heresy or other permutations of religious guilt, thereby saving the souls of sinners (and the souls of all people the heretic might influence) from eternal damnation."[12] Some read the Jewish Talmud as authorizing torture if it might save a greater number of people from harm.[13]

ARGUMENTS AGAINST THE USE OF TORTURE

Perhaps the most important argument against torture is that it does not work. Author and attorney Joshua Dratel, who has been involved in some of the Guantanamo cases, explained that the best information obtained to date from al Qaeda captives has not come from interrogations but from more traditional forms of intelligence gathering. In fact, the first al Qaeda informant walked in voluntarily to a U.S. embassy.[14] Dratel has noted that the information gained via torture of prisoners at Guantanamo Bay has not only been limited, it has actually been unreliable. The "Tipton Three," three British brothers who, in 2004, confessed to appearing in a video with Osama bin Laden, did so only under extreme duress. In actuality, all three were nowhere near Afghanistan on the date of the filming.[15] "The governments of

Nazi Germany, China, North Vietnam, Great Britain, and Israel also found pain to be an unreliable interrogation technique. As prisoners disintegrate, harden, or dissociate under pain, they tend to give inaccurate, useless, or misleading information." Despite the fact that torture has not, either in the war on terror or throughout history, proven to be very successful, "harsh and humiliating interrogation may have been embraced by the public because it is widely perceived as an 'appropriate' response. The 9/11 hijackers violated an absolute prohibition. What possible reaction could be adequate to what they did? A response that trespasses on equally sacred ground." This reasoning sees torture as "an emotionally satisfying (not useful) form of counterterrorism because it *mirrors* terrorism itself. For one thing, it is meant to terrorize."[16]

Torture is not, according to opponents, "necessary" to prevent terrorist attacks. Rather, support for it is tied to romanticized notions of the "bad boy" who, although he uses questionable tactics, saves the day. U.S. popular culture glorifies cops like Dirty Harry, who save the day despite violating the rules.

Additionally, torture alienates persons who might otherwise be recruited as informants. This is even documented in the CIA's 1983 *Human Resource Exploitation Manual,* which stated, "Use of force . . . may damage subsequent collection efforts." Many FBI reports of interrogations with prisoners in the war on terror tell of prisoners who refused to cooperate with interrogations because of harsh, abusive, or degrading treatment meted out to fellow prisoners or themselves. Some prisoners even say that their endurance of torture validated their sense of importance and the rightness of their cause. Conversely, others viewed their abuse as confirming the evil of their torturer.[17]

Another issue with using torture concerns where to draw the line. If, as proponents argue, some form of "limited torture" is authorized, how do we ensure the methods and degree inflicted will indeed remain limited? Is it possible to ensure that "case-hardened torturers, inured to levels of violence and pain that would make ordinary people vomit at the sight, will know where to draw the line on when torture should be used? They never have in the past. . . . Escalation is the rule, not the aberration."[18]

The idea of limited torture "assumes a single, ad hoc decision about whether to torture, by officials who ordinarily would do no such thing except in a desperate emergency. But in the real world of interrogations, decisions are not made one-off. The real world is a world of politics, guidelines, and directives." In reality, then, even if limited torture was approved, it would be impossible to ensure that all people charged with conducting interrogations at domestic and foreign prisons and detention centers would be able to implement them in a limited fashion. A simple reason for this is bureaucratic in nature: When a prisoner is turned over to interrogators, their job is to get as much valuable intelligence as possible from the prisoner, not to wonder whether this is a ticking time bomb case. They will work within the guidelines they are given, whatever those are. The person who decides whether the prisoner presents a genuine ticking bomb case is not the interrogator. The interrogator simply executes decisions made elsewhere. "Soldiers learn about torture not in schools, but through backroom apprenticeships. Backroom apprenticeships prove to be a very powerful method of education, gradually transforming torture techniques in the course of a century. This method of transmission is difficult to detect, a quality torturers value in an age of increased international scrutiny of human rights abuses."[19] The following quote sums up the concern about "limited" torture:

Torture plumbs the recesses of human consciousness, unleashing an unfathomable capacity for cruelty as well as seductive illusions of omnipotence. Once torture begins, its perpetrators—reaching into that remote terrain where pain and pleasure, procreation and destruction all converge—are often swept away by dark reveries, by frenzies of potency, mastery, and control. Just as interrogators are often drawn in by an empowering sense of dominance, so their superiors, even at the highest level, can succumb to fantasies of torture as an all-powerful weapon.[20]

Beyond concerns about limiting the techniques and degree of abuse perpetrated by individual interrogators, there is another concern that involves groups and organizations. "Once legitimated, torture could develop a constituency with a vested interest in perpetuating it. We have seen in recent years how the enterprise of enforcing the drug laws in the United States has made law enforcement agencies as dependent on the resulting forfeitures as the junkies are on the dope."[21]

The fiction must presume…that the interrogator operates only under the strictest supervision, in a chain of command where his every move gets vetted and controlled by the superiors who are actually doing the deliberating. The trouble is that this assumption flies in the face of everything we know about how organizations work. The basic rule in every bureaucratic organization is that operational details and the guilty knowledge that goes with them gets pushed down the chain of command as far as possible.[22]

In sum, "History's most important lesson is that it has not been possible to make coercion compatible with truth."[23]

Opponents also maintain torture violates basic moral and ethical guidelines. "Interrogators do not inhabit a world of loving kindness, or of equal concern and respect for all human beings. Interrogating resistant prisoners nonviolently and nonabusively still requires a relationship that in any other context would be morally abhorrent."

Torture aims...to strip away from its victim all the qualities of human dignity that liberalism prizes. It does this by the deliberate actions of a torturer, who inflicts pain one-on-one, up close and personal, in order to break the spirit of the victim—in other words, to tyrannize and dominate the victim. The relationship between them becomes a perverse parody of friendship and intimacy; intimacy transformed into its inverse image, where the torturer focuses on the victim's body with the intensity of a lover, except that every bit of that focus is bent to causing pain and tyrannizing the victim's spirit. At bottom all torture is rape, and rape is tyranny.[24]

The impact of torture on victims as well as perpetrators has been well documented. Further, the psychological damage to the soldiers who abused prisoners remains to be assessed. Those traumatized veterans will have medical needs.[25]

In addition to the more widely publicized criticisms of torture, an important point was made in the 1700s by Cesare Beccaria. Beccaria maintained that torture eliminates interrogators' ability to interpret body language. Intelligent interrogators can often use body language to determine if a subject is lying. "That is why physical torments ordinarily result in a loss of information. Subtle signals disappear when torture is employed to unearth truth."[26]

Rather than point to individual factors, opponents of torture often look at the issue more sociologically, addressing the social factors that contribute to its use. In 1971, Philip Zimbardo created a study at Stanford University that helps explain the function of role and setting. He designed an experiment in which some volunteers were assigned to be prisoners and others were to be guards. All were male, and all were healthy mentally and physically. Guards were given uniforms and made to look the part, while prisoners were actually "arrested" and taken to a makeshift jail, where they were booked, searched, and provided clothing in a close approximation of the real process. Within days, the experiment went bad, as guards began to torment prisoners, forcing them into solitary confinement for no reason, requiring them to do push-ups and jumping jacks, stripping them naked, dressing them in hoods and chains, and verbally berating them. One of the researchers, Craig Haney, explained, "Environments in which one group of people is given near total control over another invariably degenerate into places pervaded by mistrust and abuse."[27]

If there is any environment that emphasizes obedience, it is the military. Similarly, the military is the epitome of an environment in which one group is given almost total control over another. Those who buck this and make independent decisions are not generally viewed positively. In some cases, they are punished for not following commands. Staff Sergeant Camilo Mejia Castillo of the Florida National Guard was sentenced to a year in prison when he refused to return to Iraq. He had applied for conscientious objector status, which was pending at the time of his trial. In that application, he explained that he thought the war was "illegal and immoral" and that he had tremendous concern about the mistreatment of Iraqis. He later detailed being told to "soften up" inmates by keeping them awake for 48 hours or longer. Not knowing precisely what to do, Mejia's squad locked the prisoners in a tiny metal box and beat the sides with sledgehammers for hours.[28] One of his attorneys, Ramsey Clark, highlighted "the incredible irony that we're prosecuting soldiers in Iraq for violations of international law and we're prosecuting a soldier here because he refused to do the same things."[29]

Beyond the actual incidents of torture lie other concerns, and those are related to broader political repression. "Governments sanction torture as part of state terrorism in order to paralyze the whole population and to convince it of the omnipotence of the regime. Indeed, torture is one of the most extreme components of the apparatus of tyranny." In *Torture and Truth,* Mark Danner commented, "If the Hooded Man and the Leashed Man and the naked human pyramids and the rest shocked Americans because of their perverse undermining of the normal, they shocked Iraqis and other Arabs because the images seemed to confirm so vividly and precisely a reality that many had suspected and feared but had tried not to believe."[30] Although proponents of torture generally argue it is reserved for the most serious cases and for the worst enemies,

states that sanction torture often allow it to spread beyond a few selected targets to countless suspected enemies. When U.S. leaders have used torture to fight faceless adversaries, Communist or terrorist, the practice has proliferated almost uncontrollably. Just four years after the CIA compiled its 1963 manual for use against a handful of counterintelligence targets, its agents were operating forty interrogation centers in South Vietnam that killed more than twenty thousand suspects and tortured thousands more. A few months after the CIA used its techniques on a small number of "high-target-value" al Qaeda suspects, the practice spread to the interrogation of hundreds of Afghans and thousands of Iraqis. Modern states using torture, even in a very limited way, run the risk of becoming increasingly indiscriminate in its application.[31]

Typically, torture is used initially for the most dangerous criminals. Cultures that use torture, however, tend to expand the actions they approve as well as whom is included in the "torturable class." In the United States, as in most countries that use torture, the torturable class most often includes nonwhites. Amnesty International's 2000 report on torture acknowledges the link between racism and torture.

When a nation participates in torture, it can only expect that its enemies will do the same. "Abusive interrogation fosters an 'arms race' between interrogators and prisoners. As targeted groups learn the techniques that will be used against their members, they prepare their colleagues for what to expect. They take measures to limit the amount of damaging information that any individual can disclose. As interrogators change in reaction to the strategic moves of prisoners, the targeted organizations adapt again."[32]

Torture is counterproductive in that it often decreases support for the cause or even increases support for the enemy. Surveys found Iraqi support for U.S. forces declined 54 percent after the release of the Abu Ghraib photos. It is also likely the evidence of torture by American troops boosted insurgents.[33] "Today, the images of Abu Ghraib are used as a powerful recruiting tool for al Qaeda across the globe. Christopher Hitchens has aptly described the fallout from the photos as a 'moral Chernobyl.' Before the Abu Ghraib scandal broke, a Coalition Provisional Authority poll showed that 63 percent of Iraqis supported the occupation. One month after Abu Ghraib, the number dropped to 9 percent."[34] Historians have yet to assess whether the abuses and that shift in public opinion fostered recruitment into paramilitary forces against the effort to stabilize Iraq, but it seems likely.

In sum, it is clear that torture does not advance long-term national interests. It does not elicit reliable information; rather, the falsehoods procured may overload and confound intelligence analysts. If information is gleaned through use of torture, that evidence would not (at least ideally) be allowed in court cases. Additionally, torture alienates potential recruits and informants. Because it is so horrifying, it may enrage and mobilize the forces against which it is directed. Torture creates and sustains unhealthy collaborations between nations who torture their own peoples or who torture on behalf of others, and it makes those allies who do not torture unlikely to cooperate or to share intelligence.

The experience with torture in the war on terror has not found new value in torture; it has confirmed old lessons: torture is a fruitless, often counterproductive, use of state power. Torture's effects on the torturing society are equally destructive. Societies mobilized to torture are weakened by the vicious dehumanization that they must propagate to support the practice. Torture laws erode respect for the justice of law itself. The honor and traditions of institutions like medicine, law, journalism, and the military are tarnished by acquiescence in torture. Political reputations are diminished when the false conceit that torture can be confined to narrow licit channels is discovered. Torture responds to the barbarity of terrorism in kind. Like the terrorism it would deter, torture undermines civil societies. The rejection of either must include the forswearing of both.[35]

RECOMMENDATIONS

The International Committee for the Red Cross (ICRC) made a number of recommendations in their February 2004 report, in which they documented a number of serious violations of international humanitarian law in prisons in Iraq. Most notably, they wished to remind soldiers of their duty to, at all times, respect the human dignity of all persons held under their control in ways consistent with the Geneva Conventions and other human-rights documents. They also recommended putting into place a system by which families of persons in detention could be notified of an arrest in a timely fashion, strategies to prevent ill treatment of detainees, and policies to ensure that those charged with conducting arrests and interrogation are adequately trained.[36]

In his March 2004 report, General Taguba did not denounce many controversial interrogation techniques, but did emphasize the need for general safeguards in their use. These include limiting their use to those interrogators who are specifically trained; only conducting interrogations that are planned, deliberate actions; and ensuring the safety of detainees at all time.[37]

Recommendations by the Independent Panel from August 2004 included the following: The United States must (1) clarify its policy on the categorization of detainees, ensuring their status is consistent with the Geneva Conventions and U.S. law as well as military doctrine; (2) enable the Department of Defense to develop policy to specify the collaboration between military police and military intelligence in detention facilities; (3) As a nation, provide more specialists for detention and interrogations, all of whom must be provided significant professional development; (4) develop a new Operational Concept for detention operations applicable to the global war on terror; (5) examine the structure of the armed forces as it applies to the "new" form of warfare, ensuring a mix of active and reserve officers; (6) further develop policies and procedures for conducting interrogations and promulgate them, with training, to all personnel; (7) require participation of all those who may be engaged in detention operations in a professional ethics program; (8) establish clearer guidelines regarding the interaction between the Department of Defense and the CIA in regard to detention and interrogation; (9) As a nation, reconsider its commitment to humanitarian standards and international human-rights law, regardless of the chances of reciprocity; (10) ensure the Department of Defense works more closely with the International Committee of the Red Cross. The Red Cross must also adapt to the "new realities of conflict, which are far different from the Western European environment from which the ICRC's interpretation of Geneva Conventions were drawn"; (11) assign a new focal point within the office of the Under Secretary for Policy to specifically oversee detention policy and the interaction between DOD and ICRC; (12) review the reporting channels from the Secretary of Defense to DOD leadership to ensure bad news is effectively communicated without prejudice to any criminal or disciplinary actions that may be pending; (13) include in training for medical personnel the obligation to report any abuse, as well as more training about and enforcement of policies regarding sanitation, preventive medicine, and medical treatment for detainees; and (14) continue to study the integration of these recommendations and revise as needed.[38]

The August 2004 Fay-Jones report listed many recommendations. Among the most pertinent here are: re-emphasizing soldier and leader responsibility and accountability, including offering adequate training for personnel; releasing detainees who pose no threat and are of no intelligence value within 72 hours; adopting one Department of Defense policy on interrogation that adheres to international frameworks; hiring more Arab linguists in Iraq for better translation and culturally sensitive communication; improving training to all personnel in accordance with the Geneva Conventions; cross-training MI and MP personnel so that they have better knowledge about each other's roles and responsibilities; conducting a complete review and reorganization of the lines of authority between MIs and MPs; ensuring all personnel understand one simple reporting and record-keeping practice; and reviewing and revising the use of contracted interrogators and, when used, ensuring they receive the same training as other staff.[39]

The American Bar Association (ABA), the leading organization of lawyers in the United States, also made several recommendations in August 2004. It urged the government to immediately cease the practice of rendition and to ensure all interrogation practices are in full compliance with international standards. They called for an amendment to the U.S. torture law that would make any kind of torture, wherever inflicted, a prosecutable offense regardless of intent. The ABA also called for an independent, bipartisan commission with subpoena power that could prepare a full account of U.S. detention and interrogation practices. Its findings would be made public.[40]

Many have gone further in their recommendations. In January 2008, Admiral Mike Mullen, chairman of the Joint Chiefs of Staff since October 2007, said he would like to completely shut down the prison at Guantanamo. The biggest reason, according to Mullen, is the widespread negative image of the prison, which is damaging to the United States. Of the current population of 280 in March 2008 (it was once as large as 600), only four Gitmo prisoners are currently facing military trials. Others agree, and January 11, 2008, marked a global day of action called Shut It Down focusing on closing the doors at Gitmo. Mullen admitted he alone could not make the decision to shut the prison down, and that he was not aware of any decision to do so soon.[41] After my considerable research on the topic, I am in agreement— Gitmo has become a blight on the United States, and seems to be doing more damage than good.

Additionally, I believe we need to, as a nation, revisit how we define as torture and cruel, inhuman, and degrading treatment. This should involve people from a variety of institutions and interests, not just the military and the courts. Beyond the legal and political systems, this conversation must include academics from an array of fields, physicians, law enforcement, educators, and members of the general public. We should clarify for our nation what is and is not acceptable, and never waver based on circumstances. This is what the Geneva Conventions, the CAT, the ICCPR, and our own laws already say we are to do, and time has come for us to adhere to them. For instance, the controversial practice of waterboarding should never be authorized. Additionally, we should require all candidates for Congress or other positions in the federal government be aware of the new, clarified definitions and ensure that they vow to follow them and hold accountable those who do not. Historian Jeremy Brecher has argued similarly, saying the very first corrective process to end U.S. war crimes is "broad public repudiation of U.S. war crimes and the consequent isolation of the Bush administration from public support."[42] As Mahatma Gandhi once said, "Even the most powerful cannot rule without the cooperation of the ruled."[43]

In conclusion, perhaps Jennifer Harbury, director of the STOP (Stop Torture Permanently) program and author of *Truth, Torture, and the American Way,* summed up the point of this book best when she said:

Using sanitized language like "stress and duress" and "collateral damage" to lull the conscience of the American public does not create true security for anyone. This only leaves us, ostrichlike, with our head in the sand. Rather than averting our eyes from disturbing realities, we must take a long, hard look. Better yet, we should take that long hard look from the viewpoint of the Afghan and Iraqi people.[44]

To that, I would add only the hope that, if this book demonstrates anything, it highlights the need to examine our own domestic practices as well. Only then can we implement practices at home and abroad that treat all persons with respect and humanity. As citizens, we have a duty to be educated so that we can, when needed, demand change. As Brecher, Cutler, and Smith explained in their book, *In the Name of Democracy: American War Crimes in Iraq and Beyond,* "Where national and international institutions fail to halt such crimes, it is the responsibility of the people to do so."[45]

NOTES

1. MacDonald, H. (2006). How to interrogate terrorists. In Greenberg, K. (Ed.), *The torture debate in America* (pp. 84–97). New York: Cambridge University Press.
2. Ibid.
3. Ibid.
4. Ibid.
5. Ibid.
6. Ibid.

7. Ibid.

8. McCarthy, A. (2003, July–August). Torture: Thinking about the unthinkable. In Greenberg, K. (Ed.), *The torture debate in America* (pp. 98–110). New York: Cambridge University Press.

9. Ibid., p. 94.

10. Ibid., p. 108.

11. Dubensky, J., & Lavery, R. (2006). Torture: An interreligious debate. In Greenberg, K. (Ed.), *The torture debate in America* (pp. 162–182). New York: Cambridge University Press.

12. Ibid.

13. Ibid.

14. Ibid.

15. Dratel, J. (2006). The curious debate. In Greenberg, K. (Ed.), *The torture debate in America* (p. 111–117). New York: Cambridge University Press.

16. Ibid.

17. Hersh, S. (2004). *Chain of command: The road from 9/11 to Abu Ghraib.* New York: HarperCollins.

18. Ibid.

19. Ibid.

20. Ibid.

21. Ibid.

22. Ibid.

23. Ibid.

24. Luban, D. (2006, March). Liberalism, torture, and the ticking bomb. *Harper's Magazine.*

25. Harbury, J. (2005). *Truth, torture, and the American way.* Boston: Beacon Press.

26. Holmes, S. (2006). Is defiance of law a proof of success? In Greenberg, K. (Ed.), *The torture debate in America* (pp. 118–135). New York: Cambridge University Press, p. 122.

27. Cited in Human Rights Watch. (1997). *Cold storage: Super-maximum security confinement in Indiana.* New York: Human Rights Watch, p. 61.

28. Luban (2006).

29. Amnesty International. (2004, June 4). USA: Staff Sergeant Camilo Mejia Castillo is a prisoner of conscience.

30. Danner, M. (2004). *Torture and truth: America, Abu Ghraib, and the war on terror.* New York: The New York Review of Books, p. 29.

31. Ibid., p. 13.

32. Ibid., p. 17.

33. Zakaria, F. (2005, November 14). Psst...nobody loves a torturer. *Newsweek.*

34. Ibid.

35. Ibid.

36. The ICRC report. (2004, February). In Greenberg, K., & Dratel, J. (Eds.), *The torture papers: The road to Abu Ghraib* (pp. 383–404). New York: Cambridge University Press.

37. The Taguba report. (2004, March). In Greenberg, K., & Dratel, J. (Eds.), *The torture papers: The road to Abu Ghraib* (pp. 405–465). New York: Cambridge University Press.

38. The Schlesinger report. (2004, August). In Greenberg, K., & Dratel, J. (Eds.), *The torture papers: The road to Abu Ghraib* (pp. 908–975). New York: Cambridge University Press.

39. The Fay-Jones report. (2004, August). In Greenberg, K., & Dratel, J. (Eds.), *The torture papers: The road to Abu Ghraib* (pp. 987–1131). New York: Cambridge University Press.

40. American Bar Association report to the House of Delegates. (2004, August). In Greenberg, K., & Dratel, J. (Eds.), *The torture papers: The road to Abu Ghraib* (pp. 1132–1164). New York: Cambridge University Press.

41. Burns, R. (2008, January 14). Close Guantanamo, top officer urges. *Miami Herald,* p. 3A.

42. Brecher, J. (2005). Affirmative measures to halt U.S. war crimes. In Brecher, J., Cutler, J., & Smith, B. (Eds.), *In the name of democracy: American war crimes in Iraq and beyond* (pp. 248–259). New York: Metropolitan.

43. Ibid., p. 248.

44. Harbury (2005).

45. Brecher, J., Culter, J., & Smith, B. (2005). Conclusion. In Brecher, J., Cutler, J., & Smith, B. (Eds.), *In the name of democracy: American war crimes in Iraq and beyond* (pp. 322–329). New York: Metropolitan.

Timeline of Significant Events in the History of Torture and Prisoner Abuse

907	Five Dynasties period of China said to introduce slow slicing method of torture, or *ling chi.*
1420	First use of the torture chamber, or rack.
1478	Beginning of Spanish Inquisition, infamous for its torture techniques.
1591	William Shakespeare is thought to be the first to use the word "torture" as a verb.
1608	First execution in the United States.
1740	Frederick the Great virtually abolishes torture.
1752	Britain's Murder Act allows the public hanging of dead men on a chain, called the gibbet.
1760	First execution by hanging using the "drop" technique in London.
1764	Cesare Beccaria's *An Essay on Crimes and Punishment* denounces torture.
1772	British outlaw the barbaric practice of pressing or crushing someone to death.
1783	First public executions outside Newgate Prison in England.
1792 April 25	First guillotine used in Paris.
1876	First U.S. prison built in Elmira, New York.

1880	William Kemmler is the first to be executed by electrocution.
1903	United States obtains control over Guantanamo Bay, Cuba, at the end of the Spanish-American War.
1910	Supreme Court rules chain gangs are unconstitutional.
1924	First inmate is executed by gas chamber at San Quentin.
1931	Wickersham Commission report identifies widespread police brutality across America.
1936	Supreme Court determines that coerced confessions are unlawful in *Brown v. Mississippi.*
1941	In *Ashcraft v. Tennessee,* the Supreme Court invalidates "relay" confessions.
1943	LSD is discovered by chemist Dr. Albert Hoffman.
1945–1946	Nuremberg trials of Nazi officials.
1946	School of the Americas (SOA) opens.
1947	Nuremberg Report outlines fair treatment of and experimentation on prisoners.
	U.S. Central Intelligence Agency (CIA) is created.
	U.S. Navy launches Operation Chatter and experiments with mescaline.
1948 December 10	United Nations (UN) General Assembly adopts the Universal Declaration of Human Rights.
1949	Geneva Conventions outline rules of warfare and guidelines for humane treatment of prisoners of war, civilians, and others.
1950	*Miami Daily News* reporter Edward Hunter coins the term "brainwashing."
	CIA launches Operation Bluebird to discover useful interrogation techniques. CIA begins MK-ULTRA project designed to uncover secrets to mind control.
1953	U.S. "prison camp" school established at Chinhae, South Korea.
1954	Project QKHILLTOP inaugurated to study brainwashing techniques allegedly used by Chinese communists.
1957	*Standard Minimum Rules for the Treatment of Prisoners* approved by the UN's Economic and Social Council.
1959	Abu Ghraib prison designed in Iraq under the leadership of General Abdul Karim Kassem.

1961	Stanley Milgram conducts controversial experiment on obedience at Yale University.
1963	MK-ULTRA project officially suspended, but continues covertly.
	CIA compiles results of mind control and interrogation experiments into *Kubark Counterintelligence Interrogation Manual.*
1964	The Supreme Court rules in *Cooper v. Pate* that state inmates can sue prison administration for violation of their constitutional rights.
1965–66	Army Intelligence launches Operation X, designed to export foreign intelligence gathering and interrogation tactics to Latin American countries.
1966 December 10	UN General Assembly adopts the International Covenant on Civil and Political Rights (ICCPR).
1967	Beginning of CIA Phoenix Program, which was responsible for torture and assassinations of Viet Cong and others in Vietnam.
1968	Supreme Court rules that corporal punishment in prison is a violation of the Eighth Amendment.
March 19	U.S. soldiers massacre civilians at My Lai village in Vietnam.
1970	Abu Ghraib prison opens in Iraq.
1973	Amnesty International issues first *Report on Torture.*
1975 December 9	UN General Assembly adopts the Declaration on the Protection of All Persons From Being Subjected to Torture and Other Cruel, Inhuman, and Degrading Treatment or Punishment. In doing so, they present a detailed definition of torture.
1975	World Medical Association (WMA)'s Declaration of Tokyo sets guidelines for the medical community's involvement with torture.
	Former CIA officer Philip Agee publishes tell-all book, *Inside the Company,* documenting the agency's use of torture.
1979	UN General Assembly adopts a Code of Conduct for Law Enforcement Officials that prohibits the infliction, instigation, or tolerance of torture or cruel, inhuman, or degrading treatment or punishment.

1981	France abolishes guillotine.
1982	First inmate is executed by lethal injection.
	Rehabilitation and Research Centre for Torture Victims (RCT) opens in Copenhagen.
1984 December 10	UN General Assembly adopts the Convention Against Torture and Other Cruel, Inhuman, and Degrading Treatment or Punishment (CAT).
1989 November 20	UN General Assembly adopts Convention on the Rights of the Child.
1991	United States passes Protection for Victims of Torture Act, allowing civil suits in U.S. Court against foreign perpetrators of torture.
1992	UN General Assembly adopts WMA's *Principles of Medical Ethics,* which define torture and cruel, inhuman, and degrading treatment to be a gross breach of medical ethics.
1993	UN General Assembly adopts Declaration on the Elimination of Violence Against Women.
1994	United States ratifies the CAT with 19 reservations.
1995	U.S. federal judge finds widespread, systemic abuse perpetrated by guards at Pelican Bay prison in California.
	Congress passes Prison Litigation Reform Act (PLRA) to limit "frivolous" lawsuits by inmates.
1996	United States passes War Crimes Act (WCA) making violations of the Geneva Conventions punishable by lengthy jail terms or even death.
1997 August 9	Haitian immigrant Abner Louima is assaulted and sodomized by police in New York City.
1999	Texas prisons are pervaded by a "culture of sadistic and malicious violence," according to a federal judge.
2001 September 11	19 terrorists fly planes into the U.S. World Trade Center in New York City and the Pentagon in Washington, D.C., and hijack the subsequently downed Flight 93 over Pennsylvania, killing more than 3,000 people.
September 14	Congress grants Bush the power "to use all necessary and appropriate force against those nations, organizations, or persons

	he determined planned, authorized, committed, or aided the terrorist attacks that occurred on September 11."
September 16	Vice President Dick Cheney, in an interview on NBC's *Meet the Press,* says the United States should use any means at its disposal to win the war on terror, and claims it might need to "work the dark side."
November	The Justice Department authorizes CIA use of sleep deprivation and other "stress and duress" techniques, claiming they are not in violation of international law and regulations.

2002

January	Secretary of Defense Donald Rumsfeld approves the use of harsh interrogation tactics at Guantanamo Bay, Cuba, including intimidation with canines.
	The first group of prisoners arrives at Camp X-Ray in Guantanamo Bay.
January 9	White House Office of Legal Counsel attorney John Yoo co-authors a 42-page memo in which he concludes that neither the Geneva Conventions nor any other laws of war apply to the conflict in Afghanistan.
January 25	White House Counsel Alberto Gonzalez advises President Bush that the Geneva Conventions do not apply to Guantanamo detainees. In doing so, he refers to the Conventions as "quaint" and "obsolete."
February	President Bush issues a memorandum adopting the position advocated by Gonzalez and Yoo, and authorizes the CIA to set up secret detention camps for interrogations outside the United States.
summer	Justice Department expresses concern about the lack of useful information coming from Guantanamo detainees.
August	In a Justice Department memo, Jay Bybee offers a narrow definition of torture that includes only those acts intentionally designed to induce immense physical pain.
November 4	Major General Geoffrey Miller takes command at Guantanamo.
December	Rumsfeld approves a list of 16 controversial interrogation methods to be used at Guantanamo. This is in addition to the 17 traditionally approved methods in the Army Field Manual.

2003   Illinois Governor George Ryan commutes the sentences of 167 death row inmates, in part due to evidence of coerced confessions.

January 15	Rumsfeld rescinds December memo.
March 20	U.S. military invades Iraq.
April 16	Rumsfeld approves 24 interrogation techniques for Guantanamo.
June 26	In a letter to Ambassador Paul Bremer, Amnesty International (AI) raises concerns about abuse in U.S. detention camps in Iraq.
July 23	AI issues a report about abuse in prisons in Iraq, including Abu Ghraib. They also cite several suspicious deaths.
August	AI reports abuse at Bagram in Iraq.
August–September	Major General Geoffrey Miller is sent to Iraq to "Gitmoize" U.S. prisons.
September 8	Guards at Abu Ghraib take pictures of themselves abusing inmates.
October	The International Committee of the Red Cross (ICRC) documents abusive conditions and interrogation at Abu Ghraib.
November	Christian Peacemakers Team documents abuse in Iraq.

2004

January	U.S. Justice Department finds horrific abuse at Arizona juvenile detention centers.
January 13	Military Policeman Joseph Darby submits a CD containing photos of soldiers abusing prisoners at Abu Ghraib to the Army Criminal Investigations Division.
February	ICRC issues a report documenting abuse and recommending better policies and training for staff in interrogations.
March	General Taguba's report recommends safeguards be put in place for the most controversial interrogation tactics, but does not denounce their use.
March 19	A Justice Department memo authorizes transfer, or rendering, of detainees to other countries known to use torture for interrogation.
April	*60 Minutes* publicly airs some of the Abu Ghraib photos.
May	The *Wall Street Journal* publicly discloses the contents of the ICRC's October 2003 report on torture.
May 10	Bush publicly reiterates his complete support of Rumsfeld in the aftermath of public release of the photographs documenting abuses at Abu Ghraib.

May 24	Bush gives a speech in which he describes the incidents at Abu Ghraib as acts "by a few American troops who disregarded our country and disregarded our values."
June 8	Attorney General John Ashcroft tells the Senate Judiciary Committee that the international ban against torturing prisoners of war does not necessarily apply to suspects detained in the war on terror.
June 28	U.S. Supreme Court issues decisions in the "enemy combatant" cases, rejecting Bush administration arguments.
August	The Independent Panel and Fay-Jones reports recommend significant changes for interrogations.
2005	General Accounting Office (GAO), the investigative arm of Congress, finds widespread abuse at juvenile boot camps in the United States.
January 14	Army Specialist Charles Graner, alleged ringleader of the Abu Ghraib abuses, is convicted.
March 17	CIA Director Porter Goss testifies before the Senate Armed Services Committee that he cannot say whether interrogation techniques employed by the CIA in the aftermath of the 9/11 attacks were always in compliance with the law.
April 28	The U.S. Army Inspector General, on the one-year anniversary of the Abu Ghraib scandal, announces that no senior U.S. military officer will be held accountable. Only Brigadier General Janis Karpinski is relieved of her command and reprimanded.
September	Army Private First Class Lynndie England convicted by a military jury.
December	McCain Torture Amendment passes through Congress as part of the Detainee Treatment Act. The Amendment specifies that prohibitions against torture apply to any detainee, regardless of where he or she is held.
2006	Guards at Florida boot camp kill Martin Lee Anderson, prompting closure of boot camps in the state.
June	Supreme court rules that prohibitions on torture and cruel treatment apply to al Qaeda in *Hamdan v. Rumsfeld*.
September	Department of Defense (DOD) issues new field manual prohibiting specific techniques such as sleep deprivation, use of dogs, and waterboarding.

2007

May	Vermont becomes last state in the United States to pass a law protecting female inmates from sexual abuse by guards.
December	CIA destruction in 2005 of interrogation tapes recorded in 2002, suggesting that problematic practices were used, makes international headlines.
January	Worldwide action advocating closure of Guantanamo.

Further Readings

WEB SITES

Amnesty International, http://www.amnesty.org. International nonprofit dedicated to human-rights issues, with global campaigns against torture, violence against women, and many other topics.

Human Rights Education Association, http://www.hrea.org. Provides information about human-rights abuses and ideas for educating about human rights.

Human Rights First, http://www.humanrightsfirst.org. Devoted to documenting abuses and advocating human rights for all.

Human Rights Watch, http://www.hrw.org. Global watchdog group for human rights abuses of all varieties.

Human Rights Web, http://www.hrweb.org/legal/undocs.html. Summary of UN documents prohibiting torture and abuse and outlining basic human rights.

Program for Torture Victims, http://www.ptvla.org. Provides help services for victims of torture and coordinates awareness events.

Torture Abolition and Survivors Support Coalition International (TASSC), http://www.tassc.org. Provides support services for torture victims and advocacy efforts to end torture.

Witness, http://www.witness.org. Uses video and online techniques to document human-rights abuses and advocate change.

World Organization Against Torture, http://www.omct.org. Devoted to studying and ending torture practices worldwide.

BOOKS

Brecher, J., Cutler, J., and Smith, B. (Eds.). *In the name of democracy: American war crimes in Iraq and beyond.* New York: Metropolitan Books.

Conroy, J. (2000). *Unspeakable acts, ordinary people: The dynamics of torture.* New York: Alfred A. Knopf.

Danner, M. (2004). *Torture and truth: America, Abu Ghraib, and the war on terror.* New York: New York Review of Books.

Forrest, D. (Ed.). (1996). *A glimpse of hell.* New York: New York University Press.

Greenberg, K. (Ed.). (2006). *The torture debate in America.* New York: Cambridge University Press.

Grey, S. (2006). *Ghost plane.* New York: St. Martin's Press.

Hallinan, J. (2003). *Going up the river: Travels in a prison nation.* New York: Random House.

Harbury, J. (2005). *Truth, torture, and the American way.* Boston: Beacon Press.

Hersch, S. (2004). *Chain of command: The road from 9/11 to Abu Ghraib.* New York: HarperCollins.

Hornblum, A. (1998). *Acres of skin.* New York: Routledge.

Kelleway, J. (2000). *The history of torture and execution.* New York: The Lyon's Press.

Levison, S. (Ed.). (2004). *Torture: An anthology.* New York: Oxford.

McCoy, A. (2006). *A question of torture: CIA interrogation, from the Cold War to the war on terror.* New York: Metropolitan.

Meeropol, R. (Ed.). (2005). *America's disappeared.* New York: Seven Stories Press.

Miles, S. (2006). *Oath betrayed: Torture, medical complicity, and the war on terror.* New York: Random House.

Milgram, S. (1974). *Obedience and authority: An experimental view.* New York: Harper & Row.

Mossallanejed, E. (2005). *Torture in the age of fear.* Milton, Ontario: Seraphim.

Otterman, M. (2007). *American torture.* London: Pluto Press.

Rajiva, L. (2005). *The language of empire: Abu Ghraib and the American media.* New York: Monthly Review.

Rathbone, C. (2005). *A world apart: Women, prison, and life behind bars.* New York: Random House.

Rejali, D. (2007). *Torture and democracy.* Princeton, NJ: Princeton University Press.

Rose, D. (2004). *Guantanamo: The war on human rights.* New York: The New Press.

Valentine, D. (2000). *The Phoenix program.* Lincoln, Nebraska: iUniverse.com.

Williams, K. (2006). *American torture and the logic of domination.* Cambridge, MA: South End Press.

Williams, K. (2007). *Our enemies in blue: Police and power in America.* Cambridge, MA: South End Press.

Bibliography

Abramsky, S., & Fellner, J. (2003). *Ill-equipped: U.S. prisons and offenders with mental illness.* New York: Human Rights Watch.

American Bar Association report to the House of Delegates. (2004, August). In Greenberg, K., & Dratel, J. (Eds.), *The torture papers: The road to Abu Ghraib* (pp. 1132–1164). New York: Cambridge University Press.

American Civil Liberties Union. (2007, November 8). *Disparate advocates tell Congress to fix law that silences prisoner abuse.* Retrieved November 17, 2007, from http://www.aclu.org/prison/gen/32771prs20071108.html.

American Civil Liberties Union. (2005, December 14). *Prison conditions and prisoner abuse after Katrina.* Retrieved November 17, 2007, from http://www.aclu.org/racial justice/gen/23007res20051214.html.

Amnesty International. (2000, May). *United States of America: A briefing for the UN Committee against Torture.* New York: Amnesty International.

Amnesty International. (2001). *Broken bodies, shattered minds: Torture and ill treatment of women.* New York: Amnesty International Publications.

Amnesty International. (2004, June 4). *USA: Staff Sergeant Camilo Mejia Castillo is a prisoner of conscience.*

Argetsinger, A. (2001, September 17). At colleges, students are facing a big test. *Washington Post,* p. B1.

Bravin, J., & Fields, G. (2003, March 4). How do U.S. interrogators make a captured terrorist talk? *Wall Street Journal,* p. B1.

Brecher, J. (2005). Affirmative measures to halt U.S. war crimes. In Brecher, J., Cutler, J., & Smith, B. (Eds.), *In the name of democracy: American war crimes in Iraq and beyond* (pp. 248–259). New York: Metropolitan.

Brecher, J., Culter, J., & Smith, B. (2005). Conclusion. In Brecher, J., Cutler, J., & Smith, B. (Eds.), *In the name of democracy: American war crimes in Iraq and beyond* (pp. 322–329). New York: Metropolitan.

Brody, R. (2005). The road to Abu Ghraib. In Meeropol, R. (Ed.), *America's disappeared* (pp. 113–129). New York: Seven Stories Press.

Bruton, J. (2004). *The big house.* Stillwater, MN: Voyageur Press.

Burns, R. (2008, January 14). Close Guantanamo, top officer urges. *Miami Herald,* p. 3A.

Center for Constitutional Rights. (2005). Individual accounts of torture. In Brecher, J., Cutler, J., & Smith, B. (Eds.), *In the name of democracy: American war crimes in Iraq and beyond* (pp. 79–81). New York: Metropolitan Books.

Chinyelu, M. (2003, July 17). Defining torture: At home and abroad. *New York Amsterdam News,* pp. 5–7.

Christianson, S. (2004). *Notorious prisons.* London: First Lyons Press.

Cockburn, A., & St. Clair, J. (1999). *Whiteout: The CIA, drugs, and the press.* New York: Verso.

Conroy, J. (2000). *Unspeakable acts, ordinary people: The dynamics of torture.* New York: Alfred A. Knopf.

Crews, G. (2004). Justice and the origin of corrections. In Stanko, S., Gillespie, W., and Crews, G. (Eds.), *Living in prison: A history of the correctional system with an insider's view* (pp. 25–42). Westport, CT: Greenwood Press.

Danner, M. (2004). *Torture and truth: America, Abu Ghraib, and the war on terror.* New York: New York Review of Books.

Dow, M. (2004). *American gulag: Inside U.S. immigration prisons.* Berkeley, CA: University of California Press.

Dratel, J. (2006). The curious debate. In Greenberg, K. (Ed.), *The torture debate in America* (pp. 111–117). New York: Cambridge University Press.

Dubensky, J., & Lavery, R. (2006). Torture: An interreligious debate. In Greenberg, K. (Ed.), *The torture debate in America* (pp. 162–182). New York: Cambridge University Press.

Fay, G. (2004). AR 15–6 Investigation of the Abu Ghraib Detention Facility and 205th Military Intelligence Brigade (U). In Danner, M. (Ed.), *Torture and truth: America, Abu Ghraib, and the war on terror* (pp. 437–579). New York: New York Review Books.

Fay, G. (2004). Investigation of the Abu Ghraib detention facility and the 205th Military Intelligence Brigade. In Strasser, S. (Ed.), *The Abu Ghraib investigations* (pp. 109–171). New York: Public Affairs Press.

The Fay-Jones report. (2004, August). In Greenberg, K., & Dratel, J. (Eds.), *The torture papers: The road to Abu Ghraib* (pp. 987–1131). New York: Cambridge University Press.

Fellner, J. (2004, May 14). *Prisoner abuse: How different are U.S. prisons?* Retrieved May 1, 2007, from http://www.hrw.org/english/docs/2004/05/14/usdom8583.htm.

Finley. L. (2007) Our own Abu Ghraib? Torture of the "other" in the U.S. *War Crimes, Genocide, and Crimes Against Humanity, 2*(2).

Franklin, B. (n.d.). *The American prison and the normalization of torture.* Historians Against the War. Retrieved October 9, 2007, from http://www.historiansagainst war.org/resources/torture/brucefranklin.html.

Gillespie, W. (2004). Prisoners' rights and states' responsibilities. In Stanko, S., Gillespie, W., & Crews, G. (Eds.), *Living in prison: A history of the correctional system with an insider's view* (pp. 111–127). Westport, CT: Greenwood.

Goodman, A. (2006, May 9). Chicago's Abu Ghraib. *Democracy Now.* Retrieved January 15, 2008, from http://www.democracynow.org/206/5/9/chicagos_abu_ ghraib_un_committee_against.html.

Grey, S. (2006). *Ghost plane.* New York: St. Martin's Press.

Gutierrez, T. (2005, September 26). England convicted. *USA Today.* Retrieved January 12, 2008, from http://www.usatoday.com/news/nation/2005_09_26-england_ x.html.

Hallinan, J. (2003). *Going up the river: Travels in a prison nation.* New York: Random House.

Hallinan, J. (2005). Prisons are cruel and needlessly punitive. In Bailey, K. (Ed.), *How should prisons treat inmates?* (pp. 9–21). Farmington Hills, MI: Greenhaven Press.

Harbury, J. (2005). *Truth, torture, and the American way.* Boston: Beacon Press.

Hathaway, O. (2004). The promise and limits of the international law of torture. In S. Levison (Ed.), *Torture: An anthology* (p.199–212). New York: Oxford.

Heilpin, J. (2004, September 22). *Indian jails likened to Iraq.* Tribal Court Clearinghouse. Retrieved March 15, 2005, from http://www.tribal-institute.org/message/ 00000052.htm.

Herald Wire Services. (n.d.). CIA Chief: Methods don't include torture [Electronic version]. *Miami Herald.*

Hersch, S. (2004). *Chain of command: The road from 9/11 to Abu Ghraib.* New York: HarperCollins.

Holmes, S. (2006). Is defiance of law a proof of success? In Greenberg, K. (Ed.), *The torture debate in America* (pp. 118–135). New York: Cambridge University Press.

Holtzman, E. (2005). Watergate and Abu Ghraib: Holding war criminals accountable in the U.S. courts and Congress. In Brecher, J., Cutler, J., & Smith, B. (Eds.), *In the name of democracy: American war crimes in Iraq and beyond* (pp. 260–271). New York: Metropolitan Books.

Hopkins, E. (1972). *Our lawless police: A study of the unlawful enforcement of the law.* New York: Viking.

Hornblum, A. (1998). *Acres of skin.* New York: Routledge.

Horton, S. (2005, January 20). A Nuremberg lesson: Torture scandal began far above "rotten apples." In Brecher, J., Cutler, J., & Smith, B. (Eds.), *In the name of democracy: American war crimes in Iraq and beyond* (pp. 112–114). New York: Metropolitan Books.

Human Rights Watch. (1997). *Cold storage: Super-maximum security confinement in Indiana.* New York: Human Rights Watch.

Human Rights Watch. (2001). *No escape: Male rape in U.S. prisons.* Retrieved October 12, 2007, from http://www.hrw.org/reports/2001/prison/report2.html.

Human Rights Watch. (2006, July). "No blood, no foul": Soldiers' accounts of detainee abuse in Iraq. *Human Rights Watch, 18*(3), 1–55.

The ICRC report. (2004, February). In Greenberg, K., & Dratel, J. (Eds.), *The torture papers: The road to Abu Ghraib* (pp. 383–404). New York: Cambridge University Press.

Investigation launched on harsh prison conditions. (n.d.). Retrieved March 15, 2005, from http://www.owlstar.com.

Jempson, M. (1996). The agencies involved. In Forrest, D. (Ed.), *A glimpse of hell* (pp. 122–126). New York: New York University Press.

Johnson, K. (2004, May 20). Former BIA official urged prison fixes [Electronic version]. *USA Today.* Retrieved from: http://www.usatoday.com/news/nation/2004–05–20-indian-prisons-usat_x.html.

Johnson, R. (1998). *Death work: A study of the modern execution process.* Belmont, CA: Wadsworth.

Johnston, D. (2007, December 9). Destroyed tapes fuel new questions over CIA tactics. *Miami Herald,* p. 3A.

Jones, A. (2004). Introduction: History and complicity. In Jones, A. (Ed.). *Genocide, war crimes and the west: History and complicity* (pp. 3–30). London: Zed.

Karpinski, J. (2005). *One woman's army.* New York: Miramax books.

Kelleway, J. (2000). *The history of torture and execution.* New York: The Lyon's Press.

Klein, N. (2005, December 26). "Never before!" Our amnesiac torture debate [Electronic version]. *The Nation.* Retrieved from http://www.thenation.com/doc/20051226/klein.

Langbein, J. (2004). The legal history of torture. In S. Levison (Ed.), *Torture: A collection* (pp. 93–103). New York: Oxford University Press.

Levin, B. (2007, May). Trials for terrorists: The shifting legal landscape of the post 9–11 era. *Journal of Contemporary Criminal Justice, 23*(2), pp. 195–218.

Lewis, A. (2005, December 26). The torture administration [Electronic version]. *The Nation.* Retrieved from http://www.thenation.com/doc/20051226/lewis.

Lifton, R., & Mitchell, G. (2002). *Who owns death? Capital punishment, the American conscience, and the end of executions.* New York: Perennial.

Lockwood, M., & Alexander, R. (2005). Prisoners should not have it too easy. In Bailey, K. (Ed.), *How should prisons treat inmates?* (pp. 22–28). Farmington Hills, MI: Greenhaven Press.

Lomax, A. (2005, June 16). The *real* American gulag. *Counterpunch.* Retrieved January 21, 2006, from http://www.counterpunch.org/lomax06162005.html.

Luban, D. (2006). Liberalism, torture, and the ticking bomb. In Greenberg, K. (Ed.), *The torture debate in America* (pp. 35–83). New York: Cambridge University Press.

MacDonald, H. (2006). How to interrogate terrorists. In Greenberg, K. (Ed.), *The torture debate in America* (pp. 84–97). New York: Cambridge University Press.

Marsh, J. (2006–7, Fall/Winter). The prison guard's dilemma. *Greater Good,* p. 35.

Martin, J. (2004, August 6). Suicide triggers probe of tribal detention center. *The Seattle Times,* p. B1.

Masri, K. (2005, December 18). America kidnapped me. *Los Angeles Times.*

Mayer, J. (2005, February 14). Outsourcing torture: The secret history of America's "extraordinary rendition" program. *The New Yorker,* p. 106.

McCarthy, A. (2003, July–August). Torture: Thinking about the unthinkable. In Greenberg, K. (Ed.), *The torture debate in America* (pp. 98–110). New York: Cambridge University Press.

McCoy, A. (2006). *A question of torture: CIA interrogation, from the Cold War to the war on terror.* New York: Metropolitan.

McEntee, A. (1996). Law and torture. In Forrest, D. (Ed.), *A glimpse of hell* (pp. 1–20). New York: New York University Press.

McLaughlin, A. (2001, November 14). How far Americans would go to fight terror. *Christian Science Monitor,* 1.

Miami Herald Staff and Wire Reports. (2008, April 11). Torture methods got Cheney's OK. *Miami Herald,* p. 3A.

Miles, S. (2006). *Oath betrayed: Torture, medical complicity, and the war on terror.* New York: Random House.

Miller, C., & Caputo, M. (2006, October 14). New claims of abuse at boys camp. *Miami Herald,* pp. 1–2A.

Minton, T. (2002, May). *Jails in Indian country, 2001.* Bureau of Justice Statistics.

Morin, R., & Deane, C. (2004, May 28). Americans split on how to interrogate: Majority polled oppose using torture. *Washington Post.*

Mossallanejed, E. (2005). *Torture in the age of fear.* Milton, Ontario: Seraphim.

Myrdal, G. (1944). *An American dilemma: The Negro problem and modern democracy.* New York: Harper.

The Nazi Doctors. (2007). Retrieved January 12, 2008, from http://www.auschwitz.dk/doctors.html.

Newman, T. (2004, May 27). Prisons aren't Indians' only problem. *USA Today,* p. 12A.

Newhouse, E. (2003, January 13). *Watchdog group says prison fails to give proper treatment.* Prison Activist. Retrieved June 10, 2005, from http://www.prisonactivist.org/pipermail.prisonact-list/2003-January/006443.html.

Otterman, M. (2007). *American torture.* London: Pluto Press.

Parry, J. (2004). Escalation and necessity: Defining torture at home and abroad. In S. Levinson (Ed.), *Torture: An anthology* (pp. 145–164). New York: Oxford University Press.

Pfohl, S. (1994). Images of deviance and social control: A sociological history (2nd ed.). New York: McGraw-Hill.

Priest, D., & Gellman, B. (2002, December 26). U.S. decries abuse but defends interrogations. *Washington Post,* p. A1.

Princeton Survey Research Association. (2005, November 10–11). *Newsweek Poll.* Retrieved from http://www.pollingreport.com.

Rajiva, L. (2005). *The language of empire: Abu Ghraib and the American media.* New York: Monthly Review.

Rathbone, C. (2005*). A world apart: Women, prison, and life behind bars.* New York: Random House.

Ratner, M. (2005). The Guantanamo prisoners. In Meeropol, R. (Ed.), *America's disappeared* (pp. 31–59). New York: Seven Stories Press.

Reid, T. (2007, October 12.). Torture, starvation, and death: How American boot camps abuse boys [Electronic version]. *London Times.* Retrieved January 12, 2008, from http://www.timesonline.co.uk/tol/news/world/us_and_americas/article264 1635.ece.

Rejali, D. (2007). *Torture and democracy.* Princeton, NJ: Princeton University Press.

Riok, J, (2006, April). *Deadly restraint.* Project NoSpank. Retrieved February 11, 2007, from http://www.nospank.net/camps.

Rose, D. (2004). *Guantanamo: The war on human rights.* New York: The New Press.

Rosenberg, C. (2007, December 9). Filing: Detainee "tortured." *Miami Herald,* p. 3A.

Ross, L. (2001). Punishing institutions. In Lobo, S., & Talbot, S. (Eds.), *Native American voices,* (2nd ed., pp. 455–465). Upper Saddle River, NJ: Prentice Hall.

Ross, L. (1996). Resistance and survivance: Cultural genocide and imprisoned Native American women. *Race, Gender, and Class, 3*(2), pp. 143–164.

Rutenberg, J. (2001, November 5). Torture seeps into discussion by news media. *New York Times,* p. C1.

Saar, E., & Novack, V. (2005). *Inside the wire: A military intelligence soldier's eyewitness account of life at Guantanamo.* New York: Penguin.

Schaffer Library on Drug Policy. (1950). "Truth" drugs in interrogation. MKULTRA Hearing. Retrieved October 12, 2007, from http://www.druglibrary.org/schaffer/HISTORY/e1950/mkultra/hearing04.html.

Schlesinger, J. (2004, August). Final report of the independent panel to review Department of Defense operations. In Strasser, S. (Ed.), *The Abu Ghraib investigations* (pp. 1–101). New York: Public Affairs Press.

The Schlesinger report. (2004, August). In Greenberg, K., & Dratel, J. (Eds.), *The torture papers: The road to Abu Ghraib* (pp. 908–975). New York: Cambridge University Press.

Shue, H. (2004). Torture. In Levinson, S. (Ed.), *Torture: A collection* (pp. 47–60). New York: Oxford University Press.

Skolnick, J. (2004). American interrogation: From torture to trickery. In S. Levinson (Ed.), *Torture: A collection* (pp. 105–127). New York: Oxford University Press.

Smith, B. (2006, January 1). Sexual abuse of women in United States prisons: A modern corollary of slavery. *Fordham Urban Law Journal.*

Snepp, F. (1980). *Interval: The American debacle in Vietnam and the fall of Saigon.* London: Allen Lane.

Spinner, J. (2004, May 8). Unit's role was to break down prisoners: Reservist tells of orders from intelligence officers. *Washington Post.*

Stephens, T. (2005, May 13). A chronology of U.S. war crimes & torture, 1975–2005. *Counterpunch.* Retrieved November 17, 2007, from http://www.counter punch.org/stephens05132005.html.

Strasser, S. (2004). *The Abu Ghraib investigations.* New York: Public Affairs Books.

The Taguba report. (2004, March). In Greenberg, K., & Dratel, J. (Eds.), *The torture papers: The road to Abu Ghraib* (pp. 405–465). New York: Cambridge University Press.

Tarpley, L. (n.d.). Torture in Maine's prisons [Electronic version]. *Portland Phoenix*. Retrieved January 11, 2008, from www.portlandphoenix.co/features/top/ts_multi/documents/05081722.asp

Tetreault, M. (2006, Fall). The sexual politics of Abu Ghraib: Hegemony, spectacle, and the global war on terror. *NWSA Journal, 18*(3), pp. 33–51.

Tirado, M. (2005, February). Help for the forgotten. *American Indian Report, 21.*

United Nations General Assembly. (1975, December 9). *Declaration on the protection of all persons from being subjected to torture and other cruel, inhuman, and degrading treatment.* Adopted as Resolution 3452. Retrieved in full from the Office of the High Commissioner for Human Rights at http://www.unhchr.udhr/index.html.

United Nations General Assembly. (1984, December 10). *Convention against torture and other cruel, inhuman, or degrading treatment or punishment.* Adopted as Resolution 39146. Retrieved in full from the Office of the High Commissioner for Human Rights at http://www.unhchr.udhr/index.html.

USA Today/Gallup Poll results. (2005, January 12).

Valentine, D. (2000). *The Phoenix program.* Lincoln, Nebraska: iUniverse.com.

Vann, B. (2000, March 9). *The Abner Louima case: Three New York cops guilty in cover-up of torture.* World Socialist Web Site. Retrieved May 21, 2005, from http://www.wsws.org/articles/2000/mar2000/loui-m09_prn.shtml.

Vito, G., & Simonson C. (2004). *Juvenile justice today* (4th ed.). Upper Saddle River, NJ: Prentice Hall.

Watt, S. (2005). Torture, "stress and duress," and rendition as counterterrorism tools. In Meeropol, R. (Ed.), *America's disappeared* (pp. 72–112). New York: Seven Stories Press.

Williams, K. (2006). *American torture and the logic of domination.* Cambridge, MA: South End Press.

Wooden, K. (2000). *Weeping in the playtime of others* (2nd ed.). Columbus, OH: Ohio State University Press.

Zakaria, F. (2005, November 14). Psst...nobody loves a torturer. *Newsweek.*

Index

Abu Ghraib, 1–10, 11–13, 65, 69, 91, 98, 101, 109; investigations into, 129–37; photos of, 1–5, 114, 118, 122–37, 157
Addington, David, 6
Afghanistan, 1, 109, 116–19
Agee, Philip, 60–61
Ahmed, Ahmed Shehab, 120
Al-Arabiya, 2
Al-Jamadi, Monadel, 123–24
Al-Jazeera, 2
Al-Kahtani, Mohammed, 113–14
Al-Libi, Ibn al-Shaykh, 140
Al-Zarqawi, Abu Musab, 119
American Bar Association (ABA), 31, 159
American Civil Liberties Union, 90, 92
American College of Physicians (ACP), 128
American Gulag, 97
American Medical Association (AMA), 127–28
American Psychological Association (APA), 49–50
Amnesty International, (AI), 64, 72, 91, 109–10, 116, 133
Anderson, Martin Lee, 71

An Essay on Crimes and Punishment, 21
Arar, Maher, 139
Area 2, 80–82
Armed Forces Institute of Pathology, 124
Arpaio, Joe, 70, 100
Ashcraft v. Tennessee, 33
Ashcroft, John, 111, 138
Asphyxiation, 79
Audy Home, 96
Ausch, David, 125

Bagram, 117–19
Baker, Sean, 155–16
Bates, David, 80–81
Beale, Corey, 76
Beccaria, Cesare, 20–21, 27, 155
Belmont report, 72–73
Berg, Nicholas, 4, 7–8
Bien Hoa Mental Hospital, 56
Boot camps, 71, 96
Botched executions, 28–29
Brainwashing, 44
Brazil, 58–59
Bremer, Paul, 121
Brockway, Zebulon, 83–84
Brooks, Charles Jr., 28
Brown v. Mississippi, 25–26

Bruder, Thomas, 79–80
Bruton, James, 94–95
Bucking, 23–24
Bureau of Indian Affairs (BIA) prisons, 98–100
Bureau of Social Science Research (BSSR), 51
Burge, Jon, 80–82
Bush administration, 112–13, 131–32, 138, 141–42
Bush, George H. W., 61
Bush, George W., 4–10, 122–23, 128, 137, 141–44
Bybee, Jay, 112

Calejo, Edward, 98
Caligula, 16
Calley, William, 57
Cameron, Ewan, 47–48
Camp Delta, 116
Camp Mackall, 54
Camp Nama, 119–20
Camp X-Ray, 114–15
Carter, Jimmy, 58
Castillo, Camilo Mejia, 155–56
Cedar Woman (Catherine), 99–100
The Celling of America: An Inside Look at the U.S. Prison Industry, 69
Central Intelligence Agency (CIA), 6–7, 9–10, 37, 41–65, 120, 122–24, 130–31, 137–42
Chambers v. Florida, 32–33
Chemical torture, 20–31
Cheney, Dick, 5–6
Chinhae, South Korea, 53–54
Chirac, Jacques, 9
Chokeholds, 78
Chomsky, Noam, 59
Choy, Paul, 96
Christian Peacemaker Team (CPT), 121
Christian Science Monitor, 11
Christians, 16
Church Committee, 42
Church, Albert, 124
Church, Frank, 57
Civil War, 23–25
Clauberg, Carl, 33
Clinton Correctional Facility, 93–94

Code of Hammurabi, 20–21
Colby, William, 57
Cold War, 47, 63, 65
Condon, Richard, 51
Conroy, John, 83
Convention Against Torture (CAT), 12, 38–41, 72, 101, 110–11
Cooke, Reginald, 94
Cooper, Thomas, 86–87
Cooper v. Pate, 86–87
Corcoran Prison, 70, 93–95
Cornell University, 45–46, 48
Corrections Corporation of America (CCA), 92
Corsetti, Damien, 118–19
Coulter, Ann, 134

Daley, Richard, 80–81
Danner, Mark, 156
Darby, Joseph, 135–36
Davis, Sergeant, 3, 125
Death penalty: 12–13, 16, 28–29, 103; history, 27–29
Death Work: A Study of the Modern Execution Process, 103
Debility, Dependency, and Dread (DDD), 53
Debret, Jean, 24
Declaration of Tokyo, 39
Dedicated enemies, 9
"Democrisy," 5
Dergoul, Tarek, 115
Dershowitz, Alan, 151
Detainee Treatment Act (DTA), 142–143
Devaney, Earl, 98–100
Dilawar, 117
Dittman, Beth, 71
Dow, Mark, 97
Draconian Code, 21
Dratel, Joshua, 152
Dulles, Allen, 45

Eastman Kodak v. Kavlin, 143
Ebibillo, Tony, 97–98
Edgewood Chemical Arsenal, 45
Edison, Thomas, 28
Eighth Amendment, 40
Electroshock torture, 29

Ellis, O.B., 84
El-Masri, Khaled, 139
Elmira, New York, 83–84
El Salvador, 61
England, 16–17; courts, 20–21
England, Lynndie, 3, 125, 131, 135
Esmor Detention Center, 97
Estelle v. Gamble, 87
European law of proof, 18–20
Extreme Reaction Force (ERF), 115–16

The Farm, 53
Fay, George, 130, 133, 159
Fay Report, 133, 159
Federal Bureau of Investigations (FBI),
    10–11
519th Military Intelligence Battalion,
    118–19
Flagellus, 16
Folsom Prison, 94–95
Food and Drug Administration (FDA),
    43, 75
Ford, Gerald, 58
Ford, Misty, 99–100
Forest Hays, Jr. State Prison, 93
Fort Benning, 62
Forward Operating Base (FOB) Tiger,
    120, 135–36
Francis, Willie, 28
Frederick, Ivan "Chip," 3, 7, 124
Frederic the Great, 20
Freedom of Information Act (FOIA), 42
Furman v. Georgia, 12

Garrote, 17
Gas chamber, 28
Geneva Conventions, 6–7, 37–38, 58,
    110–11, 113, 118, 131, 142–43
Ghost Plane, 61
Ghost prisoners, 123–24
Giuliani, Rudy, 81–82
Gonzalez, Alberto, 111–12
Goss, Porter, 9
Gottlieb, Sidney, 46, 50–51
Graner, Charles, 3, 101, 125, 127,
    131, 135
Greenville Hills Academy, 96
Grey, Stephen, 9–10, 61

Guantanamo Bay, 1, 10, 109, 112,
    113–16
Gulf War, 64
Gunbar al-Yasseri, Nori, 3

Habib, Mamdou, 140–41
Hallinan, Joseph, 88–89
Hamdan, Salim, 142
Hamdi v. Rumsfeld, 142
Hamoodi, Yehiya, 126–27
Harbury, Jennifer, 160
Harman, Sabrina, 3, 124, 131
Hathaway, Oona, 40–41
Helms, Richard, 46, 53, 57
Herman, Edward, 59
Hersch, Seymour, 2, 123
Hilao v. Estate of Marcos, 143
Hillenkoetter, Roscoe, 45
Hinkle, Lawrence, 45, 48
History of torture, 15–30; Beccaria,
    Cesare, 20–21, 27; Central
    Intelligence Agency (CIA), 6–7, 9–10,
    37, 41–65, 120, 122–24, 130–31,
    137–42; European law of proof,
    18–20; Inquisition, 17; Middle Ages,
    15–20; Nazi doctors, 42–43; Nazis,
    33–35; Nero, 16
Hoffman, Albert, 43
Hoffman, Everett, 92
Holt v. Sarver, 87
House, Robert, 34
*Human Intelligence Collector
    Operations,* 143
Human Rights Committee, 9
Human Rights Watch, 95, 96, 98, 102,
    119–20, 128, 132–35
Human subjects, 58
Hunter, Edward, 44
Hussein, Saddam, 1
Hutchinson Correctional Facility, 78–79

Immigrants, 96–98
Immigration and Naturalization Services
    (INS), 96–98
Imperial Hubris, 140
Independent Panel, 132–33, 158–59
Innocent bystanders, 9
Inquisition, 17

Inside the Company, 60–61
Inside the Wire, 116
International Committee of the Red
    Cross (ICRC), 109, 121, 133, 157–58
International Covenant on Civil and
    Political Rights (ICCPR), 12, 38,
    73, 95
International Covenant on Economic,
    Social, and Cultural Rights
    (ICESCR), 38
International Police Academy (IPA), 55
Interrogational torture, 8–9
*In the Name of Democracy: American War
    Crimes in Iraq and Beyond,* 160
Ionia State Hospital, 48
Iran, 61–62
Iron Maiden, 17

Jackson County Jail (Florida), 98
Jackson v. Bishop, 87
Jacoby, Charles H., 118
Jacoby, Lowell E., 123
Janis, Irving, 43, 48
"Jihad Jerry," 125–26
Johnson, Robert, 103
Jones, Anthony, 130
Jordan, Steve, 124–25, 130
Judicial torture, 17–20
Justice Department, 6

Kandahar, 117
Karpinski, Janet, 7, 130, 133–36
Kassem, General Abdul Karim, 1
Kemmler, William, 28
Kendall, George, 27
Kennedy, John F., 58
KGB, 52–53
Khan, Majid, 10
Kimmons, John, 143
Kind and Unusual Punishments, 75
Klein, Naomi, 5
Korean War, 45–46
Krome Detention Center, 97–99
*Kubark Counterintelligence Interrogation
    Manual,* 52–53, 58, 62–63

Lagouranis, Tony, 120–21
Larned Mental Health Facility, 78–79

Latin America, 52, 58–61
Leahy, Patrick, 121
Lethal injection, 13, 28–29
Lieberman, Senator Joseph, 8
Lifton, Robert Jay, 27
Lilly, John, 47
Limbaugh, Rush, 4, 8
"limited torture," 153–54
Ling chi, 16
Lomax, Adrian, 69, 71
Longtin, Keith, 76
Louima, Abner, 79–80, 82
Lovenhart, Arthur, 34
LSD, 43, 45
Lynching, 24–26

MacDonald, Heather, 149–52
MacLaine, James, 16
Manchurian Candidate, The, 51
Manhattan Project, 44
Marcos, Ferdinand, 59–61
Maximum Security University, 70
McCain, Senator John, 4, 143–44
McGill University, 46–48
McLaughlin Group, 11
Medical personnel, 127–28
Mengele, Josef, 33
Mensah, Eric, 96–97
Mentally ill, 95–96; juveniles, 96
Metropolitan Detention Center, 102
Middle Ages, 15–20; executions, 21
Miles, Steven, 111, 127–28
Milgram, Stanley, 48–50
Military Commission Act (MCA), 143
Military Police (MPs), 7
Miller, Geoffrey, 115, 122, 132–33,
    135
Mind control, 34; drugs, 34
Miranda v. Arizona, 75–76
Mitchell, Greg, 27
Mitford, Jessica, 75
Mitrione, Dan, 60
MK-SEARCH, 51–52
MK-ULTRA, 45–48, 50–51, 58
Mohamed, Binyam, 141
Mosul, 120–121
Muehlberger, Clarence, 35
My Lai Massacre, 56–57

Naranjo, Ed, 99
The Nation, 136
National Commission on Law
    Observance and Enforcement, 31
National Institute of Mental Health
    (NIMH), 47
National Interrogation Center (NIC),
    55–56
National Security Counsel (NSC), 41–42
Naval Air Station Brunswick, 54
Naval Special warfare Squadron 7, 120–21
Navy Seals, 123–24
Nazi doctors, 42–43
Nazis, 33–35
Nero, 16
Newgate Prison, 16
Newsweek, 7, 11
Nicaragua, 62–63
North, Oliver, 4
Nosenko, Yuri, 52–53
NOVA XR-5000, 77
Nuremberg Code, 72–73
Nuremberg trials, 28, 33–34

Oberheuser, Herta, 33
Odah v. United States, 142
Office of Legal Counsel (OLC), 6–7, 41
Office of Naval Research (ONR), 50–51
Office of Public Safety (OPS), 55, 58–59
Olson, Frank, 50
One Woman's Army, 134
Operation Bluebird, 45
Operation Chatter, 42–43
Operation Paperclip, 42
Opposing torture, 152–57
Osborn, K. Barton, 56
Oviawe, Felix, 97

Palacio, Luis, 89–90
Pappas, Thomas, 124, 130
"Parrot's Perch," 23–24
Pash, Boris, 45
Pearl, Daniel, 8
Pelican Bay State Prison, 69–70, 94
Pepper spray, 30–31, 79
Philippines, 59–60
Phillabaum, Jerry, 126
Phillips State Prison, 96

Phoenix, 55–58
Pimentinhas, 58
Plotner, Kurt, 42
Police abuse, 12, 26–27
Police corruption, 81–82
Principles of Medical Ethics, 39–40
Prison abuse, 28–35, 69–75, 83–102;
    of Black Muslims, 85–87; conditions,
    12; experiments, 72–74; first prisons,
    83–84; Hurricane Katrina, 90;
    immigrants, 96–98; Iraq, 119–29;
    juveniles, 70–71, 96; medical
    attention, 71, 99–100; mentally
    ill, 95–96, 126; Native Americans,
    98–100; Oahu Prison, 88–89;
    private prisons, 92; rape, 91–94, 99;
    restraints, 90; Supermax prisons, 92;
    Texas, 83–85; women, 71, 91, 99–100
Prison experiments, 33–35
Prison Litigation Reform Act (PLRA),
    100–101
Prison overcrowding, 1–2
Project Artichoke, 45
Project X, 59–60
Protection for Victims of Torture Act, 64
Pro torture arguments, 149–152
Provincial Interrogation Center (PIC),
    55–56
Provincial Reconnaissance Units (PRUs),
    55–56
Public support of torture, 11–12

QKHILLTOP, 45–46

Ragen, Joseph, 85–87
Rajiva, Lila, 136
Rasul v. Bush, 113, 142
Ready collaborators, 9
Reagan, Ronald, 38, 58, 63–64
Recommendations, 157–60; ABA, 159;
    Fay Report, 133, 159; Schlesinger
    Commission, 122; Taguba Report,
    133–34, 158
Reese, Donald, 124
Reform the Armed Services Movement
    (RAM), 60
Rehabilitation and Research Centre for
    Torture Victims (RCT), 64

Rehidwaniya, 120
Rejali, Darius, 27
Rendition, 9–11, 109, 137–42
Report on Torture, 109
Reuben, Layton, 127
Rice, Condoleeza, 121, 138
Robertson, Wayne, 94
Rockefeller, Nelson, 50
Rockefeller Commission, 42
Roman Empire, 16, 21
Rotten apples, 82–83
Rumsfeld, Donald, 5, 114, 121,
    130–31, 133
Rush, Benjamin, 27
Ryan, George, 80–82
Ryder, Major General Donald, 2

Saar, Erik, 116
Sanchez, Ricardo, 130, 133–35
San Quentin, 28, 34
Scheuer, Michael, 140
Schlesinger, James, 132
Schlesinger Commission, 122
School of the Americas (SOA), 62–63
September 11, 2001, 4, 5, 9–10, 102,
    112, 137
Shakespeare, William, 15
Shelton, Craig, 78–79
Sing Sing prison, 24, 28, 30–31
Sivits, Specialist, 125
60 Minutes, 2, 11
Slaves, 23–25
Snepp, Frank, 56
Sohappy, Cindy Gilbert, 99
Soviet Union, 43–45
Spain, 17
Spanish-American war, 29–30
Special Access Program, 123
Specter, Arlen, 121
Stalin, Joseph, 44
*Standard Minimum Rules for the
    Treatment of Prisoners,* 73–74
Stateville Correctional Center, 34,
    85–87, 89–90
"Statue of Liberty," 3
"sweat box," 26
"sweating," 27
Stead Airforce Base, 54

Strappado, 15
Strip searches, 92
Stun belts, 78–79
Stun technology, 77–78
Supermax prisons, 12, 92
Survival, Evasion, Resistance, Escape
    (SERE), 54–55
Sylvester, Major Richard, 26

Taguba, Antonio, 2, 129, 133, 158
Taguba Report, 133–34, 158
Talion principle, 20
Tallulah Correctional Center, 96
Tarpley, Lance, 95
Tasers, 77–78
Task Force 6–26, 122–23
Taylor, Fliny, 81
Tenet, George, 137
Terroristic torture, 8
Third degree, 26–27
Tiberius, 16
Torture and Democracy, 27
Torture and Truth, 156
"Torture Memo," 112
Torture Victim Protection Act
    (TVPA), 143
Trial by ordeal, 18–20
Truth serum, 34–35
Truth, Torture, and the American Way, 160
20/20, 54

Union County Jail, 96–97
United Nations, 38
United Nations Committee Against
    Torture, 9
United Nations Convention on the
    Rights of the Child, 74
United Nation's Standard Minimum
    Rules for the Treatment of
    Prisoners, 95
Universal Declaration of Human Rights,
    12, 37–38, 73–74
Unspeakable Acts, Ordinary People, 83
Uruguay, 60–61
U.S. Agency for International
    Development (AID), 52, 59
U.S. War Crimes Act (WCA), 6–7,
    12, 111

Valdez, Frank, 70
Valent, Michael, 96
Van den Heuvel, Katrina, 136
Viet Cong, 55–56
Vietnam War, 38
Vogeler, Robert, 43
Volpe, Justin, 79–80

Wagner, Bill, 53
Warner Springs, California, 54–55
The Washington Connection and Third World Fascism, 59
Washington Post, 76
Water torture, 29–30
Watson, Kenneth, 77
Waupun Correctional Institution, 71
Weise, Thomas, 79–80
Western Hemisphere Institute for Security Cooperation (WHISC), 62–63
Westinghouse, George, 28
Wickersham Commission, 23, 31–33

Williams, Kristian, 7, 61
Wills, Garry, 4
Wilson, Andrew, 80–81
Wisdom, Specialist Matthew, 3
Wolff, Harold, 45, 48
Wolfowitz, Paul, 134
Wood, Carolyn, 122–23, 126–27
Woods, Donald, 71
Working Group, 114
World Medical Association (WMA), 39
World War I, 30
World War II, 37

Yakima Tribal Detention Center, 100
Yale University, 48–50
Yassem, Kjadeja, 129
Yoo, John, 6–7, 112–13, 142
Young, Keith, 54

Zimbardo, Philip, 155

About the Author

LAURA L. FINLEY teaches in the Department of Women's Studies at Florida Atlantic University and was formerly Director of Social Change at Women in Distress, the only domestic violence agency in Broward County, Florida. Dr. Finley is the author of *Juvenile Justice* (2007) in Greenwood's Historical Guides to Controversial Issues in America series and editor of *Encyclopedia of Juvenile Violence* (Greenwood Press, 2006).